JOHN TALBOT AND THE WAR IN FRANCE 1427–1453

JOHN TALBOT
AND
THE WAR IN FRANCE
1427–1453

A.J. Pollard

Pen & Sword
MILITARY

To the memory of E.E. Pollard and T.H. Thompson

First published in Great Britain by the Royal Historical Society, 1983
Published in 2005 in this format by
PEN & SWORD MILITARY
an imprint of
Pen & Sword Books Limited
47 Church Street
Barnsley
South Yorkshire
S70 2AS

ISBN 1 84415 247 2

A CIP catalogue record for this book
is available from the British Library.

Printed and bound in Great Britain by
CPI UK

Pen & Sword Books Ltd incorporates the imprints of
Pen & Sword Aviation, Pen & Sword Maritime, Pen & Sword Military,
Pen & Sword Select, Pen & Sword Military Classics,
Leo Cooper and Wharncliffe Local History

For a complete list of Pen & Sword titles please contact:
PEN & SWORD BOOKS LIMITED
47 Church Street, Barnsley, South Yorkshire, S70 2AS, England.
E-mail: enquiries@pen-and-sword.co.uk
Website: www.pen-and-sword.co.uk

CONTENTS

Abbreviations   vi

Acknowledgements   viii

Preface to First Edition   ix

Preface to Second Edition   xi

1. The Terror of the French: John Talbot in
   Legend and History   1

2. The Regent's Lieutenant: John Talbot at
   War, 1427-1436   12

3. Lancastrian Normandy and the Organization
   of its Defence after 1435   26

4. Marshal of France: John Talbot at War, 1436-50   44

5. Captain of War: John Talbot and his Troops   68

6. Soldier of Fortune: John Talbot and the
   Profits of War   102

7. Man of Honour: John Talbot and Chivalry   122

8. 'Le Roi Talbot': The Last Years, 1450-53   131

Appendix: Musters and counter-rolls of Talbot's
   Retinues   140

Bibliography   145

Index   155

ABBREVIATIONS

Add Ch	Additional Charters, British Library
Add Ms	Additional Manuscripts, British Library
ADSM	Archives de la Seine Maritime, Rouen
AN	Archives Nationales, Paris
Basin	Thomas Basin, *Histoire de Charles VII*, ed C Samaran, 2 vols, Paris, 1933-44.
BIHR	*Bulletin of the Institute of Historical Research*
BL	British Library, London
BN	Bibliothèque Nationale, Paris
Bourgeois	*Journal d'un Bourgeois de Paris, 1405-1449*, ed A Tuetey, Paris, 1881.
CP	*The Complete Peerage*
CPR	*Calendar of Patent Rolls*
CCR	*Calendar of Close Rolls*
Chartier	Jean Chartier, *Chronique de Charles VII*, ed M Vallet de Viriville, 3 vols, Paris 1858.
Clair	Collection Clairambault, Bibliothèque Nationale
D Len.	Collection Dom Lenoir, Archives Nationales
Duboc, 'Calendar'	Calendar of Acts enrolled in the Rouen Tabellionnage concerning the period of the English occupation compiled by M André Dubuc.
EHR	*English Historical Review*
Econ HR	*Economic History Review*
Gruel	G Gruel, *Chronique d'Arthur de Richemont*, ed Archille Ie Vavasseur, 1890
Monstrelet	*La Chronique d'Enguerrand de Monstrelet*, ed L. Douet d'Arcq, 6 vols, Paris 1857-62.
MS Fr	Manuscrit Français, Bibliothèque Nationale
NAF	Nouvelles Acquisitions Françaises, Bibliothèque Nationale

Pollard	'The Family of Talbot, lords Talbot and Earls of Shrewsbury in the Fifteenth Century', University of Bristol, Ph D Thesis, 1968.
PRO	Public Record Office, London
Stevenson, *Wars*	*Letters and Papers Illustrative of the Wars of the English in France during the reign of Henry VI*, ed J Stevenson, 2 vols in 3, 1861-4.
THAS	*Transactions of the Hunter Archaeological Society*
TRHS	*Transactions of the Royal Historical Society*
Waurin	*Recueil des Croniques par Jehan de Waurin*, ed Sir William Hardy, 5 vols, 1864-84.

ACKNOWLEDGEMENTS

The book has its genesis in part of my doctoral thesis on the Talbot family completed in 1968. Since then I have added to the substance of my work on Talbot's war career and modified my interpretation of it. During the many years in which I have been studying this subject I have built up a large debt of gratitude to many institutions and people. I would first like to record my appreciation of the financial support I have received from the Department of Education and Science and Cleveland County Education Authority. I owe much to the help given to me by the staff of all the record offices and libraries I have visited in England and France, as well as to the staff of the libraries at Bristol University and Teesside Polytechnic. All those friends and colleagues from whom I have received support, advice and assistance are too numerous to acknowledge individually, but I would like to record my longstanding indebtedness to Charles Ross and James Sherborne, especially in my salad days as a student; my appreciation of the encouragement given to me for many years by Ralph Griffiths and by Robin Jeffs, who knows as much about John Talbot as I do; my thanks to Ray Linacre who drew the maps; and my gratitude to Christopher Allmand not only for providing numerous references, but also for reading and giving expert comments on an early draft of this book. Jill Wren, who has typed and retyped the drafts and final copy of the work, and Janet Godden, who has steered it on behalf of the Royal Historical Society towards publication, have greatly eased the burden of the final stages. Finally there are two special debts. To my wife, who has lived with this work for longer than either of us realize or would care to remember, I am eternally grateful not only for assistance in proof reading, but also for her never failing support and encouragement. To Anne Curry, who is currently engaged in research on the organization of the English army in France, I am permanently indebted not only for giving me the benefit of her knowledge of French archives and their contents, but also for the way in which she has generously made available to me the transcripts of innumerable documents which I have overlooked.

PREFACE TO FIRST EDITION

Paradoxically John Talbot, first earl of Shrewsbury, overthrown and killed at Castillon in 1453, was one of the few English leaders to escape from the débâcle of the English defeat at the end of the Hundred Years War with his reputation intact if not enhanced. His fame in the fifteenth century was widespread. His death, leading a charge at massed cannon, came to symbolize the passing of an age and the end of chivalric warfare. This work is a study of the closing years of that age and of the later career of its last hero. It is not a biography of John Talbot; the personal material does not exist to enable the historian to penetrate the man's character and personality. Nor is it a full study of his life and times. Rather is it a series of studies of aspects of his career in the years 1427-53, especially in Normandy from 1435 to 1450. There are several reasons for concentrating on the period 1435-50. First, it was the most important in Talbot's career as a soldier. Before the treaty of Arras, which transformed the strategic situation in northern France,Talbot had only served for some four or five years in the war and had been overshadowed as a commander by such men as the earls of Salisbury and Arundel. After the loss of Normandy he spent less than a year in Gascony before his death. The most famous incidents in his life — his involvement in the siege of Orleans and his defeat at Patay in 1429 as well as at Castillon itself — were respectively a prelude and an epilogue to the years when he fought tenaciously but in vain to save Henry V's conquests in France. These years were unspectacular, but his contemporaries recognized that it was then that he did his sovereign greatest service. The key to Talbot's fame lies in what he did in Normandy in these years. Second, relatively little has been written or published on this phase of the war. The glorious reign of Henry V has received frequent attention and the success of John, duke of Bedford in extending and holding on to his conquests up to 1435 has been duly recognized. But the years between Bedford's death and the final expulsion of the English have for obvious reasons proved less attractive to English historians. Talbot's career provides a focal point for an attempt to make good part of this deficiency. Third, there is no shortage of sources for writing the military history of these years. The starting point is provided by the French chroniclers, especially the Burgundians, who told the stories of the gallant deeds done in the honour and glory of chivalry. But more important are the surviving administrative records of the English in France. Remnants of the English

Chambre des Comptes at Rouen and of the Chambre des Comptes at Paris (deposited in the Archives Nationales and the Bibliotheque Nationale in Paris, in the departmental archives of Normandy, and in the British Library) make possible a detailed study of Talbot's war career in these years. The documents — musters and related papers, acquittances for payment of troops, letters expediting payment for business of all kinds, registrations of sales of land and other related deeds, and royal grants of office and lands — cover most aspects of the military organization in Normandy and France. They provide invaluable supplementary information on the actual course of military operations; they shed important light on the development of English strategy; they make it possible for the historian to reconstruct the composition and, to a limited extent, the organization of individual retinues of war; and they provide useful additional information on the profits and costs of individual captains. The character of these sources has helped shape the form of this work as a series of studies; the nature of Talbot's role and his achievement, especially in Normandy between 1435 and 1450; the composition and organization of his retinues; the profitability of the war to himself; and, finally, the appropriateness of Talbot's reputation as the last chivalric hero. If the man himself cannot be brought to life, at least the many-sided character of the fifteenth-century soldier can be illuminated.

A. J. Pollard

PREFACE TO SECOND EDITION

This book began as part of a PhD thesis on the Talbot family in the fifteenth century. I started research in 1964 and the thesis was completed in 1968.[1] The thesis, supervised by Charles Ross, was one of the first in a spate of similar baronial studies undertaken by research students in the 1960s and early 1970s. I did not return to the subject of Talbot's war career until a decade later when I had the pleasure of myself supervising Professor Anne Curry in her initial, doctoral research on the organisation of the Lancastrian army in Normandy. I cannot recall now how it came about that I decided to update the relevant part of my thesis and submit it to the Royal Historical Society to be published as part of its then relatively new Studies in History series. The typescript was completed in 1980. The text therefore is at least twenty five years old, and in some parts, as essentially unrevised passages from my thesis, almost thirty five years old. I have not totally lost touch with John Talbot since then; I contributed entries on him to the *Oxford Companion to British History* in 1997, on Castillon (ten lines) to the *Oxford Companion to Military History* in 2001, and to the *Oxford Dictionary of National Biography* in 2004. It would be less than honest of me to claim that I undertook a significant amount of new research for these contributions; it would even less honest of me to claim that I am at heart a military historian. I became involved in Talbot's war career because it was the most significant element in the life of the most significant member of the Talbot family in the fifteenth century.

The text published in 1983, which is reprinted below, set out to give the most detailed narrative as yet attempted (and I believe not superseded) of Talbot's fighting in the service of the house of Lancaster after 1427 (chapters 2, 4 and 8), especially the period of continuous service in Normandy from 1434 to 1444. It also endeavoured to flesh that out by a study of his troops and the retinues of war he recruited to serve him, again with special emphasis on Normandy (ch 5); by examining his commitment to the ethics and practice of chivalry (ch 7); and by consideration of the extent to which Talbot profited or lost financially as a consequence of his engagement in the war (ch 8). The last was a subject of some intense academic debate in the 1960s. It is of little concern to historians today. The book was deliberately brief on his early career, and largely ignored him as a peer of the realm in England (for which now see the *Oxford DNB*). It was not a biography; it was a study, as the title indicates, of a military career.

A considerable amount of research has been undertaken and new work published in the intervening years. If the book were to be written now it would be longer, modified in some detail and in several ways fuller. The political and diplomatic context would need to be revisited in the light of recent revaluations of Henry VI's reign.[2] The discussion of Lancastrian Normandy, its government under English kings, and the organisation of the defence of the duchy would be transformed. I completed the book before the publication of Christopher Allmand's *Lancastrian Normandy, 1415-1450* in the same year as this slim volume came out.[3] The chapters in his work on the English settlement, on Caen as a case study, on the governing institutions, on social and economic conditions and on the French reaction would have deepened and broadened my analysis substantially.

Equally important has been the publishing of other studies of the English in Normandy and the character and implications of the English settlement.[4] In this the continuing work of Anne Curry has been of greatest importance, whether further case studies such as the settlement in Mantes, or the whole range of issues connected with military organisation in Lancastrian Normandy including recruitment, patterns of service, payment, deployment and discipline.[5] This would have yielded for me important additional detail about Talbot's movements, about his men and about his relationship with the duchy government. Chapter 5 in particular, which anyway benefited immensely from the early stages of her research, would now be considerably better informed. Professor Curry has ransacked the French archives, central and departmental, in such a way as I suspect that there is little left to find about Talbot or any of his fellow commanders in this stage of the hundred years war. Her research would also have enabled me to have provided an immensely more nuanced understanding of the social, administrative and military context of Talbot's career in Normandy. Fortunately she is now engaged in bringing all this work together in a monograph to be published by Oxford University Press, which will enable readers to fill the gaps.

Furthermore our understanding and appreciation of the way in which chivalry infused every aspect of military practice have been greatly extended since I took my first faltering steps on the subject in chapter 7. The most important figure in this respect has been Maurice Keen, whose magisterial *Chivalry* was published just a year after this book, and whose continuing work has convinced us that chivalry in all its dimensions was not a superficial, decadent gloss on war and politics in late-medieval society, but lay at the very heart of its ideals.[6] I would also have responded to Richard Kaeuper's recent and wonderfully vivid *Chivalry and Violence in Medieval Europe*. In particular I would have grasped, more fully than appears in the text, how prowess, the very physical activity of hewing and hacking, actual fighting, defined what men of chivalry actually did in war, or were valued for doing, in the fifteenth century.[7] To which one would have added David Morgan's essay on the extraordinary life and death of Lewis Robesart which drew out the importance of honour, even if the valuation of it in oneself led to defeat and death.[8]

The question of chivalry leads to the most important question of how, twenty five years later, the historian seeks to evaluate a military career such as Talbot's. There has been a recent surge in interest in medieval military history.[9] It has tended to focus on major battles and how they were fought. Andrew Ayton and J. L. Price, in pondering about the idea of military revolution from a medieval perspective, have suggested that artillery did not radically transform warfare until the second half of the fifteenth century, after Talbot's death; until then it was used on the battle field and during sieges in very much the same way as conventional and established missiles. Armies were still small - that change was yet to come as well; and fighting in the fifteenth century was usually on foot with cavalry used as shock troops, flanking manoeuvres and pursuit (and flight).[10] And so it was in Talbot's military career. The overall thesis about military revolution additionally confirms the conventional view, expressed below, that Talbot's death, charging at massed cannon outside Castillon represents the end of an era.

Matthew Bennett has stressed how difficult it is to know precisely what went on in the heat of battle during the Hundred Years War, but he has proposed that the English developed a battlefield tactic, involving the use of archers, which did themselves proud at Agincourt and Verneuil. The key factor, he argues, was discipline; the ability to hold formation when in action and especially under assault. He draws attention to the importance of the shout in unison to instil fear into the enemy, to let him know that you were still in formation and still confident even when reeling from attack. Bennett suggests that Talbot was a less than successful commander, being defeated in two major engagements, because he failed to deploy effectively the well-honed tactics which had brought victory at Agincourt and Verrneuil (at neither of which he was present).[11]

Perhaps the most significant recent contribution to the study of fifteenth-century military history has been Michael K. Jones' important reconstruction of the battle of Verneuil, subtitled 'Towards a History of Courage'. This offers a synthesis of the conventional military historian's preoccupation with tactics with an understanding of the importance of the mental outlook of the combatants as applied to late medieval warfare. In part a devastating refutation of A. H. Burne's much recycled theory of 'inherent military probability' (which was very much in vogue in 1965), the essay is also a demonstration of how chivalry worked in practice in battle. He draws attention to the ritualistic elements of the preparations in which a *journee*, a day of battle, was agreed by both sides to determine the fate of Verneuil, then threatened by the French; how honour was at stake in meeting these terms; how contemporaries drew a distinction between the prudence of the 'manly' man and the rashness of the (fool) 'hardy' man; how important it was for men in the heat of battle to be led by example by their commanders showing the prowess expected of them; and how the renown and standing of their commander, and their conviction in the rightness of their cause, inspired them to fight bravely.[12] These ideas have profound implications for one's reading of Talbot's career.

As I stressed in the book, Talbot was a man who achieved high renown despite the fact that the two major battles in which he held command were shattering defeats, one leading to his capture, the other to his death. The question remains as to how one reconciles this apparent contradiction. Bennett's criticism, that Talbot failed to use well-established tactics properly, echoes contemporary criticism that he was wont to charge recklessly at first sight of the enemy. Thomas Basin, in particular, who wrote that he normally attacked the enemy by impetuous daring rather than deliberate assault, characterised Talbot as a 'hardy' rather than a 'prudent' man, for which he deemed him to be unfitted for senior command. It is a serious charge, and one that has lain at the bottom of all those evaluations of Talbot that seek to demonstrate that the high reputation he enjoyed in his life and thereafter was undeserved. In 1981 I sought, in part, to counter this by side-stepping it, by stressing a different aspect of his career, including his loyalty to the Lancastrian cause in France, his willingness to 'soldier on', his tirelessness in relieving sieges and recovering lost places, his capacity to organise and hold the defence of eastern Normandy; in short, his refusal to give up.[13] Now I would also need to take it head on as being grounded in a misconception of what it meant to be a successful warrior in the fifteenth century.

Prowess, honour, prudence and discipline: these are the issues. There is no doubting Talbot's personal prowess. He led by example. Talbot's great valour was stressed in the citation of his promotion to the office of marshal of France in 1436. It was his prowess and renown that were frequently reiterated in both Burgundian and English sources, even though the authors knew little of the detail of how the prowess had won the renown. And so, too, we find is the case with honour. This he took most seriously, as we know, from the manner in which he pursued his complaint in the court of chivalry against Sir John Fastolf, for, as Talbot saw it, his flight from the field of Patay was both cowardly and dishonourable. This became something of a *cause celebre*. When it came to Talbot being tested, again, at Castillon, he was not found wanting. The best explanation of the course of the action of that battle is that Talbot found himself, as the result of faulty intelligence, drawn up for action with his banner unfurled before a fortified artillery park where he had expected to find only a lightly defended encampment. But having declared his intention to attack, his sense of honour determined that there was no stepping back. Tactically this proved to be unwise; a less honourable man would have withdrawn. And so he met his death honourably and not in disgrace; a point even Basin was prepared to acknowledge.

Yet the honourable assault at Castillon has been characterised as foolhardy. The question of his prudence or foolhardiness was the gravimen of Basin's criticism. Were his military actions based on calculated or uncalculated risk? As I pointed out in the book, there were several occasions in Talbot's career in which he held back from rushing at the enemy. After one of them, at Harcourt in the summer of 1449, when he refused to attack a much larger French force in the field, he was gloatingly chided in the official French memoir of the campaign, compiled by a herald who had witnessed the campaign, for his cowardice. However, all contemporary accounts of the remarkable action around Pontoise in the summer of 1441, when Talbot sought not only to hold the town in English hands but also to capture Charles VII, who for once had taken the field, suggest that Talbot was capable of tactical thinking of the highest order and knew exactly when a risk was worth taking. At least one, French, account suggests that he might have seized the king if the duke of York had been prepared to play his part in a planned pincer movement.[14] And Michael K. Jones has amply demonstrated the same capacity in the action at Avranches two years earlier. Jones' reconstruction of the relief of Avranches, demonstrating the calculated boldness of Talbot's crossing the estuary at St Michael's Bay so as to outflank and defeat the French besieging force, shows what could well be done with other engagements for which the English source material is relatively meagre.[15]

Honour, courage and prudence, it is apparent, were sometimes difficult to balance. But those engagements in which he succeeded, successful sieges and the relief of beleaguered outposts included, all depended on discipline. Talbot could not have succeeded had he not had at his call troops who were well trained, practiced in war and inspired by the renown of their captain. The cry 'a Talbot, a St George', raised loudly and in unison when his troops attacked, did indeed put fear into the hearts of those opposing him. The commendation in his letters of appointment as marshal of France in 1436 that it was in part for the maintenance of order and discipline in the army was not empty rhetoric. And it is worth noting that it was reported that he broke off an attempted siege of Dieppe in 1443 because of the lack of discipline of unseasoned troops recently recruited in England.[16]

The contemporary admiration for a man who practiced chivalry on the field of battle was well-founded. However, in the twenty first century we cannot escape the fact that we evaluate generalship not merely by the manner in which it was exercised, but additionally by the success it achieved. My judgement remains that in the decade from 1434 to 1444 he above all others was responsible for the English success in arms in Normandy, in managing to hold on to the duchy and to make possible the Truce of Tours when it might well have been otherwise. He was not alone; he fought alongside other competent commanders such as Lords Scales and Fauconberg; and he was perhaps fortunate that he did not face a concerted assault on the duchy by his enemies. But this was in the context a significant, if ultimately futile, military achievement. Of course, he failed to hold Normandy in 1449 and he was the commander in the battle in which England finally 'lost' the Hundred Years War. He was no Alexander. On the other hand Napoleon was defeated in his last battle.

Notes

1. 'The Family of Talbot, Lords Talbot and Earls of Shrewsbury in the Fifteenth Century', Bristol University, 1968, esp pp.144-213, 251-91 and 319-32 .

2. For example G. L. Harriss, *Cardinal Beaufort: a Study of Lancastrian Ascendancy and Decline* (Oxford: Clarendon Press, 1988); P. A. Johnson, *Duke Richard of York, 1411-60* (Oxford: University Press, 1988);J. L. Watts, *Henry VI and the Politics of Kingship* (Cambridge: University Press, 1996)

3. *Lancastrian Normandy, 1415-1450: the History of a Medieval Occupation* (Oxford: Clarendon Press, 1983)

4. Robert Massey, 'The Land Settlement in Lancastrian Normandy', in A. J. Pollard, ed., *Property and Politics in later Medieval English History* (Gloucester: Alan Sutton, 1984), pp. 76-96; idem, 'Lancastrian Rouen: military service and property holding, 1419-1449', in D. Bates and A. E. Curry, eds, *England and Normandy in the Middle Ages* (London: Hambleton Press, 1994), 269-86; G. L. Thompson, *Paris and its People under English Rule: the Anglo-Burgundian Regime, 1420-1436* (Oxford: Clarendon Press, 1991).

5. Some idea of the range and scale of the output is given by the following selected references, 'The first English standing army? Military organisation in Lancastrian Normandy, 1422-1450', C. D. Ross, ed., *Patronage, Pedigree and Power in Later*

Medieval England (Gloucester: Alan Sutton, 1979), pp. 193-214; 'The impact of war and occupation on urban life in Normandy, 1417-1450, *French History*, 1, part 2 (1987), 157-81; 'Sex and the Soldier in Lancastrian Normandy, 1415-50', *Reading medieval Studies*, 14 (1988), 17-45; 'The English army in the fifteenth century', in A. Curry and M. Hughes, eds, *Arms, Armies and Fortifications in the Hundred Years War* (Woodbridge: Boydell and Brewer, 1994), pp. 39-68; 'Lancastrian Normandy: the Jewel in the Crown', in D. Bates and A. E. Curry, eds, *England and Normandy in the Middle Ages* (London: Hambledon Press, 1994), pp. 235-52; 'L'administration financiere dde la Normandie anglaise: continuite ou changement', in *La France des principautes: les chambres des comptes xive et xve siecles* (Paris: CHEF, 1996), 83-1-3†; 'The organisation of filed armies in Lancastrian Normandy', in M. Stricklnad, ed., *Armies, Chivalry and Warfare in Medieval Britain and France* (Stamford: Paul Watkins, 1998), pp. 207-31; 'L'occupation anglaise du xive siecle: la discipline militaire et le probleme des gens vivans sur le pais', in J-Y. Martin, ed., *La Normandie dans la Guerre de Cent Ans, 1346-1450* (Milan and Paris: Skira-Seuil, 1999), pp. 47-9; 'Bourgeois et soldat dans la ville de Mantes pendant l'occupation anglaise de 1419 a 1449', in J. Paviot and J. Verger, eds, *Guerre, Pouvoir et Noblesse au Moyen Age* (Paris: CTHS, 2000), pp. 175-84; 'The Loss of Lancastrian Normandy in 1450. An administrative nightmare?, in D. Grummitt ed., The English Experience in France (Aldershot†: Ashgate, 2002), pp. 24-45.

6. M. H. Keen, *Chivalry* (New Haven: Yale University Press, 1984); idem, *Nobles, Knights and Men at Arms in the Middle Ages* (London: Hambleton Press, 1996); idem, *The Origins of the English Gentleman: Heraldry, Chivalry and Gentility in Medieval England* (Stroud: Tempus, 2002).

7. R. W. Kaueper, *Chivalry and Violence in Medieval Europe* (Oxford: University Press, 1999), esp. pp. 129-188; see also idem 'Chivalric Violence and Religious Valorization', in *Warriors and Courtiers: Comparative Historical Perspectives on Ruling Authority and Civilization* (Kyoto: International Research Center for Japanese Studies, 2003), pp. 489-508.

8. 'From a Death to a View: Lewis Robesart, John Huizinga and the Political Significance of Chivalry', in S. Anglo, ed., *Chivalry in the Renaissance* (Woodbridge: Boydell and Brewer, 1990), pp. 93-8.

9. See for example Helen Nicholson, *Medieval Warfare: Theory and Practice of War in Europe, 300-1500* (Basingstoke: Palgrave Macmillan, 2003) for an overview; M. Prestwich, *Armies and Warfare in the Middle Ages: the English Experience* (New Haven: Yale University Press, 1996) for the later middle ages; and K. De Vries, 'The Effectiveness of Fifteenth-century Shipboard Artillery', *Mariner's Mirror*, 84 (1998), 389-99; idem, 'The Use of Gunpowder Weaponry against Joan of Arc during the Hundred Years War', *War and Society*, 14.1 (1996), 1-16 for the fifteenth century in particular. With the exceptions of the works cited below, however, not much has focussed on the theatre of war in which Talbot was engaged.

10. A. Ayton and J. L. Price, 'The Military Revolution from a Medieval Perspective', in Ayton and Price, eds, *The Medieval Military Revolution: State, Society and Military Change in Medieval and Early Modern Europe* (London: I. B. Taurus, 1995), pp. 1-22, esp 6-7.

11. M. Bennett, 'The Development of Battle Tactics in the Hundred Years War', in A. Curry and M. Hughes, eds, *Arms, Armies and Fortifications in the Hundred Years War* (Woodbridge: Boydell and Brewer, 1994), pp. 1-20.

12. Michael K. Jones, 'The Battle of Verneuil (17 August 1424): Towards a History of Courage', *War in History*, 9 (2002), 375-411.

13. See below, pp. 67, 139.

14. See below, pp. 56-8. See also the capture of Pontoise in 1437 (p.48).

15. Michael K. Jones, 'The Relief of Avranches (1439): An English Feat of Arms at the End of the Hundred Years War', in N. Rogers, ed., *England in the Fifteenth Century: Proceedings of the 1992 Harlaxton Symposium* (Stamford: Paul Watkins, 1994), pp. 42-55.

16. See below, pp. 37, 59-60.

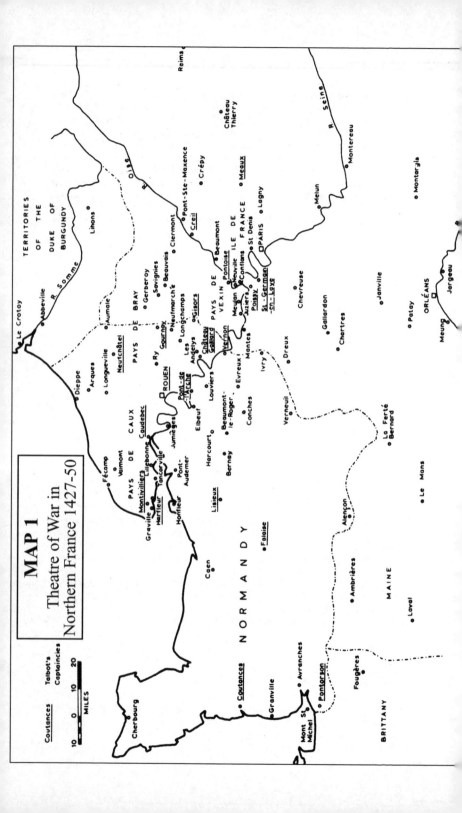

MAP 1

Theatre of War in
Northern France 1427-50

1

THE TERROR OF THE FRENCH:
JOHN TALBOT IN LEGEND AND HISTORY

In the morning heat of 17 July 1453 the vanguard of an Anglo-Gascon army launched a frontal assault on a strongly fortified French encampment near the town of Castillon on the Dordogne. The defenders outnumbered the attackers and were, moreover, safely behind a line of 250 guns of all calibres massed wheel to wheel. Such an attack was suicidal but the troops, fighting on foot and inspired by the presence of their renowned veteran commander, actually managed to establish themselves for a moment on the ramparts; there the standard bearer fell in the moment of planting the standard. But the losses from the hail of shot and ball at point-blank range were devastating and the men soon fell back. When counter-attacked they broke and fled — all, that is, except a small party around the old commander who, attempting to rally his men, was himself brought down from his horse and had his skull smashed by an axe. The commander was the legendary John Talbot, earl of Shrewsbury.[1] Widely, but erroneously, believed to be eighty years old (he was approximately sixty-six), he had, according to some accounts, gone to battle on a small white horse, wearing no armour at all. For him it was the end of fifty years of warfare and a large part of a lifetime devoted to the forlorn struggle to stave off his country's military disasters. His death was greeted with wild rejoicing in France, where his tenacity in the English cause had won him widespread respect, while his reputation for cruelty had made him feared and hated. As one Frenchman wrote, 'he had for a long time been one of the most formidable scourges and sworn enemies of France, and had proved to be her dread and terror'. In Gascony and Normandy he was to be long remembered as 'the terror of the French'. A lesser London chronicler commented shortly after his death that he was 'fierce in fight and most dred of all other in France'. Almost a hundred years later Edward Hall amplified this same epitaph:

---

[1] A H Burne, *The Agincourt War* (1956), pp. 338-45. Accounts differ on how Talbot actually met his death. I have followed Mathieu d'Escouchy, *Chronique*, ed. G du Fresne de Beaucourt, 2, (1864) pp. 36-41, who received his information from Talbot's herald. In 1874 Talbot's skeleton was disinterred and a fracture 2¾ x 5 inches was found in his skull, thus apparently confirming d'Escouchy. (W H Egerton, Talbot's Tomb', *Trans. Salop. Arch. Soc.* 8, 425).

> This man was to the French people, a very scorge and a daily
> terror, in so much that as his person was fearfull and terrible to
> his adversaries present, so his name and frame was spiteful and
> dreadful to the common people absent, in so much that women in
> Fraunce to feare their yonge children would cry — the Talbot
> cometh, the Talbot cometh.

And indeed as recently as the nineteenth century the people of
Gascony, it is reported, remembered the deeds of 'Le Roi Talbot' and
mothers still used to check their children with the cry, 'the Talbot
cometh'.[2]

By the English, Talbot was remembered more as a tireless and
devoted servant of the Lancastrian cause in France. To members of
his own class he soon came in addition to be celebrated as the last
representative of the true chivalric breed. When, shortly before 1461,
William Worcester first wrote his *Book of Noblesse*, and more so when
he revised it in the early 1470s, he had men such as Talbot in mind
when he advocated a return to the war in France as a means of reviving
the 'right noble chivalry' which he believed was everywhere in
decay.[3] The same feelings were shared by William Caxton, and one
presumes by many of his readers, when in 1484 he published his
version of Ramon Lull's *Order of Chivalry*. In his epilogue he made a
plea to his sovereign, Richard III, to use the book to spearhead a
campaign of chivalric moral rearmament. Caxton was concerned that
the 'nobel order of chivalry hath been forgotten and the exercises of
chivalry not used'. 'O ye knights of England', he bewailed,

> where is the custom and usage of noble chivalry that was used in
> those days [of King Arthur]? What do ye now but go to the
> bagnios and play at dice? Leave this, leave it and behold that
> victorious and noble king Harry the fifth and the captains under
> him, his noble brethren, th' earl of Salisbury and many others
> whose names shine gloriously by their virtuous noblesse and acts
> they did in th'onour of the ordre of chivalry.[4]

Talbot was one of those whose names shone gloriously and whose
example, if followed, would help bring England out of the decadence

[2]Chartier, 3, p. 7; C.L. Kingsford, *English Historical Literature in the Fifteenth
Century* (Oxford 1905), p. 372; E. Hall, *The Union of the Noble and Illustre Famelies
of Lancastre and Yorke* (1809), p. 230; H. Ribadieu, *La Conquête de la Guyenne*
(Bordeaux, 1866), p. 323.

[3]W. Worcestre, *The Boke of Noblesse*, ed. J.G. Nichols (Roxburghe Club, 1860), pp.
76-8. A. B. Ferguson, *The Indian Summer of English Chivalry* (Durham, North
Carolina, 1960), pp. 143-58. It is to be noted that neither Worcester nor Caxton
mentions Talbot by name.

[4]N. F. Blake *Caxton's Own Prose* (1973), pp. 126-7. See also Ferguson, *English
Chivalry*, pp. 34-8.

into which she had recently fallen. In this, the era of the 'Indian summer of English chivalry', he took on the aura of being the last of the old breed of true heroes. It was the image caught perfectly by Polydore Vergil who, coming to England in the first decade of the sixteenth century, picked up and recorded the opinion of his contemporaries:

> He was a man amongst men, of reputation in deed esteemed both for nobility of birth and haughtiness of courage, of most honourable and high renowne, who was conqueror in so many sundry conflictes, that both his name was redowted above all others and yet continueth of famous memory universally at this day.[5]

The theme of the chivalric hero, repeated by Hall and Holinshed, was taken up again by Shakespeare. In *King Henry V* Talbot is (wrongly) made one of the happy few, the band of brothers, celebrated in the St Crispin's day speech, as sharing the glory and honour of Agincourt:

> Old men forget: yet all shall be forgot,
> But he'll remember with advantages
> What feats he did that day. Then shall our names,
> Familiar in his mouth as household words,
> Harry the King, Bedford and Exeter
> Warwick and Talbot, Salisbury and Gloucester,
> Be in their flowing cups freshly remembered.[6]

But it is in Shakespeare's *King Henry VI, Part I*, that the Talbot legend reaches its apogee. Written and first performed in the last decade of the sixteenth century, this presents Talbot, the central character of the play, as a man almost alone in continuing the heroic and doomed struggle to prevent the loss of France. While the nobility bicker and squabble at home, Talbot works wonders in France until he is finally brought low by the sorcery of Joan of Arc and by the indifference of his fellow Englishmen. A wild and ferocious figure he may be, but he is nevertheless the only true embodiment of that spirit of chivalry which had made England so powerful under Henry V. This comes out most clearly in the long final scenes between the hero and his son on the field of Castillon. Twice Talbot urges his son John to flee from the field. Twice young Talbot refuses. Before the battle he cries,

> Is my name Talbot? and am I your son?
> And shall I fly? O, if you love my Mother,
> Dishonour not her honourable name,

---

[5]*Three Books of Polydore Vergil's English History;* ed. H. Ellis (Camden Soc., 1846); p. 15.

[6]*Henry V,* Act IV, Scene 3.

> To make a bastard, and a slave of me;
> The World will say, he is not Talbot's blood,
> That basely fled, when noble Talbot stood.[7]

And later in the middle of the battle, after Talbot has rescued his son, again he pours scorn on flight.

TALBOT: By me they nothing gain, and if I stay,
            'Tis but the short'ning of my life one day.
            In thee thy Mother dies, our Household's Name,
            My death's revenge, thy youth and England's fame:
            All these, and more, we hazard by thy stay;
            All these are sav'd, if thou wilt fly away.

JOHN: The sword of Orleans hath not made me smart,
            These words of yours draw life-blood from my heart.
            On that advantage, bought with such a shame,
            To save a paltry life, and slay bright Fame,
            Before young Talbot from old Talbot fly,
            The coward horse that bears me, fall and die:
            And like me to the peasant boys of France,
            To be Shame's scorn, and subject of Mischance.
            Surely, by all the glory you have won,
            And if I fly, I am not Talbot's son.[8]

And so he stays to fight and die by his father's side, all honour satisfied, and immortality assured for the name of Talbot. As Talbot himself declares in his dying speech,

> Thou antic Death, which laugh'st us here to scorn,
> Anon from thy insulting tyranny,
> Coupled in bonds in perpetuity,
> Two Talbots winged through the lither sky,
> In thy despite shall 'scape mortality.[9]

Through the device of Talbot's young, untried son emulating his father, Shakespeare (perhaps rather at the expense of the pace of the action) pushes home to his audience the true nobility of this last great hero of a bygone age. In Shakespeare's play this by now traditional chivalric image is coloured by a somewhat crude nationalism and chauvinism. Talbot is not only a true hero, but he is an English hero to boot. When the play was written England was once again in the throes of a long and costly war. It has even been suggested that *King Henry VI, Part I*, is an adaptation of another play on the subject of Talbot's heroic life

[7] *Henry VI, Part 1*, Act IV, Scene 5.

[8] *Ibid.*, Scene 6.

[9] *Ibid.*, Scene 7.

and death, written and performed to commemorate the earl of Essex's expedition to Rouen in 1591.[10] Was there a contemporary allusion in Lucy's final words on Talbot in act four, scene seven?

> I'll bear them hence: but from their ashes shall be rear'd
> A Phoenix that shall make all France afear'd.

Whether or not *King Henry VI, Part I*, began life as a Talbot play, it appears that its blend of heroism and chauvinism ensured immense popularity when it was first performed. This was attested by Thomas Nashe in 1592:

> How it would have joyed brave Talbot (the terror of the French) to think that after he had lyne 200 years in his tomb he should triumph again on the stage, and have his bones embalmed with the tears of 10,000 spectators at least (at several times) who, in the tragedian that represents his person, imagine they behold him fresh from bleeding.[11]

The Talbot legend reached its widest audience and its zenith in the Elizabethan age. Thereafter it set into a rapid decline. During the seventeenth century, as old chivalry finally became obsolete, and in the eighteenth century, as new military heroes came to the fore, so did the memory of old Talbot fade. Today, his legend, let alone his life, is familiar to only a few. In the long gallery of English military heroes he now hangs in a dark corner. Winston Churchill, an arbiter of recent popular history and an admirer of heroes great and small, dismissed him in a couple of lines in his *History of the English Speaking Peoples* and even identified someone else as commander at Castillon. And in 1960 the producer of a television adaption of *King Henry VI, Part I* happily dispensed with the character of Talbot altogether.[12] In the present century Talbot is almost a forgotten hero.

There are, in fact, solid foundations for Talbot's currently diminished standing. Warriors are no longer judged according to the tenets of chivalry. Their reputations stand or fall not on their personal prowess, but on their records as military commanders in battle. They are judged according to their strategic and tactical skills. In this respect, Talbot was found wanting even in the fifteenth century. Writing about Castillon, Thomas Basin stated that Talbot was determined to attack against the better advice of his lieutenants because, he remarked, Talbot was 'normally impelled to drive the

---

[10] *The First Part of King Henry VI*, ed. J. Dover Wilson (Cambridge, 1952), pp. ix, xvi-ii, xlviii-ix; *The First Part of King Henry VI*, ed. A.S. Cairncross (1962), p. xl.

[11] R. B. McKerrow, *Nashe* (Oxford, 1910) 1, p. 212.

[12] W. S. Churchill, *A History of the English Speaking Peoples* 1 (1956), p. 345; *King Henry VI*, ed. Cairncross, p., xli.

enemy into flight by impetuous daring rather than by a deliberate assault, thinking that his name alone would cause the enemy to take flight'.[13] This notion of Talbot's rashness and lack of tactical insight has been taken up and elaborated by most modern historians who have offered an assessment of his abilities. J. A. Tait, contributing to the *Dictionary of National Biography* in 1890, commented: 'Talbot was a sort of Hotspur, owing his reputation more to dash and daring than to any military genius. In all his long career as a commander he fought only two actions which deserve to be called battles: Patay was a rout from the beginning and Castillon a miscalculation.'[14]

This is a judgement endorsed, for instance, by Miss Ethel Carleton Williams who, in her study of John, duke of Bedford, suggested that Talbot had neither the ability to read his opponents' minds nor the skill to forestall their movements, but rather, whenever he caught sight of the enemy, dashed headlong at him regardless of the odds.[15] Of twentieth-century historians, Colonel A.H. Burne was the first to dissent from this now conventional view and attempt to vindicate the legend. *The Agincourt War*, published in 1956, appears almost to have as its main purpose the propagation of the view that Talbot was the greatest of a 'breed of mighty and illustrious leaders such as can stand comparison with those of any other century in our history', a military genius greater even than Henry V.[16] In so far as Burne drew attention to Talbot's dogged persistence and occasional dashing success in the defence of Normandy after 1435, his detailed narrative of the war provided an important balance to more critical assessments. This emphasis was taken up and developed in more detail by Reginald Brill in his unpublished Princeton University doctoral thesis some ten years later. The defence of Normandy after 1435 is here presented as Talbot's 'mission'. Talbot, Brill argued, was justifiably a 'legend in his own lifetime' because of this 'spectacular achievement' — an achievement which, he declared, reasserted the superiority of English general-ship and was tantamount to the greatest English victory (*sic*) since the days of Henry V.[17] But the larger claims of both Burne and Brill have yet to convince a generation of historians not so easily swayed by the romance of chivalry or so willing to ignore

[13] Basin, 2, p. 196.

[14] *Dictionary of National Biography*, 19, p. 322.

[15] E. C. Williams, *My Lord of Bedford* (1963), pp. 148, 170. See also the similarly dismissive views of E. Perroy, *The Hundred Years War* (1965), p. 321 and E. F. Jacob, *The Fifteenth Century* (Oxford, 1961), p. 506.

[16] A. H. Burne, *The Agincourt War* (1956), Ch. 17 *passim*, esp. p. 279.

[17] R. Brill, 'An English captain of the later hundred years war; John, Lord Talbot' (unpublished Princeton University Ph.D. thesis, 1966), pp. 1-2, 299-300.

two disastrous defeats in their search for military heroes. While recognizing the importance of Talbot's contribution to the defence of the conquest especially after 1435, the most generous recent assessment remains that he was but the ablest commander during a period of declining military power and ultimate defeat.[18]

Talbot's reputation has thus suffered since the sixteenth century. A hero of the late chivalric age, he has, with one or two notable exceptions, been cast aside by modern historians who judge their soldiers more by their results. I will return later to the questions of Talbot's capacity and achievement and of whether he actually deserved his reputation before 1600. But before considering the part played by him in the French war from 1427, it is necessary to sketch some aspects of his early life and career.

John Talbot was descended from old Anglo-Norman noble stock. Born in approximately 1387, the same year as Henry V, he was the second son of Richard, fourth Lord Talbot, who held extensive lands in the English border counties of Hereford and Gloucester.[19] His mother was Ankaret Le Strange, the eventual heiress of the Lords Le Strange of Blakemere near Whitchurch in northern Shropshire, through whom the Talbots acquired their property in that county. The Talbot family had long-established connections with the house of Lancaster. The first and second lords had been followers of Thomas of Lancaster in the reign of Edward II and the second had assisted Henry of Lancaster and Edward III against Roger Mortimer in 1330. The third lord, John's grandfather, served with John of Gaunt in Spain, where he died in 1387. John's father died in 1396, but his family of young children was well placed to benefit from the Lancastrian usurpation in 1399.[20] Almost as soon as he came of age, Gilbert, John's eldest brother and the fifth Lord Talbot, joined the household of Henry, prince of Wales. John's early career was bound up with his mother's second husband, Thomas Nevill, Lord Furnival of Sheffield, brother of Ralph, earl of Westmorland and a staunch supporter of the new régime. Part of the terms of the alliance

---

[18]M. H. Keen, *England in the Later Middle Ages* (1973), p. 403.

[19]There is no direct evidence of John's date of birth. He was said to be over thirty in 1422. More exactly one can assume that he was over twenty-one when he was summoned to his first parliament in October 1409. By the same token he was probably not yet twenty-one in October 1407, for he was not summoned to the parliament that met then, even though he had already succeeded to the barony of Furnival. This suggests a date of birth between 1386 and 1388. Such a time span is consistent with his still being in his mother's household at Christmas 1401 and his maintaining his own household at Montgomery in December 1404. Thus 1387 is unlikely to be more than a year out.

[20]*CP*, 12, Pt 1, pp. 606-7.

between the two families was his own marriage to Furnival's heiress, Maud.[21] When Furnival died in 1407, the young John — he was then about twenty years old — succeeded to his title and estates in right of his wife. It was as Lord Furnival that John took part in the pacification of Wales after Owain Glyn Dŵr's revolt, that he was first summoned to parliament in 1409, went to Ireland as Henry V's lieutenant in 1414 and first served in France in 1420. He was thus already a prominent peer of the realm when in 1422 he inherited the family title and estates. His brother had died in 1418 leaving a sole heiress who had herself subsequently died in childhood.[22] This fortuitous course of events made Talbot one of the richest peers in England on the accession of Henry VI. Some years later, in 1436, for the purpose of taxation, he declared a net income of £1,205 from lands, offices and annuities in England. This placed him among the ranks of the wealthiest laymen in England, the richest of the barons with a rated income approximately equal to that of the earls of Northumberland and Salisbury.[23] His elevation to the earldom of Shrewsbury in 1442 was as much a consequence of his wealth as a recognition of his services. Talbot's importance in Lancastrian England was enhanced in 1424 or 1425 when he married as his second wife, Margaret, eldest daughter and joint heiress presumptive of the mighty Richard Beauchamp, earl of Warwick. Talbot should never be thought of as a mere soldier of fortune. He was a rich and powerful peer of the realm, from old noble stock, linked closely by family tradition and personal ties to the Lancastrian dynasty.

Talbot spent most of his life fighting. It could be that he was blooded at the fierce battle of Shrewsbury in 1403. His elder brother fought in the company of the prince of Wales and he himself could have been alongside his father-in-law, Lord Furnival, who after the battle brought Hotspur's body back to Whitchurch for burial. The first direct evidence of John in arms comes almost eighteen months later in December 1404 when he took up command, as Furnival's deputy, of

---

[21]*CPR, 1399-1407*, p. 51; *Calendar of Fine Rolls, 1405-13*, p. 74; Shropshire Record Office, Bridgewater Papers, 75/1401-2.

[22]*CP*, 12, Pt 1, p. 518.

[23]PRO, E163/7/31; H.L. Gray, 'Incomes from Land in England in 1436', *EHR* 49 (1934), 615. See also T. B. Pugh and C. D. Ross, 'The English Baronage and the Income Tax of 1436', *BIHR* 26 (1953), 1ff. As with many fellow peers, Talbot's return for his landed income probably represented an understatement. In 1436 lands to the value of nearly £200 *per annum* were in the hands of his sons and his brother's widow. Nor did the return include lands in Wales and Ireland which Talbot held (see Pollard, pp. 315-6). It is likely, however, that his income was not as under-assessed as that of Northumberland, which was more than double that for which he was rated (Pugh and Ross, *BIHR* 26 (1953), 9).

garrisons in the fortresses of Montgomery and Bishop's Castle on the border between Shropshire and Wales.[24] He would have been about eighteen years old. Thereafter he played a prominent role in the long drawn out pacification of Wales, serving in the sieges of Aberystwyth in 1407 and 1408 and with his brother taking Harlech in 1409.[25] A few years after the suppression of the Welsh revolt, in 1414, he was sent by Henry V as his lieutenant in Ireland. Here his main task was the defence of the borders of the English lordship against the incessant attacks of the Gaelic tribes. In a series of devastating raids in 1415 and subsequent years he succeeded in bringing a degree of security to the colony not known for many a day. His successful campaigns, at a time when the Gaelic resurgence was in full flood, played a part in stabilizing the nascent Pale.[26] In his early fighting Talbot learnt much of his warcraft. It is perhaps significant that his youthful experience was in warfare against an enemy, especially in Wales, who enjoyed the support of many of the inhabitants; and that it was the kind of warfare in which no great victories in the field could be won, but in which success only came through wearing down the enemy by constant pressure. It was a kind of fighting too, especially in Ireland, where speed, surprise and terror gained the best results. He cannot have endeared himself to the Welsh and one Irish annalist wrote of him that 'from the time of Herod there came not anyone so wicked'.[27] By 1419, when he left Ireland, the image which was to stay with Talbot for the rest of his life was already formed.

From Ireland Talbot went to France to join his monarch. He was first mustered there in May 1420, and was probably present at the sealing of the treaty of Troyes and the king's marriage there on 2 June. He certainly took part in the siege of Melun (July–November), returned in triumph to England that winter and was one of the lords appointed to arrange the feast at Queen Katherine's coronation on 23

[24] J. H. Wylie, *The History of England under Henry the Fourth*, 1, (1892) p. 364; *CPR, 1401-05,* p. 262; PRO, E101/44/6.

[25] For Owain Glyn Dŵr's revolt and Talbot's role see Sir John Lloyd, *Owen Glendower* (Oxford, 1931), *passim*: G. Williams, *Owen Glendower* (Oxford, 1966); Wylie, *Henry the Fourth*; and Pollard, pp. 15-18.

[26] For an excellent analysis of medieval Irish politics and society see J. E. Lydon, *The Lordship of Ireland in the Middle Ages* (Dublin, 1972). J. F. Lydon, *Ireland in the Later Middle Ages* (Dublin, 1973) is a complementary short narrative. For fuller narratives, especially of Talbot's period as lieutenant, see E. Curtis, *The History of Medieval Ireland* (1938), esp. pp. 291-3 and A. J. Otway-Ruthven, *A History of Medieval Ireland* (1968), esp. pp. 348-56.

[27] Curtis, *Medieval Ireland*, p. 292.

February 1421.[28] After the celebrations he accompanied the king on part of his progress through England, though he left the royal entourage in his native county.[29] On 1 May he was retained once more to go to France and set sail in June. He was in the army which besieged Meaux (November 1421-May 1422) but returned to England soon after its fall to deal with pressing private matters. (He had inherited the Talbot lordship in February and his first wife died in May.)[30] As one of many captains in the great king's army he had made no individual impact on the French. But in these last two years of the reign he had shared in the glory alongside his famous monarch. When not in the field fighting the king's enemies, Talbot showed a marked propensity for disturbing the king's peace. The occasion of his being sent to Ireland may have been a quarrel with the earl of Arundel in 1413. What exactly happened we do not know, but the two were in dispute over a property called Pokmore in Shropshire. The outcome was that Henry V imposed hefty recognizances on both parties and in November arrested and committed Talbot to the Tower, where he languished until he was released and appointed lieutenant of Ireland in February.[31] While in Ireland Talbot and his brother Richard, who had become archbishop of Dublin in 1417, became involved, against James Butler, earl of Ormond, the leading resident Anglo-Irish nobleman, in a vicious feud which divided the English lordship for almost thirty years and effectively undermined Talbot's military successes.[32] Back in England in 1423 a private war sprang up in the neighbourhood of Talbot's recently inherited castle of Goodrich in southern Herefordshire between himself and John Abrahall of Gylough and Eton Tregoz in the county. Abrahall was an influential local figure who had been a royal agent and M.P. for the county in 1419. He had also been receiver-general for Beatrice, Lady Talbot, widow of Gilbert, Lord Talbot, in the year immediately preceding John's succession to the estates. The origins of the dispute no doubt

---

[28]*CPR, 1422-9*, p. 261; *Calendar of Norman Rolls*, p. 373; *Vita et Gesta Henrici Quinti*, ed. T. Hearne (1727), p. 144; Hall, *Lancastr? and Yorke*, p. 103.

[29]*CCR, 1419-22*, p. 196.

[30]PRO, E101/70/5/706; 50/1; 10/110, 116; 15/111, 114; *Calendar of Fine Rolls 1413-22*, p. 422; *Rotulorum Patentium et Clausorum Cancellariae Hiberniae Calendarium*, 1, Part 1 (Dublin, 1828), p. 225.

[31]*CCR, 1413-19*, p. 24; J. H. Wylie, *The Reign of Henry V*, 1 (1914), pp. 63-4.

[32]The Ormond feud was only finally settled in the 1440s by a marriage treaty between Ormond's daughter and Talbot's son and heir. For the course of the feud see Otway-Ruthven, *Medieval Ireland*, pp. 357-61, 370-4; Pollard, pp. 120-34, and M. C. Griffith 'The Talbot-Ormond Struggle for Control of Anglo-Irish Government, 1414-47' *Irish Historical Studies* 2, pp. 376-97.

lay in this. But such were the disturbances caused in southern Herefordshire that the inhabitants appealed to parliament for remedy.[33] In the same parliament in 1423 Talbot levelled various accusations against his Irish enemy, the earl of Ormond. When Talbot entered the circle of Richard Beauchamp, earl of Warwick by marrying his eldest daughter Margaret, he became embroiled in more feuding with Joan, the lady of Abergavenny. In one brawl between the parties before January 1426 Talbot's younger brother William was killed. A year later, a band of Warwick's followers, including Sir Hugh Cokesay, Talbot's brother-in-law, sacked Joan's manor of Snitterfield.[34] Yet another quarrel blew up, this time with Lord Grey of Ruthin, over parliamentary precedence.[35] By 1427 Henry VI's councillors must have been heartily sick of Talbot and his violent temper and they were no doubt grateful when the duke of Bedford proposed to take Talbot back to France to vent his spleen on the king's enemies rather than his own countrymen. Thus it was that on 19 March 1427 Talbot and his retinue sailed from Sandwich to do battle once more.[36]

The man whose name was henceforth to become synonymous with the defence of the English possessions in France was almost forty years old. He was a high ranking and life-long loyal servant of the house of Lancaster. Although an unruly subject, never in his life had there been, or was there to be, a breath of treason whispered about his name. He had been a companion in arms of Henry V since early manhood and had shared in the heady triumphs of that monarch's reign. And even though he had as yet fought in France for only two years, he was soon to enjoy a reputation as a fearless and fearsome fighter. In fact, much of his early experience in Wales and Ireland had equipped him for just the sort of warfare to which he was to dedicate the rest of his life.

---

[33] *Rotuli Parliamentorum*, 4, p. 254a; Salop. R. O., BP 75/1420-21; J. C. Wedgwood, *History of Parliament — Biographies of the Members of the House of Commons 1439-1509* (1936), p. 1.

[34] *CCR, 1422-9,* pp 317-18; *CPR, 1422-9,* p. 423.

[35] *Rotuli Parliamentorum*, 4, p. 312a.

[36] It is sometimes repeated, on the strength of the articles in the *Dictionary of National Biography* and *CP*, that Talbot fought at Verneuil on 17 August 1424 (see *e.g. English Suits before the Parlement of Paris, 1420-1436*, ed. Armstrong and Allmand, Camden Fourth Series 26, 1982, p.307). There is, however, no strictly contemporary evidence to support this. In all likelihood Talbot was in England, for on 1 September, being about to go to Ireland, he nominated his attorneys for his forthcoming absence (*CPR, 1422-9*, p.332; Pollard, p.143).

2

THE REGENT'S LIEUTENANT:
JOHN TALBOT AT WAR, 1427-36

When Talbot landed in France in the spring of 1427, the English still held the initiative in the war. Bedford's strategy since the victory at Verneuil in 1424 had been to continue the methodical conquest of France, advancing southwards on a broad front between the territories of his allies, the dukes of Brittany and Burgundy, by the steady reduction of land and strongholds. Although English progress had been diverted by Gloucester's adventure in Hainault (1424-25) and the defection of Brittany (1424-27), in the west the conquest of Maine had almost been completed. Bedford was planning to advance his flank in the east by the capture of Montargis before launching an attack on the valley of the Loire. But in March 1427 the implementation of these plans was being delayed by war with Brittany.[1] The Bretons had captured Pontorson in January and the earl of Warwick was endeavouring to recover it. Talbot and his reinforcements were immediately sent to assist the earl. On 8 May the Bretons surrendered and Warwick and Talbot became the new English captains.[2] In June peace was made with Brittany and the way was clear for the attack on Montargis. A well equipped army, which included Talbot's company, set siege. But the operation ended in failure and humiliation on 5 September, when Dunois and La Hire relieved the town and forced the English to withdraw.[3] On the same day Sir John Fastolf was surprised at Ambrières in northern Maine, and, encouraged by this French success, several places in the county rose.[4] Faced by this unexpected crisis, Bedford now sent Talbot to replace Fastolf in command of the English troops in Maine.

Talbot's appointment as governor of Maine and Anjou, the formal title he enjoyed as Bedford's lieutenant in the counties, was his first general command in the French wars.[5] It is as well to recall that he

---

[1] For the course of the war and diplomacy between 1424 and 1427 see A.H. Burne, *The Agincourt War* (1956), pp. 216-21; and M. H. Keen, *England in the Later Middle Ages* (1973) pp. 381-3.

[2] E. Cosneau, *Le Connétable Richemont* (Paris, 1886) p. 137.

[3] Gruel, p. 59; Monstrelet, 4, pp. 271-5; Amicie de Villaret, *Campagnes des Anglais dans l'Orléanais, la Beauce Chartraine et le Gâtinais, 1421-28* (Orléans, 1893), pp. 28-39.

[4] Cosneau, *Richemont,* p. 147; E. C. Williams, *My Lord of Bedford* (1963) p. 155.

[5] E. Hall, *The Union of the Noble and Illustre Fameilies of Lancastre and Yorke* (1809), p. 141. B. J. H. Rowe, 'A Contemporary Account of the Hundred Years War',

was almost forty years old and still virtually unknown to his French enemies as a military commander. The position in Maine was critical, for the revolt of the county threatened to undermine Bedford's general strategy. Not all of the county had in fact been conquered — a pocket around Laval in the west had never been taken. Now La Ferté Bernard and neighbouring places in the east had thrown out the English and Le Mans itself was full of treason.[6] Talbot based himself at Alençon and spent the winter of 1427-28 preparing for a spring counter-offensive. This was launched in March 1428, when, as Edward Hall wrote, he 'slewe men and destroyed castles and brent townes and in conclusion suddenly took the towne of Laval'. Having completed this punitive raid which culminated in the conquest of the western corner of the county, Talbot withdrew again to Alençon. On 25 May he was still there when news reached him that Le Mans had been taken by a French army under the commander of La Hire and that the English garrison was bottled up in the castle. Talbot immediately dashed to the rescue and early in the morning of 27 May took the French completely by surprise in a dawn assault. A terrible vengeance was then exacted on townsmen and churchmen who had collaborated with the enemy.[7] This French attack having been so decisively repulsed, Talbot was now able to retake La Ferté Bernard and its neighbouring places without opposition. By the beginning of June 1428 Maine was more securely under English control than ever before.

By his victories in Maine Talbot established himself as a leading military commander. The manner of his operations — the punitive raid, the surprise assaults on both Laval and Le Mans, and the retribution brought on the collaborators at Le Mans (the hallmarks of his style of warfare throughout his life) – made him notorious in France almost overnight. His success was appreciated too by Bedford, who granted him the lordship of Heugeville as well as lands confiscated from Robert Stafford who had lost La Ferté Bernard to the French.[8] Talbot was now a natural choice for senior command in

EHR 41 (1926), 504-13, draws attention to details in Hall not to be found elsewhere for the years 1415-29, which were taken, she suggests, from a private history written for Sir John Fastolf. Hall's account of these years thus has the value of a contemporary chronicle.

[6] For the loss of La Ferté Bernard see R. Charles, L'invasion anglaise dans le Maine de 1417 à 1428 (Mamers, 1889), pp. 57-8; reprinted from Revue historique et archéologique du Maine, 25.

[7] BL, Add Ch 579; Hall, Lancastre and Yorke, p. 141; Bourgeois, pp. 225-6.

[8] AN, D Len 4/277; JJ 174/108.

the major offensive planned for the summer of 1428. Accordingly, he was called back to Paris where he joined in a council of war with Bedford and the earl of Salisbury, who had recently arrived from England with reinforcements. At first it was decided to make Angers and the reduction of Anjou the objectives. Presumably Talbot himself, as Bedford's lieutenant for the county, favoured this plan. But in the event, Salisbury, who was taking the command in the field, carried out his alternative and more ambitious plan of attacking Orléans.[9] Although it offended chivalric sensibilities by making war on the lands of a prisoner, this objective made greater strategic sense in that it took the war more directly towards the Dauphin's own base. The advance began in July and it is to be assumed that Talbot was in the army whose triumphant march to the Loire culminated in the capture of bridgeheads at Beaugency, Meung and Jargeau.[10] It does not appear, however, that he was with the army when it began the assault on Orléans itself on 7 October or was there when operations were suspended as a result of Salisbury's fatal shooting on 24 October.[11]

The decision to renew operations and lay siege to Orléans seems to have been made towards the end of November. On 26 November Talbot and Lord Scales and their companies were ordered by Bedford to move up from Chartres to Meung. There they joined the earl of Suffolk, with whom they were henceforward associated in command of the army.[12] By 1 December the English were once again encamped before Orléans, now preparing for a winter siege. It is likely that during the winter of 1428-29 the English commanders at Orléans intended to do no more than make a start on the building of siege works, keep a watch on the city, and endeavour to intercept supplies and reinforcements. The total allied strength before the walls, including 1,500 Burgundians, was hardly more than 5,000.[13] Unless and until substantial reinforcements could be brought up, only a

[9]L. Jarry, *Le Compte de l'armée anglaise au siege d'Orléans, 1428-1429* (Orléans, 1892), pp. 77-8.

[10]Waurin, 3, pp. 240-1.

[11]R. R. Sharpe, *London and the Kingdom* 3 (1895), pp. 370-1; Williams, *Bedford*, p. 161; Burne, *Agincourt War*, pp. 226-31.

[12]BN, MS Fr 26050/997-8; BL, Add Ch 1434.

[13]Estimates of the size of the English army at the beginning of the siege vary. Jarry (*Compte*, pp. 60-63), suggested a maximum of 3,263 combatants. The most recent estimate, that of P. Contamine ('Les Armées française et anglaise a l'époque de Jeanne d'Arc', *Revue Soc. Sav. Hte. Normandie, Lettres et Sciences Humaines* 57 (1970), 16) is 3,800 men. R. Boucher de Molandon (*L'armée anglaise vaincue par Jeanne d'Arc sous les murs d'Orléans* (Orléans, 1892), pp. 134-9) suggested a total between these two.

partial blockade could be attempted. A fortified base was established at Saint-Laurent, on the north bank of the Loire to the west of the city, and work was begun on the building of a chain of forts. On the south bank of the river the English still maintained a garrison in Les Tourelles at the end of the bridge into the city. There was little action during the first three months of 1429. The only important engagement, the battle of the Herrings on 12 February, which saw the defeat of a relieving French army by Sir John Fastolf, did not involve the besiegers. In April, while the English were still awaiting reinforcements, two events took place which transformed the situation. On 17 April, following Bedford's refusal to put the city in their duke's hands as a neutral party, the Burgundian troops withdrew. And on 28 April Joan of Arc arrived with the first convoy of French supplies for the city. Two days later she returned with more supplies and entered Orléans. With her arrival the French were galvanized into action. On 3 May French reinforcements arrived and they were immediately employed to attack and destroy the isolated English fort at Saint-Loup to the east of Orléans. Three days later the French garrison launched an assault across the bridge on the English positions at the southern end. After two days of fierce fighting they were carried. On the following day, 8 May, the English commanders on the north bank, having drawn up their army in battle array before the city walls, withdrew in good order and abandoned the siege. Such is the bare record of the relief of Orléans.[14]

Because of the intervention of Joan of Arc, the delivery of Orléans has always had an aura of the miraculous. That she transformed the spirit, morale and determination of the French cannot be denied. But from the English point of view, the failure before Orléans has no need of supernatural explanation. The army attempting to take the city was too small and inadequately equipped to mount an effective blockade. The English forces in France were already seriously stretched. It was at Orléans that for the first time detachments drawn from the garrison retinues were deployed in the field on a large scale.[15] After Salisbury's death it was a major effort even to mount a partial blockade. For success the English depended on the French lacking the will to resist. That will was restored by Joan of Arc. Once the French garrison was relieved and counter-attacked early in May 1429, the English commanders had no choice but to

---

[14] The fullest narratives of the siege in English are to be found in Burne, *Agincourt War*, pp. 233-42 and, from the point of view of Talbot's participation, in R. Brill, 'An English Captain of the Hundred Years War: John, lord Talbot, *c.* 1388-1444' (unpublished Princeton University PhD thesis, 1966), pp. 92-155.

[15] Jarry, *Compte*, pp. 59-60, 171-93.

break off the siege. Little is known of Talbot's own actions during the siege. The fact that he was one of three men sharing the command was perhaps contributory to the failure. Talbot seems to have been the more active of the three. It was he who attempted, too late, to come to the defence of the fort at Saint-Loup on 3 May. And it was he who was known to Joan of Arc and to whom she addressed her summons to the English to abandon the siege. But, with his fellow commanders, he did nothing on 6-7 May to help his compatriots under attack in Les Tourelles. In reality there was little they could do.[16] The decision the commanders took to withdraw in good order ready to fight another day had much to commend it. The real turning-point came with the destruction of their army a month later.

The choice facing the English commanders in May 1429 was whether to keep their army together and to retire north ready to face any French advance, or to divide and seek to hold the remaining bridgeheads on the Loire at Beaugency, Meung and Jargeau. Fatally, they chose the latter.[17] The decision shows, perhaps understandably, that they had no awareness of the extent to which French morale had been revived by Joan of Arc. They clearly did not expect the French to follow up their success at Orléans speedily or vigorously, for by so dividing their forces they left themselves open to piecemeal attack. But, under Joan of Arc's inspiration, the French army soon appeared before Jargeau. On 12 June the town fell to a determined assault and Suffolk was captured. The French immediately turned back to attack Beaugency and Meung, which were being held by Talbot and Scales. On 15 June they appeared before Meung and, having taken the bridge, pressed on to Beaugency.

Talbot and Scales, meanwhile, had hurriedly marched north with a small force to meet Sir John Fastolf and a relieving army at Janville (16 June). According to Jean Waurin, who was with Fastolf, a heated argument took place between Talbot and Fastolf over what to do next. The more cautious Fastolf advocated withdrawal; Talbot insisted that they advance to the relief of Beaugency. On the morning of 17 June the army duly marched down to the Loire, to find a French army drawn up in battle array two miles before Beaugency. With insufficient force to take up this challenge, Talbot at last agreed that nothing more

---

[16]Both Burne, (*Agincourt War*, pp. 295-6) and Brill ('English Captain', pp. 149-53), go to some lengths to explain away Talbot's inaction during the closing days of the siege. Burne concludes that he can be 'absolved of bad leadership on that fatal May 7, 1429'. Brill goes one step further and argues that by remaining inactive Talbot showed great strategic and tactical insight.

[17]Burne, *Agincourt War*, p. 250.

could be done to save the bridgeheads and consented to retreat. But it was too late. At midday on 18 June they were resting near the village of Patay (Talbot's men had marched all but 100 miles in two days) when the French in hot pursuit came upon them. Talbot and Scales, who were holding the rearguard, had little time to form a defensive line and were overwhelmed by the first French cavalry charge. They were both captured by the archers of Poton de Xaintrailles — Talbot, according to Hall, being 'sore wounded in the back'. Fastolf with the van managed to fight his way out of the debâcle.[18] The destruction of the army which had laid siege to Orléans was thus completed and the road to Paris lay open to the victorious French. The week of 12-18 June saw the turning point in the war and the seizing of the initiative by the French. Talbot and the English were to pay dearly for his failure to appreciate that their enemies had been transformed by Joan of Arc.

Talbot was held prisoner from 1429 to 1433. The period of captivity is shrouded in mystery; it is not known where he was held, what arrangements were made for his maintenance, or even in detail how negotiations were conducted for his release. At first there was much activity on the English side to raise what was considered to be the 'unreasonable and importable raunceon' demanded by Poton de Xaintrailles. In response to a petition in parliament in 1429, the council agreed to help by requesting Bedford to set aside the royal prisoner, the sire de Barbazan, in free exchange for Talbot.[19] Negotiations to this end were cut short on 24 January 1430 when Barbazan was rescued by the French from Château Gaillard.[20] After this set-back efforts to help Talbot appear to have flagged. In March 1431, not long after the beginning of Joan of Arc's trial, Charles VII exercised his right to acquire Talbot as a prisoner of note, settling with Poton de Xaintrailles for 12,500 *reaulx* (£2,100 sterling).[21] It may be that Charles and his advisers were contemplating an exchange between Talbot and Joan, which in the event was never proposed. The outcome was that Talbot was King Charles's prisoner

---

[18] For the campaigns which culminated at Patay see Waurin, 3, pp. 288-304; Gruel, p. 198; and Hall, *Lancastre and Yorke*, p. 150. Burne, *Agincourt War*, pp. 251-60 and Brill 'English Captain', pp. 171-95, again provide the most detailed narratives in English.

[19] *Rotuli Parliamentorum,* 5, p. 338b. For other contributions made towards the payment of Talbot's ransom see below pp. 113-4.

[20] J. H. Ramsay, *Lancaster and York*, 1 (Oxford, 1892), p. 414. Barbazan had been a prisoner since the fall of Melun in 1420.

[21] AN, Chartrier de Thouars, 1 AP 175/27; M. H. Keen, *The Laws of War in the Late Middle Ages* (1965), pp. 146-7. I am grateful to Mr Roger Little for making available to me his transcript of the original document and for advising me on its significance.

when Xaintrailles himself was captured by the earl of Warwick at Savignies in August 1431. Now that Xaintrailles was a prisoner of his father-in-law, Talbot's fortunes changed. During the next eighteen months negotiations took place between the various parties which led to Talbot's release in the spring of 1433. Some kind of exchange involving Xaintrailles took place, for safe-conducts were issued on 28 May 1432 and 12 February 1433 enabling servants of Xaintrailles to visit English territories to pursue negotiations concerning the delivery of both Talbot and their master.[22] What was agreed is not known, but in the spring of 1433 Talbot was released, to be followed in July by Xaintrailles.[23] Talbot returned briefly to England where he was summoned to parliament on 24 May, but by 16 July he had agreed to return to the wars in France.[24]

The military situation in France had changed during the four years of Talbot's captivity. Whereas in 1428 the English had been planning to open the way to King Charles's capital at Bourges, now, in 1433, they were having to concentrate on the defence of their own capital at Paris. In the immediate aftermath of Patay many places to the south, east and north of Paris had fallen and in September 1429 the city itself could well have been taken. Normandy too had been invaded and Verneuil, Louviers and Château Gaillard had been lost for a time. After the capture of Joan of Arc in 1431 English fortunes had begun to revive and the boundaries of Normandy had been secured. But hopes of further recovery had been dashed in 1432 with the loss of Chartres and Bedford's failure to retake Lagny, twenty miles east of Paris on the Marne.[25] The capital remained threatened on three sides and was still vulnerable to a determined French offensive.

Talbot was not immediately involved in the defence of Paris, for shortly after landing in France he was sent to the assistance of the duke of Burgundy. Charles VII had endeavoured to detach Burgundy from the English alliance in 1429, but Duke Philip, induced by a flow of favours from Bedford, had resisted. Nevertheless, his commitment to the English alliance was noticeably waning and he ruthlessly pursued his own ends, entering truces or making war with Charles as it suited him.[26] In 1433 he had undertaken to recover various places on

[22]*Reports of the Deputy Keeper of the Public Records* 48 (1887), pp. 286, 290.

[23]*Ibid.*, p. 293.

[24]*CCR, 1429-35*, p. 244; *Proceedings and Ordinances of the Privy Council of England*, ed. N. H. Nicolas, 4 (1836), p. 167.

[25]For the course of the war between 1429 and 1433 see Burne, *Agincourt War*, pp. 261-73; Keen, *Later Middle Ages*, pp. 387-8; Williams, *Bedford*, pp. 177-213.

[26]R. Vaughan, *Philip the Good: the Apogee of Burgundy* (1970), pp 16-28.

the northern borders of the duchy lost to French attacks in 1431. In the vital cause of Anglo-Burgundian friendship, Bedford responded to requests for help in August by despatching Talbot from Paris to the siege of Pacy. After the fall of Pacy on 1 September, Talbot continued to campaign with Burgundy, assisting him to take Avallon, Cravant, Mailly and Pierre-Perthuis.[27] Having completed this successful campaign, in November Talbot returned once more to England. This was only a brief visit. Early in 1434 he was retained again by the crown for service in France, and on 10 February orders were issued for the muster of his retinue on 11 March.[28]

On his return to France Talbot was quickly promoted to high command. By 16 May 1434, when he sealed indentures as captain of Neufchâtel and Gisors, he had succeeded Lord Willoughby as lieutenant-general of the Île de France, to which was added the lieutenancy-general of the land between the rivers Seine, Oise, Somme and the sea by 20 June.[29] He thus assumed the field command for the entire eastern and northern front for the defence of Paris and Normandy. Talbot was now ranked with the earl of Arundel, who had command of the forces in the field to the west of the Seine. On landing in Normandy Talbot marched up to Paris, only pausing to reduce the minor fortress of Jouy between Gisors and Beauvais.[30] For the next eighteen months he made Paris his headquarters and was the English commander principally responsible for the defence of the city and its environs. His first main task was to clear the French from the lower valley of the Oise where Amadeo de Vignolles, the brother of La Hire, had succeeded earlier in the year in occupying and refortifying Beaumont, so threatening communications between Paris and Rouen. With the Burgundian L'Isle-Adam and an Anglo-Burgundian army in mid-May he moved against Beaumont, which was immediately abandoned. Vignolles retreated to Creil, pursued by Talbot. There he was killed in the ensuing siege and on 20 June the town surrendered.[31] According to the 'Bourgeois of Paris', Talbot returned to Paris after this success, but having received reinforcements from England he was soon out in the field again.[32] His strengthened army

[27]Monstrelet, 5, pp. 62-9; A. Bossuat, *Perrinet Gressart et François de Surienne, agents de l'Angleterre* (Paris, 1936), pp. 208-9; Ramsay, *Lancaster and York*, 1, pp. 449-50; Vaughan, *Philip the Good*, p. 66.

[28]PRO, E404/50/159; *CPR, 1429-36*, p. 353;

[29]BN, PO 2787, Talbot 9; AN, JJ 75/313; Stevenson, *Wars*, 2, p. 564.

[30]Monstrelet, 5, p. 91.

[31]*Ibid.*

[32]Bourgeois, p. 299; *CPR, 1429-36*, p. 359. On 18 June Talbot was commissioned to muster these troops when they came into his presence.

proceeded to clear the French from Pont-Sainte-Maxence, Crépy-en-Valois and Clermont before 24 August, on which date, in recognition of his achievement, Bedford created Talbot count of Clermont. The summer's operations were brought to an end by a raid up to the walls of Beauvais.[33] Thus, a campaign which began with the objective of clearing the lower Oise valley ended with the northern approaches to Paris more securely in English hands.[34]

In spite of the successes of 1434 the English hold on Paris was still tenuous. Even while Talbot had been besieging Creil, French companies had been ravaging the Île de France right up to the city gates.[35] It was important therefore that during 1435 Talbot should maintain a vigilant defence of the area. This was not to be. In February he may have been drawn away to help Arundel crush a rising of the peasantry in Caen.[36] He presumably returned to the Île de France thereafter, but in May he was, it appears, sent back to England yet again to supervise the raising of reinforcements. The evidence for Talbot's movements during the summer months of 1435 is exceptionally meagre. There is, however, no doubt that on 8 June he was retained at Westminster to serve in France with a retinue of twenty men-at-arms and 600 archers for half a year; that on the same day fourteen other captains were likewise retained; and that units of this force, which numbered over 2,500 men, were mustered on their way to France in June and July.[37] During Talbot's absence, and taking

[33]Bourgeois, p. 299; Monstrelet, 5, pp. 91-2; AN, JJ 175/67/312,313.

[34]R. Brill ('The English Preparations before the Treaty of Arras', *Studies in Medieval and Renaissance History* 7 (1970) 243-5) argues that the campaign was part of a 'higher plan' to disrupt all French offensives in that area for years to come. I can find no evidence for the kind of far-sighted strategic planning which he envisages and am convinced that the campaign had only the limited objective of making communication between Paris and Rouen more secure. Nor is it true, as Dr Brill maintains, that the success of the campaign guaranteed English control over the Vexins until 1441. Pontoise was lost early in 1436, and although regained in 1437, it is clear that for the next four years the English hold on the French Vexin was tenuous to say the least and that Creil remained an isolated outpost from 1436 until its loss in 1441. See below pp. 23, 44-5, 48-51, 54-8.

[35]Bourgeois, p. 299.

[36]C. L. Kingsford, *Chronicles of London* (Oxford, 1905), p. 137.

[37]PRO, E404/51/320, 306-19; *CPR, 1429-36*, pp. 475, 476. The indenture of 8 June has not survived, but it was seen by Dugdale (*Baronage*, 1, 329) and is copied in BL, Stowe MS 440, f 60ᵛ where it is also noted that musters were to be held at Dover on 16 July (I am grateful to Miss Curry for this information). However, another indenture has survived; one made with Bedford at Rouen on 26 March 1435 by which Talbot was retained to serve for six months in France with his personal retinue of twenty men-at-arms and sixty archers (BN, MS Fr 26059/2495). It was probably to honour the terms of this contract that Talbot retained, on a monthly basis, an auxiliary retinue to continue to serve in France while he was in England. This retinue

advantage also of the further disruption to the English defences caused by the defeat and death of Arundel at Gerberoy, on the night of 31 May - 1 June the captains of Melun and Lagny succeeded in capturing Saint-Denis, from which they harassed the environs of Paris at will. It was probably not until after Talbot's return with his reinforcements late in July that any attempt to recover Saint-Denis was possible. Even then it appears that Talbot, having been joined by Lords Scales and Willoughby, was required first to go to the relief of Orville, near Louviers, so that Saint-Denis was not invested until the last week of August. It was finally retaken on 4 October.[38]

By 4 October, however, two events had taken place which decisively altered the course of the war: Bedford died on 14 September, and Burgundy and Charles VII sealed the treaty of Arras on 21 September. The death of Bedford not only robbed the English of a capable and respected leader, but also undermined English morale and French acceptance of their régime at a critical moment. Of greater long-term significance was the treaty of Arras. The success enjoyed by Henry V and Bedford had depended to a large measure on the fact that France itself was torn by civil war. The dual monarchy, it can be argued, would not have come into being but for the assassination of John the Fearless at Montereau and the blood feud between Burgundy and Armagnac. Burgundy had been the buttress of the house of Lancaster in France. The removal of that buttress in 1435 led ultimately to the collapse of the main structure. The diplomatic revolution of 1435 spelt the end of English hopes in France.

The immediate impact of the double blow of September 1435 was that not only did the English finally lose control of Paris but that they also came perilously near to losing upper Normandy. In the autumn of 1435 a French onslaught on Normandy as well as Paris was anticipated and for this reason, after the reduction of Saint-Denis, Talbot, Scales and Willoughby withdrew to Rouen.[39] However, the attack came from an unexpected quarter and by unexpected means. The Constable Richemont, in command of the French royal army, was concentrating his effort on Paris, but he also encouraged the free companies who had been operating against Burgundy to turn their attention to Normandy. On 29 October Pierre de Rieux, Charles de

was mustered on 12 May, 20 June and 20 July, in May at Paris, presumably while under the command of his lieutenant (BN, MS Fr 25772/944, 954, 963). See also below p. 70.

[38] Bourgeois, pp. 305-8; Monstrelet, 5, pp. 125-7. See also Brill, 'An English Captain', pp. 278-85 for a detailed reconstruction of the event.

[39] G du Fresne de Beaucourt, *Histoire de Charles VII*, 3, pp. 5-6; BL, Add Ch 1460.

Maretz and others surprised and seized Dieppe.[40] In upper Normandy, Richemont no doubt knew, there was simmering popular unrest. As the author of MS Cleopatra CIV commented, 'the lond whas at that tyme ful of treson aftyr the death of the Duke of Bedford'.[41] De Rieux and his agents from Dieppe stirred up the peasantry of the pays de Caux and in mid-December they erupted in rebellion. Forming themselves into an army under Le Charuryer, and assisted by the French companies, they overran the district. In the week following Christmas Eve they took Fécamp, Valmont, Tancarville, Lillebonne, Montivilliers and Harfleur, as well as a host of lesser places. Richemont promptly sent in more French companies to reinforce them and garrison the captured places. By the beginning of 1436 there were some 2-3,000 French troops lodged in the pays de Caux as well as a peasant army on the rampage.[42] Only Caudebec remained in English hands and Rouen itself was directly threatened. The English council and commanders in Rouen were in a state of near panic. They had already sent ambassadors to England requesting urgent assistance, but winter storms seem to have cut Rouen off from London. Hearing no news, they began to wonder whether the crown was preparing to abandon Normandy north of the Seine. For a while they seemed completely paralysed. As the author of Cleopatra CIV wrote succinctly, 'men wist not what to do'.[43]

Only in the new year, when the peasant army moved on Caudebec, did the English take any action. Talbot, it appears, now took over the captaincy of Rouen and Caudebec and sent reliable reinforcements under his lieutenant, Fulk Eyton, downstream to Caudebec.[44] When the peasant army moved against the town the new garrison sallied forth and dispersed it.[45] Talbot thereupon followed up the success with two sorties from Rouen, one setting out on 4 January, the other

---

[40] Monstrelet, 5, p. 201; Waurin, 4, p. 104; Gruel, p. 106.

[41] Kingsford, *Chronicles*, p. 141. This London chronicler is an important source for the events in France between 1434 and 1443, especially 1436, about which he seems to have had first-hand information. His reliability is indicated by his statement that in January 1436 Nicholas Burdet was made Lieutenant of Rouen under Lord Talbot, which is confirmed by administrative records (e.g. BN, MS Fr 25773/1136). Basin, 1, p. 225, also commented on the readiness of the whole of upper Normandy to rise against the English.

[42] Monstrelet, 5, pp. 201-3; Waurin, 4, pp. 105-10; Gruel, pp. 106-8.

[43] Stevenson, *Wars*, p. 424ff; Kingsford, *Chronicles*, p. 140.

[44] Talbot's garrison of over 400 men in Caudebec under Eyton was mustered there on 4 January, although his captaincy did not officially begin until 14 January (BL, Add Ch 439). It contained several men associated with Talbot's personal retinue (BN, MS Fr 25772/1050).

[45] Basin, 1, p. 217.

on 10 January, in which he scattered the peasantry and set about the devastation of town and country in reprisal. The district immediately surrounding Rouen was stripped of provisions and all the cattle and sheep that could be found were driven into Caudebec and Rouen. The town of Lillebonne was sacked.[46] Thus, with the utmost brutality, the peasantry was cowed and the hinterland of Rouen secured against a future attack. After this show of strength the French troops retired to their newly captured places. During January, Talbot's garrison in Rouen was reinforced by hastily recruited *creus* in readiness for the next French move.[47] It came at the end of the month when an attempt to surprise the city, relying on help from inside, was made by a small force of some 1,000 men under the command of La Hire and Xaintrailles. When they arrived before Rouen they found the city on its guard and so withdrew to the village of Ry, ten miles to the east, where they encamped. At dawn on 2 February the garrison of Rouen, probably led by Scales, issued out, surprised and totally routed the French. La Hire and Xaintrailles escaped, but several French captains were taken prisoner and a great number of horses and most of the baggage were seized. The immediate threat to Rouen was over.[48]

During February the centre of action shifted to Paris. Saint-Germain-en-Laye, controlling the route south of the river from Rouen to Paris, had fallen in December 1435. On 20 February Pontoise, which commanded the northern road, fell when the population rose against the English.[49] At the same time, the first reinforcements under Sir Henry Norbury with nearly 1,000 troops at last landed from England. Some troops, including part of Talbot's own personal

---

[46]Basin, 1, pp. 217-9; Kingsford, *Chronicles*, p. 140.

[47]*Ibid.*; BN, MS Fr 25772/1052-57. These companies were mustered at the end of the month. At the same time, Talbot's garrison at Château Gaillard was increased from thirty-five to sixty-five men and the garrison at Gisors reinforced with one hundred men under Sir Thomas Hoo (BL, Add Chs 6875, 94; BN MS Fr25772/1051, 2).

[48]There is considerable confusion in the sources over this action. Monstrelet recounts the story no fewer than three times as taking place on different dates in 1436 and 1437 (5, pp. 204-5, 281-2, 297-8). Waurin only tells it twice — set once in January 1436, once in January 1437 (4 pp. 112-14, 216-19). Although there are slight variations in detail, it is clear that both accounts refer to the same event. Brill ('An English Captain', pp. 311-14), ignores the repetitions and confidently places the action in January 1437. The reliable author of Cleopatra C. IV, however, offers an independent account of the same action which clearly places it on Candlemass 1436 and I have therefore followed this date (Kingsford, *Chronicles*, p. 140). The accounts of who actually led the English attack also differ. Monstrelet/Waurin give Kyriell in the first report; Talbot, Scales and Kyriell in the second. Cleopatra C. IV reports that Scales alone 'hadde a full fayre distresse' at Ry and that he returned to Rouen with a good crop of prisoners.

[49]Chartier, 1, pp. 217-18.

retinue, perhaps escorting Louis of Luxembourg, could thus be sent to the threatened capital.[50] But after the fall of Pontoise it was virtually cut off. Richemont made the town his base for the siege, which was begun in March. Early in April the English, possibly Talbot himself, were at Mantes, collecting a convoy of supplies to send into Paris, but this was unable to penetrate the French lines. On 13 April the city fell. On 17 April the English garrison, which had retired to the Bastille, treated to surrender and marched back to Rouen.[51] With Paris in his hands, Richemont was now free to concentrate on Normandy. But in fact no very decisive action was mounted. La Hire and Xaintrailles, having recovered from their discomforture of three months previously, surprised and took Gisors early in May. The garrison was shut up in the castle and sent to Rouen for help. Talbot dashed to the rescue on 7 May before Richemont had sent up reinforcements. Surprised once again, La Hire and Xaintrailles fled once more in confusion.[52] Shortly after this action, Richemont, having heard from sympathisers in Rouen, planned another attempt on the city. He gathered an army at Gerberoy, including contingents from the French forces in the pays de Caux, but he abandoned the operation on hearing more news from the city. Certainly the English there were now fully on their guard. Talbot had not ceased to reinforce the city so that during the summer there were over a thousand troops defending it. Not being able to mount a full siege, Richemont took his forces to the now isolated English outpost of Creil, upstream from Pontoise. But the siege there was abandoned at the end of June, as the Constable's attention was drawn to the operations around Calais.[53] Meanwhile, the duke of York and a powerful army of 5,000 men had at last landed in Normandy.[54] The emergency was finally over. There is no doubt that if the French had been able to mount a concerted campaign against eastern Normandy and Rouen in the early months of 1436 they would have recovered them. As it was, their sporadic and unco-ordinated thrusts nevertheless came near to success. For a while the whole English command had been paralysed. But once Talbot and Scales recovered their nerve,

[50]*CPR, 1429-36*, p. 525; Kingsford, *Chronicles*, p. 140; AN, K 64/1/32, 34; 10/15. Following the arrival of these reinforcements, Scales went to the south-west borders of the duchy. He was at Vire early in March dealing with a peasant rising (*Chronique du Mont St Michel*, 2, p. 76).

[51]Gruel, p. 113; Basin, 1, pp. 227-9; Bourgeois, pp. 311-18; Chartier, 1 pp. 220-8.

[52]Monstrelet, 5, p. 231; Gruel, p. 124.

[53]Gruel, pp. 124-6. For musters of the many companies in Rouen during the summer see BN, MS Fr 26061/1814, 2871, 2869, 2897; 26062/3092; Clair 201/8445/47; PO, Talbot, 15, 17, 18; BL, Add Ch 7892.

[54]Kingsford, *Chronicles*, p. 141; R.A. Griffiths, *The Reign of King Henry VI* (1981), p. 201.

their speed of action in dealing with these thrusts and their vigilance in the defence of Rouen saved the day.

Between the autumn of 1435 and the spring of 1436 the position of the English in France had been transformed. They had been on the defensive since 1429 and had lost ground. But until 1435 they had continued to entertain the hope that they would still be able to give substance to Henry VI's possession of the crown of France. And until that year the duchy of Normandy, the heart of the English conquests in France, had been given effective protection by Maine, Paris and, above all, by the alliance with Burgundy. The Burgundian defection and the loss of Paris not only made the implementation of the dual monarchy inconceivable, but also left Normandy, especially eastern Normandy, desperately vunerable to French attacks. The new circumstances led to a complete re-appraisal of English diplomatic and military objectives. The retention of Normandy rather than the claim to the whole kingdom of France was now to become the central aim of the English war effort. The war was entering a new phase in which Talbot was to acquire a prominence he had hitherto not enjoyed.

3

LANCASTRIAN NORMANDY AND THE
ORGANIZATION OF ITS DEFENCE AFTER 1435

Henry V, whose ambitions and aims grew in step with his success in arms, had been prepared, before the treaty of Troyes, to settle for the possession of Normandy in full sovereignty. On his deathbed he is reported to have instructed his councillors not to make peace unless the French were prepared at the very least to cede Normandy to his son.[1] At Arras this had been put forward as a sop to the French. It is not clear, however, whether in 1435 the English were thereby implying that they would surrender the claim to the throne. In a memorandum presented to Philip of Burgundy in the autumn of 1436, Hue de Lannoy commented that it was unlikely that a general peace could be achieved without the transfer of Normandy to the king of England.[2] There remained in England a vociferous party led by Gloucester which insisted long after Arras on nothing but all-out victory. But after 1437, the peace party, led by Cardinal Beaufort and encouraged perhaps by the young king who was beginning to assert himself, cautiously moved to a more flexible position. During the abortive negotiations in 1439, the culmination of two years of diplomacy, the English began with an uncompromising insistence on full rights to the kingdom of France. Eventually, in reply to a French offer of a truce in which Henry VI kept Normandy but abandoned the claim to the throne and performed homage for his French possessions, Beaufort, the chief negotiator, responded with the proposal that in the cause of peace England would be satisfied with the possession of Normandy in full sovereignty. The title to the throne would not be surrendered, but the English would be prepared to divide possession of the kingdom of France.[3] At this point negotiations collapsed. In the following year Beaufort, in the face of fierce opposition from Gloucester, took the gamble of releasing the duke of Orléans,

[1] Monstrelet, 4, p.110; J. J. N. Palmer, 'The War Aims of the Protagonists and tne Negotiations for Peace', in *The Hundred Years' War*, ed. K. A. Fowler, (1971), pp. 69-71.

[2] R. Vaughan, *Philip the Good* (1970), p. 105.

[3] Palmer, 'War Aims', p.71; C. T. Allmand, 'The Anglo-French Negotiations, 1439', *BIHR* 40 (1967), esp. p. 27; and 'Anglo-French Negotiations of 1439', *Camden Miscellany* 24 (1972). Although the principal negotiations were a failure, the English did succeed in making a truce with Burgundy, for which see R. Vaughan, *Philip the Good* (1970), pp. 107-10.

England's most valuable prisoner, in the cause of promoting a division of France. The move failed. Thereafter, at the negotiations of Tours in 1444 and London in 1445, the possession of Normandy (as well as of Gascony) in a divided France remained the basic English demand. In the event it was as unrealistic as the demand for the possession of all France. For while the least that the Lancastrians would settle for was a compromise in which they took a share of the kingdom, the most that the Valois would offer was, as has recently been said, a feudal settlement which preserved its integrity.[4] There was no bridging this gap.

If with hindsight one can see that even the Beaufort peace plan was doomed to failure, one must not therefore belittle its significance. It seemed to represent a feasible objective, which held out the prospect of an honourable end to the war, and would probably have been accepted by all but the most diehard of 'hawks'. Certainly there is no evidence to suggest that Talbot was opposed to it. But for it to have any chance of success the English had to be negotiating from a position of strength. It was absolutely vital that they should show a strong military hand and preserve the integrity of the Lancastrian duchy of Normandy. Talbot played a crucial role in the years leading to the truce of Tours in 1444 in ensuring that these military objectives were met. He was, without doubt, the most important of the English commanders in the field and the successful retention of Normandy for a further fifteen years after the treaty of Arras owed much to him. Before recounting what happened on the field of battle, however, it is necessary to put Talbot's role in perspective by assessing the strength of the opposition, the nature of the English presence in Normandy, the size and organization of the English army in the duchy and Talbot's place in the structure of command.

It must be borne in mind that English success in retaining Normandy in the decade after Arras was in part the consequence of French weakness. France was still a divided realm and Charles VII's court was riddled with intrigue, which came to a head in open rebellion in 1440. Charles VII may himself have been too cautious and timid to take immediate advantage of his opportunity. But the resources available to him from his divided and devastated kingdom were meagre and it took time for financial reform under the guiding hand of Jacques Coeur to take place. His army was a collection of independent companies mostly living off the land and controlled by competing magnates, over which it was as yet impossible to impose central

---

[4]Palmer, 'War Aims', p. 71.

control. The free companies only occasionally came together under the banner of the king's commander-in-chief, the Constable Richemont, and then soon dispersed. Various efforts to impose central control and maintain a disciplined standing army before 1445 failed.[5] Moreover, the necessity of fighting on two fronts — in Normandy and Aquitaine — led to dissipation of the war effort. Thus, despite the new diplomatic advantage, the French were for several years unable to mount an all-out offensive on Normandy. The English, on the other hand, were entrenched in the duchy where they had built up a powerful administration, and had established a disciplined and centrally-controlled army, led by experienced captains prepared to fight a long and costly war in defence of territory in which they had a personal stake.[6]

After Bedford's death in September 1435, the royal council in England was faced with the problem of finding a governor who had both the stature to represent the full majesty of Henry VI and the capability to exercise command. Gloucester was the obvious candidate, but he was unacceptable to the powerful Beaufort faction. There was as a result a series of compromises and stop-gap arrangements. The first solution was to appoint the young Richard, duke of York. His indenture was sealed in February 1436 and his commission ran for a year from 1 May. Although he had the stature, his youth and inexperience were all too obvious. The powers given him as 'Lieutenant general et gouverneur de nostre royaume de France et duchée de Normandie' were limited. York's appointment was possibly only intended to last until a more appropriate one could be made. As it was, York's commission was not renewed in 1437. He was succeeded by the veteran earl of Warwick whose commission was dated 16 July 1437. Warwick, who negotiated more advantageous terms than those enjoyed by York, arrived in Normandy in November. But he was, as he himself admitted, 'full farre from the ease of my years'. He died in office at the end of April 1439. There then followed a long interregnum as the king and his council sought to find a candidate acceptable to all parties; it was ended with the appointment of York in

[5]The standard work on Charles VII is still G. du Fresne de Beaucourt, *Histoire de Charles VII*, 6 vols (Paris, 1881-91). For a recent discussion of aspects of the reign see M. G. A. Vale, *Charles VII* (1974). P. Contamine (*Guerre, état et société à la fin du moyen âge* (Paris, 1972), pp. 234-75) discusses authoritatively the problems in French military organization between 1418 and 1445.

[6]See especially E. M. Burney, 'The English Rule in Normandy, 1435-1450' (unpublished Oxford University B.Litt. thesis, 1958); R. A. Newhall, *Muster and Review* (Harvard, 1940) and C. T. Allmand, 'The Lancastrian Land settlement in Normandy, 1417-50'. *EconHR* 2nd ser, 21 3 (1968). Lancastrian Normandy is to be studied in greater depth than in the following paragraphs in a forthcoming work by C. T. Allmand.

July 1440. York was now appointed for a second term of five years and was able virtually to dictate his own conditions of service. But it was not until a year later that he actually arrived in Normandy.[7] Between Bedford's death in September 1435 and York's arrival on his second tour of duty in July 1441 there had been a resident governor of Normandy for less than three years out of nearly six. And even then the resident governor had either been young and inexperienced or old and in declining health. Thus, over these years considerable responsibility for the administration and defence of the duchy rested on the shoulders of the ducal council, and especially the chancellor, Louis of Luxembourg. Luxembourg had been chancellor of France since 1425 and had been Bedford's right-hand man in his final years. In 1433 he had been entrusted with the administration in France when the duke visited England. In April 1436 he commanded the final defence of Paris and then retired to Rouen. He was elected archbishop of the city in October 1436, became a cardinal in 1439 and was rewarded with the bishopric of Ely. By then he had taken out letters of denizenship in England. His pre-eminence and indispensibility in the administration of the duchy were recognized in May 1439 when he was put at the head of the commission appointed formally to rule the duchy until the arrival of Warwick's replacement.[8] Luxembourg was assisted by a council and civil administration staffed largely by Frenchmen. This too had been Bedford's policy, which was continued after his death. These senior French civil servants were vital to the maintenance of the English position in Normandy. They provided a necessary link with, and example to, the people of Normandy. Above all they were a daily testimony to the legitimacy of Lancastrian rule in the duchy. It had been Bedford's policy (and it still remained the Lancastrian claim) that Henry VI ruled in Normandy as its legitimate duke as well as its king. A deliberate appeal was made to Norman particularism. Norman customs, laws and procedures were maintained. A special conciliar court was established at Rouen as an alternative to the parlement of Paris. A university, in rivalry to the University of Paris, was established at Caen. More symbolically the castle of Rouen, largely demolished by Philip Augustus after his conquest of Normandy in 1205, was rebuilt as a physical embodiment of the new

[7] See A. Marshall, 'The Role of English War Captains in England and Normandy, 1436-61' (unpublished University of Wales M.A. thesis. 1974), Ch 1 *passim* and Burney, 'Normandy', pp. 124-37 for detailed discussion of the governors appointed between 1436 and 1440 and their powers.

[8] See C. T. Allmand, 'The Relations between the English Government, the Higher Clergy and the Papacy in Normandy, 1417-1450' (unpublished Oxford University D.Phil. thesis, 1963), pp. 149-74 for a full discussion of Luxembourg's career. Also Burney, 'Normandy', pp. 24-9.

Anglo-Norman duchy.[9] A largely French administration was part and parcel of the presentation of the Lancastrian régime as the natural and legitimate government.

How the people of Normandy actually viewed the Lancastrian dynasty is hard to determine. Many landowners, churchmen and merchants had a vested interest in its survival. The mercantile community benefitted from the close ties with England and its dealing in military supplies. In the early days of the conquest choices had had to be made and those who had accepted, and had collaborated with, the new authority had powerful incentives to remain loyal. Many had been granted, or had later purchased, land which had been confiscated from men and families who remained loyal to the Valois; this was property which Charles VII, in the edict of Compiègne in 1429, had declared should be returned to its previous owners.[10] There was also a liberal sprinkling of new English settlers. Large fiefs had been granted to English noblemen; smaller properties in town and country had been acquired by men who had come over in the rank and file of the army. In the wake of the conquest there had thus been created a new Anglo-Norman nobility and gentry — some English, some French by birth — who had a large stake in the survival of the Lancastrian duchy.[11] In its short history the Lancastrian duchy adopted a character of its own as a province of France under the authority of the king of England, sustained perhaps by a positive identification with Norman separatism.

Whether any sense of identification with the Lancastrian régime extended to the peasants and country people is hard to tell. The effect on them of the conquest and the continuing war was baleful. The devastation of the countryside and the general poverty of the duchy, especially after 1435, is clearly revealed by the evidence, literary and documentary. Thomas Basin wrote that he had seen for himself 'the Vexin, both French and Norman, Beauvaisis, Caux ... absolutely deserted, uncultivated, abandoned and overgrown with brushwood'.[12] Famine and possibly even plague added to the woes of the common people. The year 1438-39 saw one of the worst famines in the whole of the later middle ages. As a result of these scourges, it has been

[9] Allmand, 'Relations', pp. 124ff.; B. J. H. Rowe, 'The *Grand Conseil* under the Duke of Bedford, 1422-35', in *Oxford Essays in Medieval History presented to Herbert Edward Salter* (Oxford, 1934); A. Dubuc, 'Le Tabellionnage Rouennais durant l'occupation anglaise', *Bulletin philologique et historique* (1969 for 1967), esp. pp.805-7.

[10] C. T. Allmand, 'The Aftermath of War in Fifteenth-Century France', *History* 61 (1976), esp. pp. 345-6; P.S. Lewis, *Later Medieval France; the Polity* (1968), pp.67-70.

[11] Allmand, *Econ HR* (1968).

[12] Basin, 1, p.87.

calculated that by 1450 the population of eastern Normandy was less than a third of its size before the Black Death. Many villages were deserted and several institutions were impoverished or forced to sell lands because after 1435 they could find no tenants.[13] There can be little doubt that all classes of country people suffered immensely. The peasants thus had little cause to love the English. In 1434 and 1435 there were widespread peasant risings in the pays de Caen and the pays de Caux. Ruthlessly put down by the English, the suppression of these revolts spread destruction even further and fuelled popular resentment. In the pays de Caux the situation was exacerbated by the entry of French companies who lived off the land.[14] Many country people, it is believed, fled and joined the bands of brigands which infested the forests and woods, especially of eastern Normandy. The brigands, who presented a vexing problem to the administrators of Lancastrian Normandy throughout its existence, have continued to trouble their historians. Brigandage was endemic in Normandy before the conquest and thus, it has been argued, the problem facing the Lancastrians was merely one of chronic lawlessness and disorder.[15] But others, especially among French historians, have maintained that the brigands after 1417 were mainly partisans who kept up a spirited resistance to the English occupation. As the most recent student of the question has concluded, 'L'occupation anglaise en Normandie n'a jamais été acceptée par tous les habitants .... Les "brigands" dont les textes parlent si frequement sont, en depit des affirmations recentes d'une école anglaise, presque tous des résistants'.[16] There may well have been partisans amongst the brigands, but even if they were primarily common robbers and highwaymen, their numbers, the failure of the government to eradicate them and the general lack of security in country districts could only have further damaged the effectiveness of Lancastrian rule and its reputation. And if we add to the problem of the brigands, the excesses of the English soldiers which, despite a tight discipline, still inevitably occurred, and the impact of growing numbers of discharged soldiers roaming the countryside and living off the land,[17] one is perhaps justified in

[13] G. Bois, *Crise du féodalisme: économie rurale et démographie en Normandie orientale du début du 14e siècle au milieu du 16e siècle* (Paris, 1976), pp. 299-300: Bois heads his discussion of the economy between 1435 and 1450, 'Hiroshima en Normandie'.

[14] Basin, 1, pp. 215-17; Chartier, 1, pp. 172-5; C. L. Kingsford, *Chronicles of London*, (Oxford, 1905), pp. 139-40.

[15] B. J. Rowe, 'John Duke of Bedford and the Norman Brigands', *EHR* 47 (1932), pp. 583-99.

[16] R. Jouet, *La Résistance à l'occupation anglaise en Basse-Normandie 1418-1450*, Cahiers des Annales de Normandie 5 (Caen, 1969), esp. p. 157.

[17] Lewis, *Later Medieval France*, pp. 71-4 and below p. 35.

concluding that, despite all Bedford's and Luxembourg's efforts, the Lancastrian régime did not win the hearts and minds of the majority of the Norman people.

Regular taxation to pay for the war and maintain a standing army could not have helped to endear the Lancastrian régime to the Normans. True to the concept of a separate province under the rule of the English king, Normandy was expected to pay for its own defence. Not only was this a logical extension of the Lancastrian appeal to legitimacy, but it also appealed to the pocket of the English taxpayer. Consequently, the Estates of Normandy met frequently (usually three times a year) to vote supplies for the maintenance of garrisons and such campaigns as were necessary for the defence of the duchy. During the 1420s the people of Normandy did indeed pay for their protection by the English army. But after the crisis of 1429-30, when the war returned to their own frontiers and the duchy became progressively impoverished, less and less of the sums needed could be supplied by the Estates. Although they continued to vote a regular annual supply for garrisons, approximately £33,000 sterling *per annum,* and to make special grants for specific operations, as for instance in the case of about £11,000 sterling voted in June and July 1440 for the recovery of Harfleur,[18] after 1435 military operations in Normandy could only be sustained with financial assistance from England. This took two forms. It came in the payment for six months of reinforcements sent from England. After 1435 such reinforcements were sent over annually. And it came in the payment of special subsidies to the governor. In 1440 York negotiated the payment of an annual sum of £20,000 from English sources, as a supplement to the Norman revenues, to cover his troops' wages. In November 1441 the council in England calculated that this was approximately a third of the total revenue he should have received to pay for his army. By the time York took up his second command it was recognised that Normandy could no longer be defended without substantial and regular charge to the English taxpayer, amounting to about half a combined lay and clerical subsidy a year.[19] This was more than the commons were prepared to vote year after year, and much more than the English council, hard pressed from several other quarters, could afford to assign every year to Normandy.[20]

---

[18]For discussion of Norman revenues see C. de Beaurepaire, *Les États de Normandie sous la domination anglaise* (Evreux, 1859) and Burney, 'Normandy', Ch II *passim*, esp. appendix, p.4.

[19]Burney, 'Normandy', Ch III, *passim*, esp. pp. 98-9, 108-9.

[20]M. H. Keen, *Later Middle Ages,* pp. 428-9; Burney, 'Normandy', pp. 107-8.

The moneys raised with increasing difficulty in both Normandy and England were spent on maintaining an army of over 6,000 men. For the third quarter of 1436 it mustered 6,627 combatants. In November 1441 the establishment was estimated to be 6,200. It was primarily a garrison army. In 1436 there were thirty-eight separate garrisons, but in addition there were nine personal retinues which escorted and accompanied the three field commanders, the master of the ordnance and senior civilian officials.[21] The indentures of service for these garrisons and other retinues were renewed annually. The prime responsibility for the defence of Normandy thus rested with a standing army, the majority of which was posted in garrisons throughout the duchy. Contingents from these garrisons were regularly mobilized to take the field to resist French incursions and to lay siege to French enclaves.[22] But operations in the field did not depend entirely on them. Every year armies of reinforcement were sent from England and these joined the garrison contingents to take part in campaigns. At the end of their six-month commission, however, these armies were disbanded. The size of these armies during 1437-1442 varied between 2,700 and 800. On average they represented an addition of about a quarter to the fighting strength of the standing army every year.[23] Yet the permanent strength of that army remained static, and even declined slightly over the period. Some of the captains in armies of reinforcement are known not to have stayed in Normandy after the expiry of their contracts. In 1436, for instance, York was accompanied by the earls of Suffolk and Salisbury and Lord Fauconberg as his principal captains. Only Fauconberg stayed in Normandy. Most of the rank and file would seem to have returned to England in 1437 with their captains. Only a few could have stayed in the Norman army to replace men who died, deserted, or retired to England.[24] As will be illustrated below in the case of Talbot's retinues, the bulk of the standing army was made up of soldiers who had made

---

[21] BN, MS Fr 25773/112. This document is reproduced in Marshall, 'English War Captains', pp. 282-4. Also Burney, 'Normandy', p. 109.

[22] See Newhall, *Muster and Review, passim.*

[23] From figures given by J. H. Ramsay, *Lancaster and York,* 2 vols (Oxford, 1892) and Exchequer warrants for issues, PRO, E404.

[24] See PRO, E404/52/196, 208, 211, 266. York's 1436 army is discussed by M. R. Powicke in 'Lancastrian Captains' in *Essays in Medieval History presented to Bertie Wilkinson,* ed. T. A. Sandquist and M. R. Powicke (Toronto, 1969), pp. 371-82. A comparison between the muster of the retinue Fauconberg took to France in 1436 and his retinue two years later and subsequently suggests that very few even of his men stayed on in Normandy with him. See BL, Add Ch 11932; BN, Clair 185/24/6854; 40/6866. Cf. the author of Cleopatra C IV's comment that in the autumn of 1437 'the Duke of York cam into England *with all his men*' (Kingsford, *Chronicles,* p. 144 - my italics).

their career in the ranks or even settled in the duchy. Native-born Normans and other nationals were also recruited to the army, although it was laid down that no more than an eighth of the establishment of any force should be of 'foreigners'.[25] It was, in line with the general policy towards the duchy, an Anglo-Norman army. Discussion of the declining interest of the English upper classes in the war in its later stages too often fails to take this into account. The main burden of the war after 1420 was carried by the army in Normandy, led by professional captains, many of relatively humble birth. The role of reinforcements from England, although of increasing importance as the years went by, was essentially auxiliary. The wholesale commitment of the English aristocracy on the field of battle was not required. This is not to deny that as the defence of the duchy came to rely more directly on English assistance after 1440, so it became more difficult to recruit soldiers in England. In 1442 the council found it had to alter the relationship of men-at-arms to archers in retinues raised in England from 1:3 to 1:10, and this, as it has often been observed, no doubt reflected the growing difficulty the government had in persuading men of substance to serve abroad.[26]

The army which bore the brunt of the fighting in Normandy and in which Talbot held senior command had evolved a complex organization. Initially created, like all late-medieval English armies, as an expeditionary force supplied by private individuals serving in the retinue of, first, King Henry V and, then, Bedford, it evolved by the late-1430s into an army centrally controlled and administered by the ducal council and the offices of the Norman treasury and receiver-general. The first stages by which this occurred naturally followed the placing of Henry V's army into garrisons after the conquest of the duchy. An elaborate system of muster and review was developed by Henry and Bedford by which the payment of the troops was supervised. As it became apparent that the garrisons were permanent and the problems involved in ruling the conquered lands revealed themselves, the administration of the army became more complex. An elaborate code of discipline was evolved and its terms were written into all indentures, and procedures were established to deal with breaches of the regulations. Frequent changes in captaincies, the modification of garrison establishments to meet changing strategic requirements, and the system of forming and reinforcing armies in the field with

[25] Newhall, *Muster and Review*, pp. 113-22, esp. p. 120. In April 1438 Talbot was paid for four Normans who had been in his garrison retinue in Rouen in 1437 because the authorities had satisfied themselves that he had not had more than one-eighth who were of foreign nationality (BN. NAF. 1482/147).

[26] See especially Powicke, 'Lancastrian Captains'. M. H. Keen, *Later Middle Ages,* p. 406, makes a similar point to mine.

contingents drawn from garrisons required an efficient, centralised secretariat. Once the army became permanent, financial, disciplinary and military necessity demanded a complex bureaucracy.[27] Whilst Bedford lived the army was still looked upon as his personal retinue and his captains were his personal followers. During the six years after his death, when there was no established governor in the duchy, even this element was temporarily missing. The council, under the dynamic leadership of Luxembourg, administered it as a department of state. The governor was still commander-in-chief and retained an important element of control over patronage, but he was himself a servant of the state and not, as Henry V or Bedford had been, the personification of the state itself. After 1441, however, when York took up his second governorship with wide powers, he reasserted the personal authority implicit in the post and recruited the army leaders into his household and personal following, thus reverting to a more traditional relationship with his men.[28]

By York's time the military organization was beginning to show signs of strain. Captaincies, which were granted as a form of patronage as well as for military reasons, were frequently held *in absentia*. Men like Talbot could hold six or more posts at one time, and although lieutenants were appointed to take actual command, with the growing practice of appointing life captaincies or captaincies for a term of years, the control of the central adminstration over discipline and order was undermined. Absenteeism was one abuse which Richard of York declared it to be his intention to correct.[29] The central command also found it increasingly difficult to form armies for field service from garrison contingents and to keep such armies up to strength. Thus, it came to call more on *creus* recruited from the less reliable gangs of discharged soldiers living off the land.[30] Morale generally was ebbing as the war dragged on and the opportunities for

[27] See Newhall, *Muster and Review*; B. J. H. Rowe, 'Discipline in the Norman Garrisons under Bedford', *EHR* 46 (1931), 194-208; C. T. Allmand, *Society at War* (Edinburgh, 1973), pp. 57-62.

[28] These changes in English military organization are discussed in greater detail by A. E. Curry, 'The First English Standing Army? Military Organization in Lancastrian Normandy, 1420-1450', in *Patronage, Pedigree and Power in Later Medieval England*, ed. Charles Ross (1979), pp. 202-7.

[29] Stevenson, *Wars* p. 590. For Talbot's captaincies see below pp. 40, 49, 51, 53, 72, 141-4.

[30] As, for example, in the campaign for the recovery of Tancarville in 1437, the military arrangements for which are discussed by Newhall, *Muster and Review*; pp. 143-6, and in the abortive attempt to recover Louviers and Conches during the winter of 1440-1, for which see the musters of the *creu*, BL Add Ch 6949. BN MS Fr 25775/1490. Soldiers living off the land without wages were becoming an increasing problem in the late 1430s. Where they came from is not clear.

profit dwindled. Profit from war, as we shall see below in Talbot's case, was still a dominant personal motive for many individual soldiers. An army which ceased to offer sufficient opportunity for profiteering, however efficiently administered, was bound to lose its appetite for war. Thus, however much it had shown its worth over the years, by 1440 the efficiency of the army was declining.

The supreme military commander of the army was the lieutenant-general and governor of the duchy, but he rarely took actual command of his troops in the field. Bedford had set the precedent for this. And between 1435 and 1441 circumstances were such that it was inevitable that the field command should be delegated. Bedford had established the practice of dividing the *pays de conquête* into military zones, each under the command of a lieutenant-general. One was the Île de France, of which Talbot had been lieutenant-general since 1434. Late in 1435 this command seems to have been taken over by Lord Willoughby.[31] Normandy was divided into two zones, roughly the same as upper and lower Normandy, east and west of the Seine. Since 1434 Talbot had been 'Lieutenant-General for the conduct of the war between the Seine, Oise, Somme and the sea', as it was usually styled. In 1435 Lord Scales had become lieutenant-general of western Normandy or of the lower march, as he was often styled, in succession to John, earl of Arundel.[32] Talbot's position as the field commander of eastern Normandy was reaffirmed and enhanced during the winter of 1435-36. In January 1436 he assumed the captaincy of Rouen, an office earlier held by Bedford and to which Talbot was officially appointed on 21 April. This high command was held in addition to the captaincies of the strategically important Gisors and Neufchâtel on the eastern border of the duchy which he had held since 1434, and of Caudebec and Château Gaillard which he took over after Bedford's death. Talbot remained in command of eastern Normandy until the truce of Tours. As such, he was a divisional commander only.[33] The crucial question is whether he was also given a more general command of the whole army. In one document dated 20 May 1436 he was described as 'Lieutenant-General for the king of the conduct of the war'. This was after York's appointment as governor and it is possible that Talbot acted for a short

[31] BN, PO 2787, Talbot, 9.

[32] AN, JJ 75/313; BL, Add Ch 1460, 6880.

[33] BN, MS Fr 26061/2812; 25771/894; PO 2787, Talbot 9; AN, K 64/1/34; BL, Add Ch 439, 6875, 7980. R. Brill ('An English Captain of the later Hundred Years' War, John, Lord Talbot' (unpublished Princeton University Ph.D thesis, 1966), pp. 272-3 and 417) asserts that Talbot as lieutenant-general was *de facto*, if not quite *de jure*' leader of the English army in the field.

while as York's official military deputy pending his arrival. More significantly, on 9 May 1436 his status and remuneration were permanently enhanced by his appointment as one of the marshals of France.[34]

The marshalcy was in part a reward. Scales was already seneschal of Normandy, a position to which he had been appointed by Bedford in 1435, and the marshalcy of France now gave Talbot an equivalent title and a slightly more generous salary than that of Scales.[35] But the post was something more than a recognition of seniority and a reward for good service. In the early-fourteenth century the marshal had jurisdiction over all those taking royal wages for the time they were on the march in the host. His responsibility had been to maintain discipline, but in time he came to take over the muster and review of the troops. In the military hierarchy he came to be subservient to the constable, and in the French army in the fifteenth century the marshalcy had consequently suffered a loss of prestige. There were traditionally two marshals of France, although Charles VII had as many as four.[36] In 1421 Henry V had appointed two Frenchmen, Antoine de Vergy and Jean de la Baume, to replace the marshals who remained loyal to the Dauphin, subsequently Charles VII. The duke of Burgundy had already appointed his own marshal of France, L'Isle Adam, in 1418, and this was eventually confirmed by Bedford in 1432. But L'Isle Adam, with his master, had deserted the English cause in 1435, so that there was in 1436 good reason for the appointment of an Englishman.[37] Talbot's commission and the terms of his appointment are particularly revealing as they indicate a development and extension of the traditional role of the marshal. The preamble cites Talbot's celebrated valour and his great diligence in the past and daily, both in the recovery and defence of France and in the maintenance of order and discipline in the army. Accordingly, the king declares that 'nous avons créé, constitué et établi, et par ces presentes faisons, créons, constituons et établissons l'un de nos mareschaulx de France pour icelui office avoir exercer et tenir par nostre dit cousin de Talbot'. The duties of the office, it continues, are

---

[34]BL, Add Ch 3781; D Len 26/193-4. On 21 December 1436, in an acquittance for the wages of his personal retinue in February, he was styled 'late lieutenant of the king' (AN, K 64/10/15).

[35]BL, Add Ch 6880. Scales received £1,600 livres tournois *per annum*, Talbot £2,000.

[36]College of Arms Library, R 26, ff30-33b; P Contamine, *Guerre, Etat et Société à la fin du moyen age* (Paris, 1972), pp. 198-200; K. A. Fowler, *The Age of Plantagenet and Valois* (1967), pp. 119-20.

[37]College of Arms Library, R 26, ff33, 33b.

threefold. First, and significantly so, Talbot is to undertake such military enterprises as he judges would be profitable for the recovery of France and the defeat of the French. Secondly, he is to carry out the muster and review of all soldiers taking part in such sieges, raids (*osts*) or other actions. And finally, he is to exercise the jurisdiction pertaining to the marshalcy — that is, in cases between soldiers and in cases between soldiers and civilians.[38] This is a significant extension of the role of marshal. For the first time, as it is employed by the Lancastrians, the marshalcy is regarded first and foremost as a field command in the modern sense. It thereby anticipates later French practice by well over a century, for it was not until after the suppression of the constableship in the later sixteenth century that a marshalcy in France took on its modern form. Indeed, a description of a marshalcy of France in the early-eighteenth century offered by an English herald sums up what could well have been Talbot's new role. 'The marshals of France', he wrote, 'are the king's lieutenants in the army and commanders in chief, if there be not present any prince of the blood or other famous general to whom the king commands them to be subject, in which case they are only lieutenants-general for them'.[39]

As marshal, Talbot would appear henceforth to have had precedence over his fellow field commanders. As the only marshal active in Normandy and France, it has been suggested that this also gave him the powers of the constable and made him *de facto* the supreme military commander.[40] This does not in fact appear to have been the case. First, the powers of the constableship seem to have been vested in the governorship of Normandy. Secondly, the system of independent commands appears to have been maintained. Scales remained in command of western Normandy until the truce of Tours, and his position in the south-west march was consolidated by his possession of the captaincies of Domfront, St. Lô and Vire. William Nevill, Lord Fauconberg, who came to Normandy with York in 1436, replaced Lord Willoughby at the end of the year as a field commander, becoming lieutenant-general for the central-southern border zone between the Seine and the Loire. From 1436 to 1441 he was captain of Verneuil and Évreux, the strategic centres of his command.[41] In

---

[38]D Len 26/193-4.

[39]College of Arms Library, R 26, f31d.

[40]Fowler, *Plantagenet and Valois*, p. 120; Brill, 'An English Captain', pp. 297 and 417; H. Talbot, *The English Achilles* (1981), p. 108.

[41]BL, Add Ch 1485; A. Marshall, 'English War Captains', pp. 248, 275.

defending their zones from French raids, both seem to have acted quite independently of Talbot. From time to time, however, one or both of them joined forces with Talbot for the recovery or relief of various places and only on these occasions did Talbot presumably take command according to the powers vested in him as marshal. Thirdly, it was the case that during one period (and possibly two) after 1436 Talbot was superseded by a lieutenant-general for the conduct of the war. In 1437 and until he returned to England with York in the autumn, Richard Nevill, earl of Salisbury was York's lieutenant-general with probable military responsibility.[42] And from the summer of 1439 until the autumn of 1440 between Warwick's death and York's second term of office, John Beaufort, earl of Somerset was in overall military command as 'Lieutenant-General for the matter of the war in the realm of France and the duchy of Normandy'. Somerset was a prince of the blood, the nephew of Cardinal Beaufort, the highest ranking peer than resident in Normandy and a contender for the governorship. It was not in fact until 1441, when York made Talbot his lieutenant-general for the conduct of the war, that we can be certain that the latter assumed the role of commander-in-chief of the army.[43] And finally, the costly dispute over his authority as marshal in Normandy with Humphrey, duke of Gloucester, which appears to have begun early in 1440, led to Talbot's virtual suspension until it was resolved two or three years later.[44] The marshalcy of itself could not have made Talbot the military supremo. Nor can we assume, as some appear to have done, that Talbot had any special voice in determining strategy or initiating military operations.[45] This lay in the hands of the governor of the duchy and his council. Two comments made by the author of MS Cleopatra C.IV illustrate this quite clearly. In the autumn of 1437 York, he tells us, would have attempted to relieve Montereau, then being besieged by the French, but 'his counsell would not counsell him thereto' because he had been discharged from the governorship. A month or so later his successor 'the erll of Warwyk made ordenance be the counsell' for the relief of Le Crotoy' and sent theder the lord Talbot, the lord ffacombrig' and

---

[42] BL, Add Ch 1171; E. Cosneau, *Le Connétable de Richemont* (Paris, 1886), pp. 266-7.

[43] Stevenson, *Wars,* 2, p. 304. Waurin, 4, p. 257, mistakenly describes Somerset as full governor of the duchy.

[44] College of Arms Library, WH. ff312-14. For a fuller discussion of this see below pp. 107-8.

[45] E.g. Brill, 'An English Captain', p. 300, where Talbot is described as 'tactical chief of staff and operational commanding general', and recently D. Seward, *The Hundred Years' War* (1978), pp. 236-40, where, reflecting Burne, Talbot is made the English leader.

many others.[46] Talbot was a member of the council and thus had a voice in military planning, but it would be wrong to imagine that he carried greater weight than others. Indeed, in so far as any one man seems to have stamped his views on strategy during the period 1436-1441 it was Louis of Luxembourg; he played as prominent a part in military affairs as in civilian affairs, even taking to the field himself on occasion.[47] Talbot was primarily an executant, not a planner, of military operations.

In reality, such authority as Talbot enjoyed for much of this period owed as much to the force of his personality and his personal connections as to his official position. The duke of York who, as the newly sworn lieutenant-general and governor of Normandy, had been one of those advising Henry VI to appoint Talbot as marshal, was already paying him an annuity of £100 when he went to the duchy.[48] That there was a special relationship between the two is revealed by several sources. On 22 November 1436 York took over the captaincy of Rouen, but then immediately came to the unusual arrangement of appointing Talbot as his deputy with the title of keeper and governor of the castle, town and bridge of Rouen on behalf of the duke, with all the rights, profits and duties of the captaincy. The change of command thus seems to have been titular only, and even this was forgotten by the garrison controller who twice named Talbot as his captain in 1437.[49] Moreover, between 16 November and 28 December 1436 all the men-at-arms and half of the archers of Talbot's personal retinue were seconded to act as York's bodyguard ('estre entour la personne du Monseigneur le duc d'york').[50] Although York soon returned to England, Talbot was hardly less close to his successor Warwick. Talbot's father-in-law, who had made it clear to the council in England that he was 'full farre from ... the continual laboure off my person att sieges and daily occupation in the warre',[51] relied equally heavily on the marshal of France. When the governorship was in commission between 1439 and 1441, Talbot carried less weight, but York's return was clearly accompanied by a revival of Talbot's

---

[46]C. L. Kingsford, *Chronicles of London* (Oxford, 1905), pp. 143, 144. See also AN, K66/1/26 from which it is apparent that Somerset, Beaufort, Talbot and Fauconberg jointly planned the siege of Harfleur in July 1440.

[47]Allmand, 'Relations', pp 162ff. Miss A. E. Curry has also drawn attention to the continual involvement of the English council in the conduct of the war between 1435 and 1441 (*Patronage Pedigree and Power*, p. 205).

[48]PRO, E163/7/31.

[49]BL, Add Ch 6911; BN, MS Fr 25774/1245, 6.

[50]BN, PO 2787, Talbot, 21.

[51]Stevenson, *Wars*, 2 part 1 pp. 1xv-1xxi.

influence, with his annuity doubled to £200, a return to the captaincy of Rouen and his appointment as lieutenant-general for the conduct of the war.[52] Talbot, of course, did not have an exclusive position of trust. In late 1437, for instance, Fauconberg and his personal retinue acted as Warwick's bodyguard.[53] Nevertheless, under both York and Warwick, Talbot seems to have remained the most favoured of the three field commanders.

Finally, it must be borne in mind that Talbot figures so prominently in the chronicle accounts of the fighting because he happened to be the commander responsible for English arms in the principal theatre of the war. French companies maintained pressure on all the borders of Normandy; but much of the southern front was protected by the deep buffer zone of Maine. Only in the far south-west around Avranches and Granville were the French persistent in their attacks.[54] The eastern front, however, was vulnerable to attack both from the Constable Richemont, who concentrated his forces in the Île de France, and from the duke of Burgundy in Picardy. Moreover, from the end of 1435 French companies were lodged in the pays de Caux. Thus, as we shall see, the English war effort after 1435 was concentrated on the defence and recovery of eastern Normandy. It may be that Talbot was retained as commander of this critical zone because of his special qualities, but the fact remains that his responsibility for the war up to 1441 was limited principally to this area. One can only conclude, therefore, that until 1441 Talbot was but the most prominent, the most renowned and the most favoured of a team of three commanders in the field. Only after 1441, when he was made lieutenant-general for the conduct of the war and subsequently created earl of Shrewsbury, was he given authority over his fellow commanders and a general field command over the whole army.

By 1441, however, English control of Normandy was visibly crumbling. One argument put before the council during the negotiations in 1439 drew attention to the worsening conditions in the *pays de conquête*. The land was poverty-stricken and deserted, the French population was turning against the English, the burden of the war would fall increasingly on the English, the organization of the army was collapsing and captains were more concerned with their own

---

[52]BN, Clair 202/8479/12, MS Fr 25763/743; BL, Add Chs 470, 1209.

[53]BL, Add Ch 442.

[54]Especially in 1436-7 and after 1441. See *Chronique du Mont St Michel*, ed. S. Luce, Société des anciens textes français (Paris, 2 vols, 1879-83).

profit than with the king's cause.[55] These same complaints were repeated in official circles in the following year. The English council stated in its explanation of the release of Orléans, 'that that is left of the cuntrey there to the kyng and in his obeissance is there devoured, deserted, and destroyed to the uttermoste'. And at the same time it recognised that 'ther is growen and spradde in his people a noyse and grutching'. So impoverished was Normandy, the council argued (with some exaggeration), that whereas a few years ago the Normans bore the cost of defence, it now fell wholly on the English. In June of the same year the council in Normandy wrote despairingly to England complaining of the low morale and unwillingness to fight in the army. At the same time the duke of York, who was recruiting in England, found 'there beth but few captains as of knights and squyers that wollen go'. No wonder, as the English council concluded in 1440, it was 'thought to the kyng nought expedient but necessarie to hym to entende to the paix'.[56] Paradoxically, just as the policy of seeking a peace based on the existence of a separate Lancastrian duchy of Normandy was determined, so the condition of the duchy and its internal strains made it unlikely that even this solution, regardless of whether it was acceptable to the French, would work. It was a case of too little, too late. Nevertheless, if peace were to have any chance of realisation, it was imperative that the English maintain their hold on the duchy. This probably explains the minor revolution of 1440-42 whereby, at the beginning of York's second administration, the government of Normandy was anglicised. This was a policy which had been advocated by Sir John Fastolf at the time of the treaty of Arras. Then he had argued 'that the king ordeine in this lande sufficient counseille of Englisshe menne, expert and knowing them in the werre ... and not it to be demened so moche be the Frenshe counseile as hit hathe be done heretofore'.[57] York, who had already negotiated a handsome annual subsidy from England to help pay for his wars, carried out this change in 1442. The number of Frenchmen on the council was reduced to two, a return to the position of the early days of the conquest, and Luxembourg's personal influence was curtailed. In the place of Frenchmen, York promoted veteran English captains, including Talbot.[58] From 1442 there is no mistaking the fact that Normandy was being governed by Englishmen. No doubt York thereby gained a more effective control of affairs, but the change was

[55] Allmand, *Camden Miscellany* 24 (1972) 140-1 and Allmand, *BIHR* 40 (1967), 25.

[56] Stevenson, *Wars,* 2, pp. 451, 456, 457, 603.

[57] *Ibid.,* 2, p. 585.

[58] Burney, 'Normandy', pp. 98-9, 134-6; Allmand, 'Relations', pp. 141-2.

nevertheless a confession of failure and a sign of desperation. It tore away the veil of legitimacy and revealed starkly the true face of the English presence — that of an occupying foreign power. After 1442 there were few pretences left. In the last resort the Lancastrian possession of Normandy had always depended on might and might alone. The English would keep their conquered duchy only so long as Talbot and his fellow commanders could successfully defend it in the field.

4

MARSHAL OF FRANCE:
JOHN TALBOT AT WAR, 1436-50

The years from 1436 to the truce of Tours saw a long, wearying and finally abortive struggle to recover ground lost in the emergency of 1435-36. English strategy as it evolved was uncomplicated. It was intended, first, to recover and hold the eastern borders of Normandy, especially to control the route down the Seine valley to Rouen. In this respect possession of Pontoise and control of the lower Oise valley were especially important, for not only did the town protect the road into Normandy, but it also posed a direct threat to Paris. Equally important, but not as easily executed, was the desire to hold on to as many of the English outposts in the Île de France as possible. The garrisons in Montereau, Montargis, Meaux and Creil were not entirely self-sufficient, so that from time to time convoys of supplies had to be escorted to them from Normandy. But they were a nuisance to the French and the operation of recovering them diverted enemy attention from Normandy itself. Thirdly, the English had to recover the lost enclave in the pays de Caux. Finally, from time to time, French or Burgundian territory was raided in an aggressive gesture, primarily (one suspects) to maintain morale by offering the opportunity for plunder rather than as part of any grander strategy.[1] The implementation of this strategy in eastern Normandy, like French efforts to advance further in the duchy, was seriously hampered by the devastated condition of the countryside. The land was so hard fought over that it became extremely difficult to mount any operation involving large numbers of troops. Basin concluded that conditions were so bad that it was almost impossible to maintain an army of as few as 1,000 to 1,500 horsemen.[2] In 1440, for instance, a French army attempting to relieve Harfleur, then under siege, had to abandon the

---

[1]It will be seen that I disagree fundamentally with the hypothesis offered by Reginald Brill, initially in his doctoral thesis, especially pp. 288-92, 413-4 and 458-9, and subsequently in *Studies in Medieval and Renaissance History* 7 (1970). In short, this maintains that Bedford devised in 1433 and 1434, and his commanders, especially Talbot, instituted, a strategy of 'defensive-offensive' or 'frontier-and-balance' warfare, as elaborated by Fastolf in his memorandum, with the purpose of taking the war to the French until 1441. M.G.A. Vale, 'Sir John Fastolf's 'Report' of 1435: A New Interpretation Reconsidered', *Nottingham Medieval Studies* 17 (1973), 78-84, has already offered a devastating criticism of Brill's use of the memorandum and his excessive claims for the supposed strategy.

[2]Basin, 1. pp. 249-51.

attempt after ten days because of the almost total lack of supplies. In 1441 York advanced beyond the Oise in the direction of Paris with an army of over 2,000 but, as Basin commented, 'n'y pouvant trouver ni vivres ni paysans, sauf de très rare, il fut rapidement forcé par la famine et le manque de tout de retourner a Rouen sans avoir rien fait'.[3] It was well nigh impossible, therefore, to maintain armies of sufficient strength long enough in the field to achieve a decisive victory. There were, therefore, no great battles. Conditions themselves dictated a war of attrition. This was nowhere more so than in the pays de Caux, where first the peasant rebels, then the English reprisals, and finally the undisciplined French garrisons reduced the district to a virtual desert.[4] Every summer between 1436 and 1443 an English army took up the laborious task of reducing piecemeal the places in French hands, often, as at Tancarville (1437) and Harfleur (1440), maintaining long sieges in appalling conditions. In fact, the recovery of the pays de Caux was never completed, for the English effort finally petered out before Dieppe in 1443.

For a while after 1436 the English enjoyed a series of encouraging successes. York's army immediately set about the recovery of the pays de Caux, retaking Fécamp, reoccupying Lillebonne and destroying several minor castles and fortresses.[5] Talbot operated in the Île de France, being 'before Saint-Germain-en-Laye' in August, and possibly penetrating as far as the gates of Paris.[6] Having taken stock and redeployed his forces in the autumn,[7] York and his council determined on a new campaign. It was decided in the middle of one of the hardest winters that men could remember to launch a surprise attack on Pontoise, the key to the Seine valley between Rouen and Paris which had been lost in February 1436. At the end of January an army was mustered from elements of York's troops and placed under Talbot's command. It first marched up the Eure valley and took the town of Ivry and then swung north and east down to the Seine, where it

[3] Monstrelet, 5, pp. 421-2; Basin, 1, p. 267.

[4] Chartier, 1, pp. 174-5. Late in 1436 the Constable Richemont visited Dieppe, 'pour mettre ordre es gens d'armes qui gastoient tous', apparently without lasting success (Gruel, p.126).

[5] Monstrelet, 5, pp. 271-2; Basin, 1, pp. 249-51; BL, Add Ch 6900. Fécamp appears to have changed hands three times during the year. Monstrelet confuses the sieges of Fécamp in 1436 and Tancarville in 1437 (5, p. 297).

[6] Bourgeois, p. 327.

[7] In November and December York and his council renewed contracts with the captains (for nine months only) and carried out a review of the army. Talbot surrendered the captaincy of Château Gaillard at this time (R.A. Newhall, *Muster and Review* (Harvard, 1940), pp. 73, 133-4).

MAP 2   Eastern Normandy and the Île De France –

The Treaty of Arras, 1435

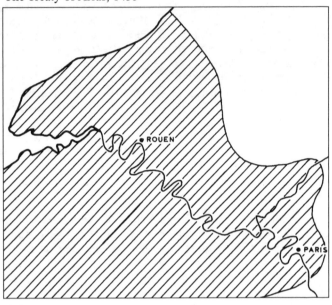

Autumn, 1440

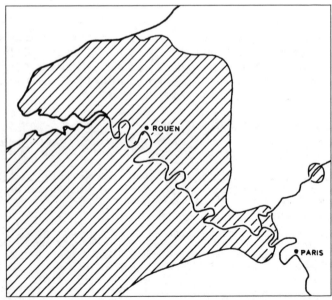

Territory under English Domination

Summer, 1436

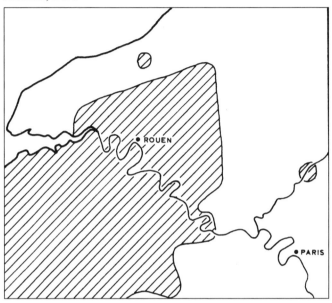

The Truce of Tours, 1444

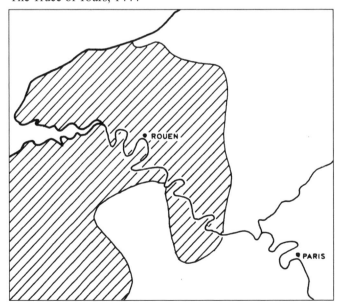

surprised Pontoise at dawn on 13 February 1437. It is worth giving some detail of this action because it exemplifies the kind of dramatic exploit which won Talbot the admiration of his contemporaries.

There was no question of attempting to take such a strongly fortified town by siege in the middle of winter; it had to be taken by surprise. Talbot and his army arrived before Pontoise on the night of 12 February. It was Mardi Gras and the garrison was celebrating. The river Oise was frozen solid, so the English assault parties could cross at will and avoid the carefully guarded bridge which controlled access to the town. Just before dawn a small advance party disguised as peasants coming to market and led by John Sterky, a man-at-arms in Talbot's personal retinue, crossed the river and approached the town gates from the French side and were let in. Meanwhile, the main assault party, camouflaged with white sheets and blankets, quietly slipped across the ice and took up positions beneath the walls with their scaling ladders. As the sun came up the men in the town raised the cry of 'Talbot, St George' and the walls were scaled from the outside. The sleepy garrison was taken completely by surprise and scarcely a blow was struck in defence. The captain, L'Isle Adam, and the French leaders fled virtually in their night clothes, leaving behind a rich haul of booty, including a vast store of grain.[8] Having won a town so brilliantly and cheaply, Talbot took a force further up stream and on the night of 16-17 February attempted a similar surprise of Paris, but the garrison was alerted and Talbot quickly withdrew.[9] A few days later he raided French-held territory north of the Oise, penetrating as far as Beauvais. Garrison contingents were called out and mustered at Les Andelys on 23 March. The enlarged army consolidated the gain of Pontoise by mopping up French-held towns and fortresses in the Vexin, in a triangle between Gisors, Mantes and Vernon. Early in April it moved south of the Seine and took Chevreuse, and thus, having completed a most succesful late winter campaign, Talbot returned in triumph to Rouen.[10] As long as Pontoise could be held, the route from Paris into Normandy would be securely defended.

Talbot's next operation was, in contrast, a routine but vital revictualling expedition to Meaux which was completed before the

---

[8]Chartier, 1, pp. 233-5; Bourgeois, pp. 329-30. Modern reconstructions are to be found in A.H. Burne, *The Agincourt War* (1956), pp. 282-3 and Brill, 'An English Captain of the later hundred years war: John Lord Talbot c1388-1444', (Unpublished Princeton University Ph.D thesis, 1966), pp. 320-3.

[9]Bourgeois, pp. 329-30.

[10]BL, Add MS 28315/2; G. du Fresne de Beaucourt, *Histoire de Charles VII,* 3, p.10; Ramsay, *Lancaster and York,* 2 (Oxford, 1892), p. 2. Talbot had returned to Rouen by 20 April (BL, Add Ch 3802).

end of June.[11] He then turned his attention to the task of continuing the reconquest of the pays de Caux. On 12 July he was before Baudemont, near Tancarville, probably making a reconnaissance,[12] for by the end of the month, even though York was daily expecting to be relieved by the earl of Warwick, it was decided to lay siege to Tancarville. Tancarville, on the north bank of the Seine between Caudebec and Harfleur, was an obstacle that had to be cleared before the recovery of Harfleur itself could be tackled. Orders were sent out for garrison contingents to gather at Jumièges in the week following 7 August. The devastated condition of the country did not help the besieging force, but Talbot persevered and Tancarville eventually fell early in November. The town's surrender may well have been hastened by Warwick's arrival, for his fleet, delayed by bad weather for eleven weeks, eventually sailed into the Seine on 8 November.[13] Warwick's arrival led to a reallocation of Talbot's captaincies. He surrendered Rouen (to Warwick himself), Caudebec and Gisors, but he gained Gournay, Falaise, Vernon, Creil and Meaux in the course of the following year. The latter two were important English outposts which Talbot now took over as a personal responsibility.[14] There was little slackening in Talbot's employment. Close on the fall of Tancarville, he was sent to the rescue of Le Crotoy, which was being besieged by the duke of Burgundy. Talbot personally led a bold crossing of the Somme at the ford of Blanche Taque under the eyes of the besieging army and then, unmolested by that army or by the duke himself, who was at Abbeville, he led his men on a profitable raid into the relatively unspoiled country of western Picardy. With Talbot thus creating terror and destruction in its rear, the besieging army abandoned its position and retreated in confusion. After about ten days Talbot re-crossed the Somme, Le Crotoy was relieved, and his army returned to Rouen loaded with booty.[15] No sooner had they returned than word came that Montargis was under siege and on 20 December Talbot and Fauconberg were ordered to collect a new relief

[11] BN, Ms FR 26065/3630.

[12] BN, Ms FR 26063/3217, 20.

[13] Newhall, *Muster and Review,* pp. 143-6; C.L. Kingsford, *Chronicles of London* (Oxford, 1905), pp. 143-4. For discussion of the army before Tancarville see below pp. 71-2. On 27 November Talbot received wages for 886 men for fifteen days' service in defence of an unnamed fortress, probably Tancarville. William Minors, who had commanded a company during the siege, was later captain there (BL, Add Chs 1472, 3861).

[14] BN, MS Fr 26065/3760, 26064/3406; Clair 201/8457/58, 8465/70; BL, Add Ch 12009.

[15] Waurin, 4, pp. 231-40; Kingsford, *Chronicles,* p. 144. Talbot was ordered to the relief of Le Crotoy before 20 November (BL, Add Ch 3830).

force at Conches and Évreux. But before they set out its commander, François de Surienne, came to terms with his besiegers and handed over the town. Nevertheless, Talbot and Fauconberg still kept their army in readiness, being at Évreux from the last weeks of January until March 1438.[16] Eventually, an alternative occupation was found for the soldiers in the reduction of the small fortresses of Longchamps and Neufmarché in the pays de Bray, which was completed by 19 March. The two commanders still kept the field and in May they were dispatched on a routine revictualling operation to Creil and Meaux.[17] On returning from this, and having been joined by Sir Thomas Kyriell, Talbot set out on what was becoming an annual campaign in the pays de Caux. The garrison contingents were mustered in Rouen on 17 and 19 June and the army then marched north to recover Longueville and several lesser places commanding the approaches to Dieppe. Having completed this, Talbot and Kyriell moved westward to the neighbourhood of Harfleur, for on 20 and 31 July and 10 August their troops were mustered at Montivilliers and Graville.[18]

Although unrecorded by any of the chroniclers, siege appears to have been laid before Harfleur by both land and sea, for a squadron of eight ships blockaded the port at the same time. This attempt may well have been linked with the arrival of the newly released comte d'Eu, who had been made captain-general of eastern Normandy by Charles VII and had arrived to take command of Harfleur, only to face a revolt by the French garrison. It is conceivable that Talbot and Kyriell were seeking to take advantage of this. If so, this plan came to nothing and the siege seems to have been abandoned after the naval squadron fell into French hands on the last day of August.[19] Harfleur was to remain in Charles's hands for another two years. But Talbot continued campaigning until the end of the year: in October he set out from Rouen on some unknown secret enterprise and on 18 December, with the aid of treachery from within the town, he succeeded in surprising and recapturing Saint-Germain-en-Laye.[20] Christmas 1438 brought to an end for Talbot three years of almost constant campaigning. They were years of important achievements. From the dark days of Christmas 1435, when it seemed that all eastern Normandy would be lost, the English had recovered and successfully defended the eastern

[16]BN, PO 2787 Talbot 25; Clair 201/8443/44; MS Fr 25774/1286; BL, Add Ch 11973; A Bossuat, *Perrinet Gressart et François de Surienne, Agents de l'Angleterre* (Paris, 1936), pp. 266-7.

[17]BL, Add Ch 11991; BN, Clair 202/8417/8,9; MS Fr 25774/1322.

[18]BN, MS Fr 25774/1322, 1348, 1349, 1391, 1393; Monstrelet, 5, pp. 340-1.

[19]Kingsford, *Chronicles,* p. 145; Monstrelet, 5, pp. 346-7.

[20]BL, Add Ch 3855; Bossuat, *Gressart et Surienne*, pp. 270-1.

frontier; they had regained most of the pays de Caux with the exception of Harfleur and Dieppe and their immediate neighbourhoods; and they had managed to hold on to all but one of the strategic outposts. Talbot, as lieutenant-general of eastern Normandy, had played an important part in all this. It was not just his dramatically successful strikes against places such as Pontoise but also his willingness to spend week after week in the saddle dealing with the less spectacular tasks of sieges and relief convoys which had led to this improvement in English fortunes. Thus, on the field of battle he had done all that could be asked of him to make it possible for the English government to reopen negotiations with the French in another effort to secure an honourable peace.

1439 was to prove a crucial year. For Talbot it was to see a substantial diminution of his influence and authority in the duchy. In the first four months of the year he seems to have spent his time with the ailing Warwick, who died on 30 April.[21] In the arrangements made after the earl's death, Talbot saw the favoured position he had occupied over the past few years crumble. Although he and his fellow field commanders, Fauconberg and Scales, were appointed to the commission established to rule Normandy until the arrival of a new governor, they were all three placed under the earl of Somerset who, as 'Lieutenant-General of the King for the matter of the war', assumed responsibility for leading the campaigning throughout the duchy.[22] There is reason to believe, as we shall see below, that Somerset superseded Talbot as senior field commander in eastern Normandy. Certainly the latter soon lost most of his captaincies, including all those in eastern Normandy itself.[23] How Talbot felt about this eclipse we do not know. The record suggests that he swallowed his pride and accepted the situation, for he continued to serve in Normandy under Somerset's command as diligently as before.

During the summer of 1439, while Cardinal Beaufort prepared for the peace negotiations, English military operations were for the most part suspended. The one important task was to keep possession of those fortresses — Creil, Meaux, Pontoise and Saint-Germain-En-Laye — which Beaufort was prepared to offer to the French. Consequently, on 21-23 June Talbot was at Vernon gathering supplies and a small escort with which to revictual Pontoise.[24] A more

[21] On 22 and 26 April Talbot was in Rouen with Warwick (BL, Add Ch 443).

[22] BL, Add MS 11,542/78 and above p. 39; Stevenson, *Wars*, 2, p. 204.

[23] By the summer of 1440 Talbot held only the captaincy of Lisieux (Stevenson, *Wars*, 2, pp. 317-9).

[24] BN, MS Fr 26066/400; BL, Add Ch 445.

serious situation was created when, on 20 July, with the negotiations at Gravelines at their height, the Constable Richemont laid siege to Meaux. Somerset immediately organised a relief force and led a strong army under his best captains, Talbot, Scales and Fauconberg, to the rescue. They did not arrive in time to save the town, which was taken by assault on 12 August; but they were able to destroy some of the French siege works and to reinforce the stronghold of the 'market' into which the garrison had retired. Everything in their power was done to secure this position. The French, who refused a challenge to fight, retreated into the town, whilst the English destroyed the siege works and transferred a quantity of captured cannon to the market. Having left 500 fresh troops under Sir William Chamberlain in the garrison, the relief force returned to Rouen.[25] Chamberlain, however, proved to be an irresolute captain and before the end of August he entered into negotiations with Richemont to surrender his charge on 15 September if no more reinforcements arrived. Talbot and Fauconberg were already busy organising a second relief column in Rouen on 27 August and moved forward to Vernon a few days later. But the march to Meaux was for some reason delayed and Talbot did not arrive there until 16 September, the day after Chamberlain had surrendered, much to the anger of the military command in Rouen. Finding Meaux in French hands, Talbot fell back on Pontoise, where he was residing on 5 October.[26] Somerset had in fact left Rouen before the end of August and returned to England, both to collect reinforcements and perhaps to further his claim to be created full governor. His brother, Edmund Beaufort (who was also Talbot's brother-in-law), appears to have been left in Normandy as his deputy.[27] It was Beaufort who led the army, with Talbot and Scales, which went to the rescue of Avranches in December after Richemont, fresh from his success at Meaux, had turned his attention to the western borders of the duchy. On the night of 22-23 December, Beaufort, Talbot and Scales surprised Richemont in his camp and completely routed him.[28]

In February 1440 Somerset returned to Normandy with an army of over 2,000 men.[29] He was joined by Talbot and a company of 1,200 troops who had been mustered at Bernay on 7 February, and at the

[25]Monstrelet, 5, pp. 387-90; Chartier, 1, pp. 249-50; Gruel, pp. 151-4.

[26]BL, Add Ch 568, 447.

[27]*Proceedings and Ordinances of the Privy Council of England,* ed. N.H. Nicolas, 5 (1836), p. 387. It was Beaufort, for instance, who had ordered over one hundred men from the Norman garrisons to join Talbot before Harfleur; they were paid on 25 September (BN, Clair 201/8469/75).

[28]Gruel, pp. 155-7; Chartier, 1, pp. 250-52.

[29]J. H. Ramsay, *Lancaster and York,* 2, p. 28.

beginning of spring they set out on a raid into the Santerre district of Picardy. It was probably this that was referred to on 21 March when Somerset was said to be in command of almost 3,000 troops newly raised for the recovery of certain places. Folville and Lihons were captured and, after raids deep into Picardy, a rich haul of plunder was taken.[30] The purpose of these raids into Burgundian territory was perhaps to keep pressure on Burgundy to sign a separate truce with England. Having completed this successful foray, the army turned towards Harfleur and Montivilliers, which were to be the chief objectives of the summer campaign. There is some doubt as to the date at which the siege of Harfleur began. Waurin stated that it opened at the beginning of April, but there is good reason to believe that the full English army did not appear before Harfleur until July. Certainly Talbot, who played a prominent part, was still at Honfleur on 26 June.[31] And although Somerset may perhaps have originally planned to take command, it was eventually decided that his brother Edmund should lead the besieging army.[32] The siege, when it eventually began, was most thorough, the town being completely cut off by land and sea. The French held out until October, when a determined effort to relieve the town was made by a force under the comte d'Eu. But the French attack on the section of the siegeworks commanded by Talbot was beaten off and the attempt was abandoned. This sealed the fate of Harfleur and towards the end of the month the garrison surrendered. [33] Talbot was immediately made its new captain.

Talbot had retired to Honfleur by 22 October, but he was soon called out into the field yet again, for during the siege of Harfleur a second French army had advanced from the south and occupied and refortified Louviers and Conches. From 29 November, therefore, he was at Pont-Audemer collecting troops for the recovery of those places.[34] It appears that, after the fall of Harfleur, both Somerset and his brother had returned to England,[35] and so it seems that Talbot,

[30]BN, MS Fr 26066; AN K 65/1/5; Monstrelet, 5, pp. 405-9; Waurin, 4, pp. 266-73.

[31]Waurin, 4, p. 274; BN, Clair 201/8471/77. Other units, however, were mustering before Harfleur on 26-28 June (BN, Clair 201/8469/73, 6; 8471/78; 202/8473/1).

[32]On 28 June Somerset, Fauconberg and Scales were operating in the neighbourhood of Avranches and Granville (BL, Add Ch 6945).

[33]Monstrelet, 5, pp. 418-24; Waurin, 4, pp. 274-85; Basin, 1, pp. 251-3; Chartier, 1, pp. 259-60.

[34]BL, Add Ch 453; Basin, 1, pp. 253-5; Gruel, p. 161; *Chronique du Mont-St-Michel*, ed. S Luce, Société des Anciens Textes Français, (Paris, 1879), p. 41, BN, MS Fr 25775/1455-69.

[35]York had been appointed Governor on 2 July 1440. It is possible that, disappointed in their ambitions for high office in Normandy, the Beauforts returned to England in a fit of pique.

Fauconberg and Scales resumed their role as independent divisional commanders until the arrival of Richard of York. Since the failure of the peace negotiations and the loss of Meaux in 1439, things had not gone too well for English arms. The recovery of Harfleur had been effectively neutralised by the establishment of the French salient based on Louviers and Conches. Now, throughout the winter of 1440-41, as the three divisional commanders joined forces to attempt to recover this land, the first ominous signs of exhaustion appeared in the English war effort. French possession of Louviers was a particular nuisance because it enabled them to cut the line of the Seine between Rouen and Pontoise. Yet during the winter the English army was unable, or unwilling, to attack the town. By 19 December the army had moved to Elbeuf. On 3 January Talbot had moved over to Lisieux, of which place he was then captain, where he recruited a *creu* which he had brought back to Elbeuf by 15 January. Here the army lingered for some two months while its strength dwindled. Originally planned to be 2,400 strong, it was reduced to 1,600 on 1 January and actually mustered 929 combatants on 26 March, by which date it had returned to Pont-Audemer. In April it moved up to Pont-de-l'Arche, again threatening Louviers, where it stayed until mid-May, still venturing nothing.[36] Having failed in this plan to reduce Louviers and Conches over the winter, Talbot decided to return to the pays de Caux for the recovery of Dieppe and, between 17 and 27 May, he set off with a sizeable train of ordnance.[37] But he was almost immediately called back by the news that the French were advancing in strength towards the Oise valley under the command, for the first time, of King Charles and that they had already laid siege to Creil. Talbot was back at Pont-de-l'Arche on 27 May gathering supplies for the relief of Creil, only to hear that the town had fallen on 24 May.[38] The relief column, however, was kept together to succour Pontoise, towards which the French next advanced.

The campaign for possession of Pontoise in 1441 was the last full-scale operation undertaken by either side before the truce of Tours. It took on additional significance because of the presence of King Charles at the head of the French army; this made it, for the English, more than the defence of a strategically placed outpost of the conquest,[39] for they

[36] See BL, Add Chs 1201, 3006, 3910-7, 1494, 6947, 6949, 8007; BN, MS Fr 25775-6/1455-1520 for the large number of surviving musters of this force.

[37] BN, MS Fr 26068/4346, 48, 51; Stevenson, *Wars,* 2, p. 463.

[38] Monstrelet, 6, pp. 5-6; Chartier, 2, pp. 15-17; Bourgeois, pp. 359-60.

[39] Since its recapture in 1437, the English had paid special attention to Pontoise. Richemont had tried unsuccessfully to storm the town in 1438. It had been constantly

saw the opportunity of inflicting a decisive defeat in pitched battle on the king himself. Despite the obviously growing exhaustion, the presence of the king stimulated the English command to one last great effort to turn the tide of war. The siege was opened on a grand scale on 6 June.[40] A few days later Talbot moved forward from Pont-de-l'Arche to Vernon, which he made his headquarters for the supply of Pontoise. The council in Rouen was greatly concerned at the situation. 'Close upon the feast of St John' (24 June), it wrote to England bewailing the failure of Richard of York to arrive, and giving news of the siege:

> Your chief adversary and his son have begun the said siege before that town, and how long it can hold out against them we cannot say. For they have a great body of troops, and are wonderfully well provided with all kinds of necessaries and requisites for the war, and their spirits are raised and stimulated to a great pitch of pride on account of the conquest of Creil. Lord Talbot is at Vernon, waiting for all the troops that can be raised to go with him, to do his best at the siege, by God's help. Whatever diligence has been done, or whatever commands have been issued in your name of any Captains or troops by showing them your need, they have indifferently *(petitement)* obeyed. It is a great misfortune for you, our sovereign lord, that the said Lord Talbot has not a sufficient strength, for he has a high notable desire to do the best he can for you against your said enemies.[41]

The council did not expect much of a half-hearted and under-strength army. Nevertheless, on 22 June Talbot did in fact succeed in entering Pontoise with supplies and reinforcements under Lord Scales, who took charge of the defence. On 24 June Talbot retired to Mantes, then to Rouen, where he collected more supplies which were probably delivered to Scales before the end of the month.[42]

At the beginning of July York made his long awaited appearance with a strong army of fresh troops and he set out for Pontoise almost

revictualled from Normandy and by 12 January 1440 a substantial power of artillery had been installed. In August 1440 the garrison had been heavily reinforced in case the French army, then preparing to relieve Harfleur, should make an attempt on it. See Bourgeois, p. 344; BN, MS Fr 26066/800; PO Talbot, 2787/35; AN, K 66/34/1.

[40] The main contemporary accounts are to be found in Basin, 1, pp. 263-77; Chartier, 2, pp. 22-7; Gruel, pp. 167-71; Monstrelet, 6, pp. 6-24 and Waurin, 4, pp. 314-48. Beaucourt, *Charles VII,* 3, pp. 180ff provides the best modern account. See also Burne, *Agincourt War,* pp. 293-301 and Brill, 'An English Captain', pp. 420-44.

[41] Stevenson, *Wars,* 2, pp. 603 ff.

[42] Waurin, 4, pp. 322, 24; Basin, 1, p. 262. Beaucourt, *Charles VII,* 3, p. 181 states that Fauconberg was also left in Pontoise, but he was in fact mustered with the rest of the army at Juziers on 13 July (BN, MS Fr 25776/1528).

immediately. He and Talbot joined forces and mustered their combined army at Juziers on 13-14 July. They were then ready to bring King Charles to battle. On 16 July they entered Pontoise unopposed. After revictualling the town, the English drew up in battle array and proclaimed to King Charles, who had retreated to the left bank of the river, their intention of crossing. About two days later they succeeded in forcing a passage upstream above Beaumont. But Charles had no intention of fighting, and himself recrossed the river, leaving a strong garrison in a bastille opposite Pontoise; and after crossing the Seine as well, he made his way to Poissy. This left the English to fortify the left bank and the bridges across the river, whilst Talbot marched down towards Conflans to keep an eye on King Charles. Without clearing the French from the bastille, York and Talbot set out once more in pursuit of Charles on about 24 July and recrossed the Oise at Heuville.[44]

The events of the last week of July are by no means clear. It appears that one purpose in crossing to the right bank of the Oise was to cut off French communications between Poissy and Pontoise. York, or some of his men, met a supply column and in the skirmish that followed the English suffered serious casualties. Chartier, Gruel and Waurin all agreed that York at this point decided to return to Rouen,[45] but Basin adds that Talbot suggested a final scheme whereby Charles could be caught. This envisaged Talbot crossing the Seine at Mantes and surprising Charles at Poissy, whilst York would wait north of the river to cut off his retreat. All the chroniclers agree that Talbot carried out the raid on Poissy, probably at dawn on 27 July, and Chartier supports Basin in suggesting that the aim was to capture Charles, though he narrowly failed to do so.[46] (In his anger he sacked the town.) Charles escaped to Conflans, but he was not intercepted by York, who had almost certainly left the region. If Basin's report of a 'pincer' movement is correct, it seems probable that York rejected it and took no part (as other accounts witness) in Talbot's raid on Poissy.[47]

[43] BN, MS Fr 25776/1528, 9; AN, K 67/1/23-28.

[44] See Beaucourt, *Charles VII*, 3, pp. 183-7 for a detailed reconstruction of these events.

[45] Chartier, 2, pp. 25-6; Gruel, p. 170; Waurin, 4, p. 338.

[46] Basin, 1, pp. 266-8; Chartier, 2, p. 26.

[47] Brill does not discuss the events of this week. Burne, *Agincourt War,* pp. 298-9, accepted Basin's account as it stands. To highlight his description of the attempt to ensnare King Charles he takes a detail from Chartier's account (2, p. 25) – namely, that York arrived too late only to see the French marching by in the distance – which refers not to this episode, but to the earlier attempt to intercept French supplies moving from Poissy to Pontoise. Basin simply states that York was not able to intercept Charles.

Both sides were exhausted. The supplies around Pontoise and in the Île de France had long been consumed and the lack of food and fodder seems to have been the chief factor in restricting the campaign to ten days. King Charles retired to St Denis, whilst York, after leaving Scales and Fauconberg in a much strengthened Pontoise, arrived back in Rouen on 1 August, his troops haggard, starving and exhausted. Talbot resumed his earlier role of collecting supplies and organized a fresh convoy at Elbeuf.[48] Although the attempt to bring King Charles to battle had failed, for the time being Pontoise was secure. But King Charles, having rested his troops, decided to renew the siege and on 16 August he appeared once more before the town. Talbot moved up to Pont-de-l'Arche before 20 August and on 22 August slipped into Pontoise, avoiding the French who had tried to block his route. Fauconberg and Scales were then relieved, for when Talbot quitted Pontoise on 24 August Lord Clinton was left as captain. Talbot retired only as far as Mantes, where he continued to watch Pontoise and maintained the flow of supplies to the town. He himself went there on at least two occasions, on 29 August and 6 September, accompanied by only a small section of his personal retinue.[49] With the lines of communication thus kept open, it was clear that Charles would never be able to reduce the town by siege before winter and so he decided to take it by assault. On 16 September 1441, after a heavy artillery barrage, the suburb around the church of Notre Dame was taken and three days later the town fell to a general assault; Clinton was captured after a brave and vigorous defence.[50]

King Charles VII had won a pyrrhic victory. Although the English had eventually failed to save Pontoise, by their stubborn resistance they had prevented any further advance into Normandy. For this they owed much to Talbot's vigour, courage and indefatigability, for over the whole summer he had overcome the indifference of many of the English soldiers, the appalling conditions, and harrassment by the French in Louviers,[51] difficulties which perhaps partly explained the

[48]Basin, 1, p. 266; AN, K 67/1/29, 31, 32; BN, MS Fr 26068/4335; Beaucourt, *Charles VII,* 3, p. 187.

[49]AN, K 67/1/33, 37, 39-41; BN, MS Fr 25776/1532, 3; Beaucourt, *Charles VII,* 3, pp. 188-90. Musters were held at Pont-de-l'Arche from 20 August. Scales and Fauconberg gave acquittances for receipts of supplies in Pontoise between 22 and 24 August.

[50]Beaucourt, *Charles VII,* 3, p. 191.

[51]The French garrison of Louviers established a fort at St Pierre du Vouvray on the Seine, from which they effectively cut communications and the passage of supplies by river from Rouen to Mantes. On 29 July, for instance, the council arranged for food and powder to be sent to Pontoise, but warned against using the river route to Mantes because of enemy action (E. Cosneau, *Le Connétable de Richemont* (Paris, 1886), p. 323; BN, MS Fr 26068/4335).

comparative brevity of York's active participation. Talbot had amply demonstrated his skill with a small mobile force in conditions which hampered the movement of large armies. It was a quality recognized by the 'Bourgeois of Paris' who, commenting on the events of 1441, wrote that the English had one captain, named Talbot, who would face and hold his ground against King Charles and of whom indeed 'il sembloit au semblant qu'ilz monstroient que moult le doudtassent, car touzjours eux eslongnoient de lui XX ou XXX lieves, et il chevauchoit parmy France plus hardiment qu'ilz ne faisoient'.[52]

Nevertheless, it is clear that during the previous year the hard effort in atrocious conditions had begun to take its toll. Fauconberg had been unable to prevent the establishment of a new salient from the southern borders of Normandy reaching to the river Seine itself or the additional loss of Beaumont-le-Roger and Évreux in 1441. Talbot, despite all his efforts, had equally been unable to prevent the loss of Creil and Pontoise. Since the recovery of Harfleur, the English position in Normandy had undoubtedly worsened. There was an air of desperation about Talbot's efforts to capture the wily King Charles in July. It was almost as though he recognized that Normandy could now only be saved by such a *coup*. If he was tired and beset by doubts, he nevertheless soldiered on. Indeed, York's return meant personal promotion for him. He was made lieutenant-general for the conduct of the war and at Michaelmas 1441 he was reappointed to the senior captaincy of Rouen. There seems little doubt that York was now prepared to rely on Talbot in military affairs and placed the defence of the duchy formally in his hands.[53] After the fall of Pontoise, Talbot spent most of his time in Rouen. He was absent for a week in October and between 18 November and 28 December, the controller of the garrison recorded, he carried out 'certaines entreprises a l'encontre les adversaires du Roy' with some of the garrison men; but the chroniclers are silent and administrative records throw no further light on these activities. Perhaps they amounted to another abortive move against the Louviers-Conches salient.[54] On 18 February he sailed from Harfleur with a deputation of Norman councillors to plead for more assistance. The result was that while in England (his first visit since 1435) he was commissioned to recruit an army of 2,500 men. But he had difficulty in raising this force in a war-weary England, having to be content with retinues with a ratio of ten archers to every one man-at-arms instead of the customary three to one. As its record

[52]Bourgeois, p. 359.

[53]Chartier, 2, pp. 17, 32; BN, Clair, 202/8479/12; MS Fr 26763/734; BL, Add Ch 470, 1209.

[54]ADSM, Fonds Danquin 11/89.

of service was to show, this was one of the poorest armies yet sent over to France. On 20 May 1442, not long before returning to Normandy, Talbot was created earl of Shrewsbury.

The newly created earl and his army landed at Harfleur, where the men were mustered on 15 June 1442.[55] They were joined by Lord Fauconberg and certain garrison contingents before opening the campaign, the original objective of which was, once again, the French enclave south of the Seine. On 14-16 July the army was at Pont-de-l'Arche and from there it marched down to Conches. Operations were made more difficult by the presence of a French army under Dunois to the south, which attacked Gallardon in an effort to draw Talbot away from Conches. But the siege of Conches was not abandoned. The town surrendered before 7 September and after a garrison of 270 men had been installed under Thomas Pigot, there was still time to save Gallardon.[56] Having achieved this, Talbot returned to the Louviers sector, where he was stationed at Gaillon on 13 September. But the garrison of Gallardon soon compounded with the French, much to Talbot's anger. It was probably because of Dunois's continued presence and sallies made by the garrison of Évreux, all of which hampered his operations, that Talbot now decided to abandon any attempt on Louviers and Évreux and to retire north of the Seine for an attack on Dieppe.[57] Consequently, in preparation for a siege of this, the last French enclave in the pays de Caux, the army and a large column of ordnance and supplies gathered at Jumièges during the last days of October. It consisted of 600 men raised from the garrisons and the remnant of those who had come over from England in the summer. Its total size, one chronicler estimated, was 1,500 men. This somewhat insufficient force marched to Dieppe early in November, the fort of Charlesmesnil being reduced en route. Talbot had little hope of maintaining a full siege and blockade and so on reaching the town he decided to concentrate his men and artillery on the hill known as the Pollet overlooking the port from the east, and to attempt to reduce it by bombardment. He had not been there long before the ubiquitous Dunois appeared with 1,000 men and took command of the defence.[58] To add to his troubles, Talbot now seems to have faced a mutiny in his army. The author of MS Cleopatra C. IV commented:

[55] ADSM, Fonds Danquin, 3/3/17; BN, PO Talbot 2787/42; Clair 202/8478/5; Stevenson, *Wars*, 1, pp. 430-1; *CPR, 1441-6*, p. 106; Ramsay, *Lancaster and York*, 2, p. 42; *CP*, 11, p. 701.

[56] PRO, E101/54/2; BN, MS Fr 25776/1573-5, 51, 91; AN, K 67/12/67-77; BL, Add Ch 469. Musters were taken at Conches on 17-20 August. Thomas Pigot and 270 men of Talbot's army were installed in the town before 7 September.

[57] Monstrelet, 6, pp. 58-9; Stevenson, *Wars*, 2, pp. 331-2.

[58] BN, MS Fr 25776/1586-91; BL, Add Ch 144; Chartier, 2, pp. 36-8; Waurin, 4, p. 372; Monstrelet, 6, pp. 60-61.

> the erll of Shrewsbury leyd sege by watyr and lond to Depe; and
> kept it a whyle till he ferd so foule with his men, that thei wolde
> not longer abyde with him; and so he whas fayne to high away
> thense to Rooen.[59]

Talbot did indeed retire to Rouen, but he left five hundred veterans
under the command of Sir William Peyto in the bastille constructed
on the Pollet.[60] The London chronicler's story, possibly picked up
from returning troops, probably refers to Talbot's relationship with
the raw recruits he brought over in June, whose six-month period of
contract was now at an end and who may well have refused to
continue in service. It is quite probable that Talbot had no choice but
to leave a token force before Dieppe during the winter with the object
of bringing a new, and hopefully better, army to continue the siege in
the following summer.

It is evident that the successful prosecution of the war in Normandy
now depended squarely on the annual supply of reinforcements from
England. This had been recognised in York's terms of appointment.
The estates of Normandy could no longer be relied upon to pay the full
wages bill of the garrisons, let alone to finance effective field
campaigns. It was thus essential that if Dieppe were to be taken in
1443 York and Talbot would have to receive the usual annual
reinforcements. In fact these, and all the English effort for this year,
were diverted to Somerset, who was appointed to an independent
command in France. Moreover, not only were the troops not
forthcoming, but the council refused to pay York the £20,000 which
was essential for the payment of the troops already in Normandy.[61] So
it was that in June 1443 Talbot returned to Westminster, not to
Dieppe, to plead with the English council. On 21 June he was assured
that Somerset's appointment implied no disrespect to York. On 8 and
13 July he secured trifling grants in York's favour and assurances of
support for the force before Dieppe, including the somewhat insufficient posting of a solitary ballinger to his army's assistance. Early
in August he returned to Normandy, virtually empty-handed.[62] A few

[59] Kingsford, Chronicles, p. 150.

[60] According to the Chronique du Mont-Saint-Michel, 1, p. 43, the fort was 'garnies .
. . des meilleurs gens.' Talbot was still at Dieppe when he mustered on 28 November,
the day on which Dunois arrived. He left part of his personal retinue in the fort under the
command of Sir John Ripley. Chartier's information is remarkably accurate. He gives
the size of the English force left on the Pollet as 500-600. In January 1443 it was
mustered at 500, in February and March at 550, and in May and June at 570 (BN MS
Fr 25776/1570, 89, 1612, 28, 39).

[61] E.M. Burney, 'The English Rule in Normandy, 1435-1450' (unpublished Oxford
University B. Litt. thesis, 1958), pp. 101-2, 137-8; Ramsay, Lancaster and York, 2, p.
50.

[62] Kingsford, Chronicles, p. 151; Proc. Priv. Council, 5, pp. 289, 290, 298, 301, 306.

days later, on 14 August, the isolated bastille at Dieppe fell to the vigorous assault of the Dauphin, who had arrived with a powerful army of relief. According to Waurin, 300 of the English were killed. The rest were taken prisoner, including Sir William Peyto, Sir John Ripley, one of Talbot's bastard sons and several men of Talbot's personal retinue.[63] Talbot's and York's bitterness and their disillusion with the English council were probably intensified by the disastrous failure of Somerset's chevauchée into France which, it had been argued, would relieve the pressure on Normandy. By the end of 1443 it was apparent that the war could not continue for much longer.[64] With the humiliating failure to retake Dieppe and his own personal retinue decimated there, Talbot no doubt welcomed the moves for a truce that were initiated early in 1444. The duke of Suffolk was appointed to treat with Charles VII in February and he passed through Rouen on his way to Tours in March. On 8 April Talbot became a conservator of a preliminary truce covering Vendôme and Le Mans. On 28 May the general truce for two years was sealed.[65] Talbot could now look forward to the peaceful enjoyment of his Norman estates and other less onerous duties, such as acting as godfather at the christening of York's daughter Elizabeth in Rouen cathedral in September. It is almost certain that in January and February 1445 he, as well as his countess, was in the party that went to Nancy to collect Margaret of Anjou for her journey to England and was fêted there for several weeks. In March this splendid entourage travelled to England via Paris and Rouen.[66] Thus, Talbot returned in state to England. On 12 March he was reappointed lieutenant of Ireland[67] and his long period of service in Normandy came formally to an end.

The English war effort ground to a halt in the early 1440s. Not even Talbot could escape the general exhaustion which then set in. With neither side having the will or the capacity to continue the fight, a truce was the only logical outcome. The truce of Tours gave both sides the opportunity to recover and build up their strength for a renewal of

[63]Chartier, 2, p. 39; Basin, 1, p. 289; Waurin, 4, pp. 381-2.

[64]In the far south-west of the duchy Lord Scales was faring equally badly. In November 1442 he had lost Granville and throughout 1443 endeavoured unsuccessfully to recover it (*Chronique du Mont-Saint-Michel*, 2, pp. 146-65; Kingsford, *Chronicles*, p. 151).

[65]Ramsay, *Lancaster and York*, 2, pp. 58-60; Bossuat, *Gressart et Surienne*, p. 281.

[66]Ramsay, *Lancaster and York*, 2, pp. 61-3; Beaucourt, *Charles VII*, 4, p. 92. On 17 August 1444 Talbot's attorney was paid £100 towards his expenses in escorting the queen (PRO, E403/753, m10).

[67]*CPR, 1441-6*, p. 345.

the fighting. There was no chance of it leading to a final peace treaty. This was revealed at the negotiations at Westminster in 1445, where once again efforts to come to terms collapsed after the English refused to surrender their claim to sovereignty in Normandy and Aquitaine and the French refused to allow a partition of the kingdom.[68] In practice the truce only benefited the French. Charles VII completed the reform of his army, welding by means of the *ordonnance* of 1445 a standing army out of the unoccupied men-at-arms from the various independent companies that had so far fought the war, and he continued to build up the power of his artillery. When war was reopened, Charles was ready for the first time to make a concerted onslaught on Normandy.[69] On the other hand, the truce hastened the disintegration of the English administration in Normandy. There was no economic recovery. It has been doubted whether the truce brought an overall financial advantage. The crippling cost of the war was removed, but the Norman exchequer had to pay out substantial sums as *appatis* and compensation.[70] At the same time, the more relaxed conditions of truce led to a speedy disintegration of the administration of the army. After 1445 there was no resident governor. Little by little, Basin commented, the English failed to pay their troops and maintain order. Troops thus took to living off the land, which incensed the French population and encouraged the spread of brigandage.[71] The extent of the anarchy may have been exaggerated by Basin, but there can be little doubt that the administrative system established at the beginning of the conquest was collapsing and that several English captains, such as Roger, Lord Camoys, had become virtual free-booters.[72] In the event, the truce proved disastrous for the English. Rather than being used to recuperate and build up strength, it became the cause of further disintegration. By 1449 the English army was in no position to renew the war.

Yet amazingly it was the English who precipitated the renewal of war by the seizure of Fougères on 24 March 1449. The explanation for this extraordinary act is complex and can only be briefly summarized here. It was born out of English efforts to find in Brittany a committed ally against France to replace Burgundy. This in itself was a not unreasonable diplomatic objective. In the long run it was only

[68] J.J.N. Palmer, 'The War Aims of the Protagonists and the Negotiations for Peace', in *The Hundred Years' War*, ed. K.A. Fowler (1971), p. 71.

[69] Contamine, *Guerre,* pp. 234-75 provides the authoritative discussion of the reforms.

[70] Burney, 'Normandy', pp. 85-6.

[71] Basin, 2, pp. 53-7.

[72] Bossuat, *Gressart et Surienne,* p. 320.

through the support of such an ally that England would be likely to retain Normandy. But the chances of clinching this diplomatic coup were slender. The dukes of Brittany had maintained a studied neutrality in recent years and the present duke, Francis I, was unlikely to change that stance. English hopes were pinned, therefore, on his ambitious and dissident brother Gilles, an anglophile, and a pensioner and sworn liegeman of Henry VI. In 1446, however, Francis I, who had recently done homage to Charles VII, arrested and imprisoned his brother. The English demanded his release and soon began plotting to secure it. It was in fact an unfortunate time, for the news of the cession of Maine, by secret treaty and with no *quid pro quo,* angered opinion in both England and Normandy. Suffolk and his fellow councillors were therefore desperate to salvage some credibility as well as to revive their floundering Breton diplomacy when they hatched the plot to seize Fougères as a bargaining counter in exchange for Gilles. Suffolk and the English council seem to have convinced themselves that, notwithstanding Duke Francis's homage to Charles VII, an attack on Fougères could be kept as a matter solely between Henry VI, as king of France, and Brittany. It was indeed a desperate gamble carried out by a failing ministry seeking a quick and easy success without giving much heed to the likely consequences.[73]

Talbot was as implicated in the conspiracy as anyone else in high office in 1447-49. Indeed, the English government's Norman policy was totally subordinated to the Fougères plot in these years. The Spanish free-lance, François de Surienne, was recruited to carry out the actual raid. In 1447, Edmund, marquis of Dorset and earl of Somerset, who was about to be created duke of Somerset, had been governor of Maine and was one of those who had lost financially by its cession; he was now appointed governor of Normandy. York, who had hoped to have his commission renewed, was sent to Ireland, and Talbot, who had been in Ireland in 1446-47, was brought back to support Somerset. Talbot and Somerset, brothers-in-law, were described by one witness at the subsequent French enquiry into the Fougères affair as men who worked in close partnership ('sont alliez ensemble') and were to all appearances in complete agreement. When they crossed to Normandy in May 1448 they must have been fully conversant with the plot.[74] Talbot was given virtually independent

[73] M.H. Keen and M.J. Daniel, 'English diplomacy and the sack of Fougères', *History* 59 (1974), 375-391, *passim;* M.G.A. Vale, *Charles VII* (1974), pp. 115-19.

[74] *Dictionary of National Biography,* 55, p. 322; Bossuat, *Gressart et Surienne,* p. 322; *Histoires des regnes de Charles VII et de Louis XI par Thomas Basin,* ed. J. Quicherat (Paris, 1859), 4, p. 314.

command of lower Normandy, which included the march with Brittany, and made Falaise, of which town he became captain, his headquarters in or before the beginning of July. Talbot's role was to provide the military support for the raid. Troops withdrawing from Maine, where they had finally surrendered to the French in March, were redeployed near the Breton border, and in the summer Talbot and Surienne attempted to restore some order and control over the soldiers stationed in the area.[75] Preparations were clearly being made for a possible war with Brittany. In the autumn Talbot attended the peace conference which secured the continuation of the truce with France.[76] During the winter the final preparations for the attack on Fougères went ahead. The marshal of Talbot's troops at Falaise told Cardinot Roque, another who gave evidence at the subsequent enquiry, that a great enterprise was being planned, of which he could not speak. At the last moment Talbot appears to have advised Somerset against going ahead. Perhaps he knew in his heart that if it led to any general outbreak of war, the English army would be overwhelmed. In the event, Surienne's attack on 24 March was a total success, and Somerset and Talbot were reported as being very pleased that it had turned out so well.[77] Certainly Talbot, still at Falaise, immediately set about supplying and victualling the town (at the same time helping himself to a share of the plunder).[78] Having completed this, he retired to Rouen to join Somerset and wait upon events. Immediately after the sack of Fougères, the duke of Brittany appealed to King Charles for assistance and, in May, Charles sent troops to take Pont-de-l'Arche, Conches and Gerberoy in retaliation. Somerset's response early in June was to send Talbot to Pont-Audemer 'acompaigne de grant nombre de gens des guerre' while last minute negotiations were conducted at Louviers.[79] At this conference the English maintained, as they had done before, that they could not discuss the Fougères affair with the French because it concerned only Henry VI and Duke Francis, who was Henry's liegeman. Finally losing patience and at length convinced that he had every right on his side, King Charles declared war in July 1449.[80] The seizure of

[75] Bossuat, *Gressart et Surienne*, pp. 317-19; Keen and Daniel, *History* 59 (1974), 378. Talbot and his personal retinue were mustered at Falaise on 2 July and again on 27 December (AN, K 68/29/6; BN, MS Fr 25778/1830).

[76] Beaucourt, *Charles VII*, 4, pp 312-19; T. Rymer, *Foedera, Conventiones, Litterae etc*, 5, Pt 2, p. 7.

[77] *Histoires*, ed. Quicherat, 4, pp. 304, 307.

[78] *Ibid*., pp. 306-18.

[79] BL. Add MS 11,509, f 12. I am grateful to Miss Curry for this information.

[80] Keen and Daniel, *History* 59 (1974), 376, 388-9; Vale, *Charles VII*, p. 118.

Fougères, far from gaining a much needed triumph for the English, precipitated the renewal of the war against France for which they were so totally unprepared. It was an act of monumental folly which gave King Charles the very justification he needed to launch the final attack on Normandy.

Two French armies, under the counts of Dunois and Eu, well equipped with guns and siege engines, attacked independently. Dunois opened his advance by taking Verneuil on 19 July. Strategically, the one English hope was to attack the divided armies at the very beginning of their advance. This Talbot threatened to do. When Dunois appeared before Verneuil the garrison appealed for help and Talbot moved forward from Pont-Audemer with a relief force. Dunois marched to meet him and the two armies came up against each other between Beaumont-le-Roger and Harcourt on 31 July. Talbot placed himself in a strong defensive position, but Dunois refused to attack. Unwilling to attack himself, Talbot withdrew during the following night and ignominiously returned to Rouen, not only allowing Dunois to continue his advance but also leaving the unprotected Pont-Audemer to fall to the army under Eu on 12 August.[81] Thenceforward the English remained rooted in Rouen until the French appeared before its walls. Talbot may not have had a very large army at his disposal, but regardless of size it was probably the poor quality and morale of his troops which caused him to be so hesitant. And perhaps even he felt that resistance was useless. At all levels the English no longer had the will to resist. When Rouen was finally attacked in October by the combined French armies under the command of King Charles himself Talbot at last showed a spark of his old vigour and daring. The French managed to scale the walls on 16 October, but Talbot personally led a determined counter-attack and repulsed them.[82] Three days later, however, the citizens turned against the English who retreated to the castle, leaving the city to the French. Here, in the fortress, a stand was attempted, but King Charles brought up such a power of artillery that resistance became pointless. Somerset attempted to negotiate an honourable surrender, but after ten days he was forced to accept King Charles's terms. These dictated that he was to surrender eight hostages, including Talbot, as surety that not only Rouen but also the entire pays de Caux would surrender in fifteen days. The hostages were handed over and Somerset marched out to Caen.[83]

[81] *Narratives of the Expulsion of the English from Normandy,* ed. J. Stevenson, Rolls Series 32 (1863), pp. 57-62, 258-61.

[82] *Ibid.,* pp. 295-6.

[83] *Ibid.,* pp. 296ff. For the treaty of surrender, see Stevenson, *Wars,* 2, pp. 607-18.

Talbot's years of service in Normandy thus came to an end. He was at first held at Rouen, paying a courtesy visit to King Charles, who lodged at St Katherine's monastery. In the company of his fellow hostages, the ladies and other notables, he also witnessed the formal entry of the king into the city on 10 November from a window overlooking Notre Dame. When the formalities were concluded he was transferred to Dreux and, because Harfleur and other places under his lieutenants refused to surrender, he was kept prisoner. In fact, he was not released until 11 July 1450, when his garrison at Falaise surrendered, and then only on condition that he undertook a pilgrimage to Rome, which he had given the king to understand was his wish.[84] And so he left Normandy for the last time.

After 1448 Talbot appears but a shadow of his former self. Robert Blondel, in his account of the expulsion of the English from Normandy, expressed the opinion that he was broken in spirit.[85] And he may well have been right. Talbot, as much as anyone, was responsible for the disaster. Yet it is remarkable that his reputation was in no way damaged by the events of 1449. The French themselves paid it a compliment by insisting that he should be removed from the theatre of war. It was perhaps this very fact, and the manner in which Somerset had to accept his surrender as a hostage, that saved his reputation. One of the poems produced in 1450 attacking Suffolk's régime inferred that, if free, he would still have been able to save Normandy, for Suffolk was said to be responsible for the fact that

> he is bounden that our dore should kepe, that is Talbot our goode dogge.[86]

Two years later, when York accused Somerset of responsibility for the loss of the duchy, Talbot was carefully ignored. York too may have been subscribing to the current image of Talbot as the frustrated hero. It is ironic that although he did little to enhance his reputation in the last year of the occupation, Talbot came to be regarded as the thwarted champion of England.

Looking back over the whole decade, it is the case that Talbot achieved little success after the recovery of Harfleur in 1440. How then is one to assess this stage of his career? The lack of success after

---

[84]*Narratives*, ed. Stevenson, p. 319; Beaucourt, *Charles VII*, 5, pp. 18, 23-4; Stevenson, *Wars*, 2, pp. 629, 735-42, esp. p. 738 for Clause 4 of the treaty in which Talbot agreed to go to Rome.

[85]Blondel devoted Chapter 30 to reflections on Talbot's conduct early in the campaign; he came to the conclusion that Talbot had lost all his old violent energy (*Narratives*, ed Stevenson, pp. 60-2).

[86]*Political Poems and Songs*, ed. T. Wright, Rolls Series 14, Part 2, (1861), pp.22, 224.

1440 was not his alone — it was a consequence of the general English exhaustion. By the same token, neither was the relative success in preserving eastern Normandy in English hands between 1436 and 1439 his alone. It was the success of the whole army and of the complex military command of which he was but a part — a success, moreover, which was only achieved against an enemy unable and unwilling to prosecute the war with any determination. Much has been made of Talbot's capacity for the sudden surprise attack, with his mobile column constantly on the alert to pounce on an unsuspecting enemy, dashing here, there and everywhere. There is no doubt that Talbot did excel in the tactics of surprise, that he could on occasion move across country at great speed, and that he did have a talent in small-scale actions in command of small bands of men, as may be witnessed in the Pontoise campaigns of 1437 and 1441. But too much can be made of this as the normal pattern of his soldiering. The reality was more humdrum. Most of the time Talbot was engaged in routine and often tedious military actions. There were the three months spent sitting before Tancarville, the five months spent kicking his heels in the neighbourhood of Louviers in 1440-41, and there was the incessant organising and convoying of supplies to revictual this or that threatened outpost of the conquest. These actions, just like the occasional plundering raids, were part and parcel of the ordinary routine of any commander in the fifteenth-century wars in France. The remarkable thing about Talbot is that, like his comrade-in-arms Lord Scales, he was prepared to soldier on, in ever worsening conditions and with ever diminishing prospects of eventual victory. In the last resort, it is Talbot's willingness to carry on year after year in the same unspectacular toil which is the most notable feature of his military career after 1435. And it is this seemingly selfless service in a dying cause for his lord and sovereign which made a lasting impression on his contemporaries. It was not that Talbot was outstandingly successful, but that he went on doing his best for the Lancastrian cause in France until all was finally lost.

5

CAPTAIN OF WAR: JOHN TALBOT AND HIS TROOPS

John Talbot, as senior field commander in the defence of Normandy after 1435, retained large numbers of troops in his service. At the siege of Tancarville in 1437 not only did he have the general command of operations, but he also personally recruited and led nearly 1,700 men, the greater part of the besieging force.[1] Throughout the three years 1436-39 he was the personal captain of well over 1,000 troops, almost one-fifth of the Lancastrian army in Normandy, in half a dozen or more retinues.[2] He was captain of fewer after 1440, but still in 1441-44 he was retaining approximately 600 men a year in five companies, which represented approximately 10 per cent of the armed forces in Normandy. In terms of men personally retained by him, Talbot was without doubt the most important of the captains of war in the years between Arras and Tours. Who were the men who thus served under Talbot's banner and how and where did he recruit them? This is a question that has not been answered for any of the captains in Normandy after 1435. The rank and file of the army, the men-at-arms and archers who made up the retinues serving in Normandy over a period of thirty years and more, have in fact received but scant attention from historians. R.A. Newhall delineated authoritatively the administrative structure by which they were controlled[3] and more recent research has amplified our knowledge of the captains and lieutenants in the service of the successive governors of Normandy between 1436 and 1450,[4] but the composition of the greater part of the army has remained largely unexplored.[5] At one time it was assumed that the rank and file were drawn from indentured retainers and dependents of the captains at home. A connection was drawn between the rise of the contract army in the fourteenth century and the development of the indentured retainer as a means of recruiting

---

[1] R.A. Newhall, *Muster and Review*, (Harvard, 1940), pp. 143-6; BN, MS Fr 25774/1241.

[2] In the last quarter of 1436 he was captain of 1,341 men in a total army strength of 6,627 (BN, MS Fr 25773/1112).

[3] Newhall, *Muster and Review, passim.* See also the pioneering work of L. Jarry, *Le Compte de l'armée Anglaise au siège d'Oriéans, 1428-9* (Orléans, 1892), pp. 15-50.

[4] A. Marshall, 'The Role of English War Captains in England and Normandy, 1436-61' (unpublished University of Wales MA thesis, 1974).

[5] Miss A.E. Curry is currently undertaking a study of this subject.

followers in England. A noble captain, it was argued, when retained to serve abroad in France, recruited his company from amongst his own indentured retainers, whose contracts specifically included such service.[6] But studies of certain prominent noblemen have shown that this was not in fact the case. It has for some time been recognized that only a nucleus of the retinues taken out of England by great magnates such as John of Gaunt or Richard of York, and but a fraction of those of lesser peers, were life retainers or annuitants.[7] And if this is so for retinues coming out of England, one can hardly expect to find a higher proportion of English retainers amongst those retinues maintained in Normandy, sometimes for many years at a stretch, by those captains entrusted with the duchy's defence after 1435. If not recruited from their English affinities, whence did the captains draw their troops? As we shall see, Talbot retained a few men, both as lieutenants and captains as well as men-at-arms, from his English affinity, but most of the men who served in his various companies were recruited in Normandy itself. By 1435 captains like Talbot were recruiting most of their soldiers from amongst the body of resident veterans of the war which was by that time established in the duchy.

Talbot was the captain of several different kinds of retinue. As we have seen, the English army in Normandy was principally a garrison army. Talbot as one of the leading captains was given the custody of many castles and towns for which he had to supply retinues. But, more important, as one of the field commanders and marshal of France, he maintained his own personal retinue which accompanied him wherever he went. In addition, in times of crisis or when leading an army in the field, he was frequently captain of a *creu*, or retinue of temporary re-inforcements. And, moreover, on at least two occasions he was commissioned to recruit re-inforcements in England and bring them over to Normandy. In these armies, as with the occasional field army, he subcontracted with captains to supply their own retinues. And in the garrisons in which he was rarely resident, he employed lieutenants to take actual command. Thus, we need to consider the men who were Talbot's own captains and lieutenants as well as the rank and file of his retinues. But before undertaking this analysis it is necessary to comment in more detail on the different kinds of retinue.

The most important of these retinues was the band of men which acompanied him permanently. This retinue came to be distinguished

[6] A. E. Prince, 'The Indenture System under Edward III', in *Historical Essays in Honour of James Tait*, ed. J. G. Edwards *et al.* (Manchester, 1933), pp.283-97.

[7] G. A. Holmes, *The Estates of the Higher Nobility in Fourteenth-Century England* (Cambridge, 1957), p. 80; K. B. McFarlane, 'Bastard Feudalism', *BIHR* 20 (1945), 165 and *The Nobility of Later Medieval England* (Oxford, 1973), pp. 102-4.

as 'la compagnie et retinue de Monseigneur de Talbot a lui ordonne estre sa personne sur les champs' or occasionally 'ordonne pour la conduite de sa personne sur les champs'. An early retinue so styled was that which accompanied him during the siege of Orléans in 1428-29, for which one muster roll has survived.[8] Although not so styled, for the purpose of this study one may reasonably include in this category the retinue which he first took to Normandy in 1420, for which again one muster roll has survived.[9] By the middle of the 1430s this specifically styled personal retinue seems to have become the special privilege of the lieutenants-general who, like Talbot, were given specific field command. It was always kept distinct from garrison retinues and was clearly something of an élite corps. Before 1441 it usually numbered twenty men-at-arms, Talbot himself included, and sixty archers (a total establishment of eighty men), although during the spring and summer of 1436 it was enlarged to thirty men-at-arms and ninety archers.[10] On another occasion, during the summer of 1435, Talbot was commissioned to raise an auxiliary retinue of twenty men-at-arms and sixty archers, 'oultre et pardessus vint hommes d'armes et soixante archiers qu'il a pour la conduite de sa personne'.[11] At michaelmas 1441, after his promotion to the general field command of all Normandy, the establishment of the personal retinue was increased to 120 men-at-arms and 360 archers, but by 1448, perhaps in line with his more limited responsibility for lower Normandy, it was reduced to fifty-four and 162.[12]

From time to time and for various reasons the personal retinue was divided. On the first occasion, in February 1436, one-third was sent to reinforce Paris, whilst the remainder stayed in Rouen with Talbot.[13] It was immediately after this splitting of the retinue that the Rouen section was reconstituted and temporarily enlarged. In the autumn of 1436 a section of the personal retinue, now back to its normal size, was seconded to the personal service of Richard of York.[14] In 1440,

[8] BN MS Fr 25768/318.

[9] PRO, E101/70/50/1.

[10] BN, NAF 8602/23; MS Fr 26061/3092. All the muster rolls make it clear that Jarry was correct in his statement that 'L'homme d'armes represente dans ces citations, une seule personne, un seul nomme, un seul combattant; c'est donc une individualité isolée, une simple unité' (L'Armée anglaise, p. 26).

[11] BN, MS Fr 25772/944, 963, musters for May, June and July. The monthly musters indicate that the auxiliary retinue was a temporary expedient. For the circumstances surrounding this see above p. 20.

[12] BN, MS Fr 25776/1559; NAF 21289/201.

[13] AN, K 64/1/32; 10/15.

[14] BN, PO 2787, Talbot, 21.

during the siege of Harfleur, half of the retinue was seconded to Fulk Eyton, and at the height of the crisis over Pontoise in August 1441 a quarter of the men was left for a short while as a detachment to reinforce the garrison.[15] In the early months of 1442, when he returned to England to raise re-inforcements, Talbot was only acompanied by the nucleus of his much enlarged personal retinue. Of those that remained in Normandy, there is record of fifty-eight lances and 181 archers serving for ten days in the field under Lord Fauconberg and of sixteen men being placed in the garrison of Rouen. The retinue was reunited, however, on Talbot's return to Normandy and campaigned together for the remainder of the season.[16] Finally, in 1448-49, on the eve of the final loss of the duchy, the personal retinue was divided on a more formal and permanent basis. According to an order dated 21 July 1449 to the treasurer of Normandy to set in motion the payment of Talbot's wages, his contract stipulated that he was to command forty men-at-arms and 120 archers 'pour nous servir sur les champs' over and above the fourteen men-at-arms and forty-two archers 'a lui ordonne pour estre entour de sa personne et a l'accompaigner en notre service et ses autres charges'. This division had clearly been in existence since July 1448, when a muster of the smaller force on its own was taken. The larger troop was mustered separately, but in two parts, at Falaise on 28 December 1448; but by 19 June 1449, when an all-out invasion of Normandy by Charles VII was expected at any time, it had been widely dispersed. Thirteen men-at-arms and thirty-two archers were at Arques, twelve men-at-arms and twenty-eight archers at Mantes, thirteen men-at-arms and forty-eight archers were at Falaise and two men-at-arms with twelve archers had been sent to reinforce the garrison of his own castle of Longempré.[17] Four months later Talbot was surrendered to the French as a hostage and the personal retinue in Normandy was finally disbanded. Only one indenture for this retinue is known to have survived, but as many as thirty muster rolls, ranging from 1421 to 1448, are in existence and twenty-six of them fall in the years 1435-48.[18] These provide the basis for a detailed study of the composition of what must have been one of the 'crack' companies in the English army.

---

[15] BN, NAF 8606/64; MS Fr 25776/1533.

[16] BN, PO 2787, Talbot, 44; MS Fr 25776/1559.

[17] BN, NAF 21289/201, 8606/102; MS Fr 25778/1830; AN, K 68/29/6.

[18] The indenture, dated 26 March 1435, was for six months only (BN, MS Fr 26059/2495). The musters are listed in Appendix I. References to Talbot's indentures for his personal retinue in 1436 and 1441 are to be found in BN, MS Fr 26062/3002, 25776/1558.

Considerably larger numbers of men than those retained in the personal retinue were retained in the various garrisons of which Talbot was captain. Between 1420 and 1450 he held at least twenty-five captaincies in seventeen or more town and fortresses.[19] The most he held concurrently was seven between 1436 and 1439, including the most important charge of all, Rouen. His largest garrison retinue was 400 men in Caudebec in 1436; the smallest was sixteen men in Poissy in the preceding year. None was permanent and the number of places in his charge fluctuated, so that although he held six or seven before michaelmas 1439, in the first part of the following year he held none. The longest he held any one place was Harfleur, from its recapture in the autumn of 1440 to its final loss to the French in 1450; the shortest appears to have been Pontorson for six months in 1427. The only garrisons he seems to have captained personally were those in Rouen in 1436 and 1441-43 and in Falaise in 1448-49. This was largely because these towns were his military headquarters. For the rest his duties were exercised, and his rights protected, by lieutenants, the names of twenty-four of whom are known. Indentures for just six of these captaincies are known to have survived,[20] but there are in existence some eighty-six muster and counter-rolls for these garrisons.

Talbot could command more men in *creu* than in garrisons, but by their very nature these retinues were less permanent. When Rouen was under threat in the early months of 1436, he reinforced the garrison with at least fourteen separately recruited retinues ranging in size from fifteen to 156 men. In May 1436 there were as many as 900 men over and above the regular garrisons of the city, which at the beginning of the year totalled over 100 men.[21] In the campaigns of 1437 to 1441, led by Talbot for the recovery of towns in the pays de Caux or the defence of places on the front line, the government had frequently to make up the deficiencies in the contingents from garrisons by raising *creus*. In the summer of 1437, for instance, Talbot was given the command of an army of 2,000 men for the recovery of Tancarville which was to be formed by calling out 1,200 from garrisons and raising 800 personally. The army was to gather at Jumièges in the week following 7 August, but insufficient notice had

[19] See Pollard, Appendix IV, pp. 421-3 and Marshall, 'English Captains', Appendix II, pp. 225 ff.

[20] The indentures are: Gisors, 20 October 1434 (BN, MS Fr 26058/2372); Gaillard, 20 October 1434 (BN, MS Fr 26058/2387); St-Germain-en-Laye and Poissy, 20 October 1434 (ADSM, Fonds Danquin, 9 (T); Neufchâtel, 16 May 1434 (BN, PO 2787, Talbot, 9); Meaux, 8 October 1438 (BL, Add Ch 12009); Falaise, 1 January 1438 (BN, MS Fr 26064/3406).

[21] BN, MS Fr 25772/1053, 4, 6, 7; 25773/1062, 1091-5, 1100, 1145; 26061/2824, 71, 97; NAF 8606/51; Clair 201/8463/66.

been given to many garrisons and in anticipation of their non-appearance Talbot was commissioned to recruit replacements, substituting three archers for every man-at-arms if necessary. Consequently, he collected a *creu* of thirty-four men-at-arms and 604 archers. For the other part of the force Talbot subcontracted with eight captains, but this still left him short and so he raised a second *creu* of twenty-four men-at-arms and 104 archers.[22] In June 1440 he had recourse to another *creu*, this time of only four men-at-arms and twenty-three archers in default of garrison men, for the siege of Harfleur. By 25 September it had swollen to twenty-two men-at-arms and eighty-one archers. In January 1441, when Talbot was turning his attention to the recovery of Louviers and Conches, he enrolled a *creu* of twenty-one men-at-arms and 118 archers. By May 1441 the numbers in this *creu*, which had been kept in the field throughout the winter and spring, had grown to fifty-five men-at-arms and 170 archers. *Creus* like this, though large in size, were never more than temporary. They were also drawn from the large pool of unemployed soldiers often described in the muster as 'gens des champs qui nagaires vivoyent sans gages sur le pays et nestoient daucunes garnisons ou retenues ordinaires'.[23]

Finally, there are the reinforcements which Talbot raised in England. We know nothing of the composition of the retinues recruited in 1434,[24] but the muster roll of the army raised in 1442 has survived. By May Talbot had entered into contracts with thirty-five captains, for at the beginning of the month Sir Henry Clifford was ordered 'to goo in this present voiage with our cousine the lord Talbot into our realm of France, sithen the appointment of the retinue of the saide lord Talbot and the making of his endentures'.[25] The muster of the army, taken on its arrival at Harfleur on 15 June, has left a record, though it is damaged. Although intended to be 2,500 strong, the total strength was in fact 2,228, of whom only a tenth were men-at-arms. Talbot himself was accompanied by a personal retinue of thirty men-at-arms and 300 archers. The names of twenty-nine captains are discernible and they are not a very distinguished crew. Only three can be positively identified as having seen previous service in France and the only man among them of noble birth was Sir Henry Clifford, the heir to Lord Clifford. It is in fact difficult to identify the majority of the

[22]BN, MS Fr 25774/1241; Newhall, *Muster and Review*, pp. 143-6.

[23]BN, NAF 15543/143; Clair 2020/8474/2; MS Fr 25775/1490; BL, Ad Ch 6949.

[24]Talbot was paid for 140 men-at-arms, of whom three were knights, and 780 archers (PRO, E101/54/2). In May he was said to be captain of 200 men-at-arms and 600 archers (BN, MS Fr 26054/1534.

[25]Stevenson, *Wars*, 1, p. 430.

captains, such are their obscure origins.[26] This, and the presumably unavoidable alteration in the ratio of men-at-arms to archers from three to one to ten to one, is ample demonstration of the difficulties Talbot faced in recruiting his army in an England increasingly unwilling to support the war. What happened to most of this army we do not know,[27] but after the termination of its six months' contract it ceased to exist and any who stayed in Normandy were absorbed into the general administration and, with the exception of his personal element, ceased to have any further contact with Talbot.

Although these various retinues were composed predominantly of Englishmen, there was a scattering of French and other nationalities among them. From 1434 captains were discouraged from recruiting more than one-eighth of their men from the native population.[28] Musters of garrisons usually specified the Normans and other nationalities, but this was not done with the personal retinue. Judging from the names, however, Talbot did retain a number of Normans in his personal retinue. About half a dozen of the forty-six men-at-arms who are known to have served in this retinue in the years 1439-41 would appear to have been of French origin. Among the archers, one may presume that Jean de Mantes, Jean de Meaux and Jean du Mans were all of French birth, but their fellow countrymen do not appear to have formed a high proportion in their ranks. It was otherwise in the *creu*. Again judging by the surnames, a quarter would appear to have been French in 1437, a third in 1441 and as many as half in 1440. The net was also thrown wider than France itself. In 1428 there was a lance named Hans Duchesman, in 1429 a Michael de Luxembourg, in 1437 a Jean de Baytmont dit Lombart and in 1448 an Anthony Hunne in the personal retinue, described as a Dutchman. Finally, in 1436 there were even six archers who were 'natifs du pays d'Italie'.[29] But on the whole the retinues were made up overwhelmingly of Englishmen.

In considering all these retinues it becomes apparent that Talbot, as their captain, could not have had any close or special connection with the vast majority of them. Whether raising reinforcements on behalf of the crown in England, or gathering together a *creu* to make up the numbers of an under-strength army in the field for the recovery of a town, or even putting together a garrison in one of several places of which he had the command at any moment, Talbot was acting more as

[26] J. H. Ramsay, *Lancaster and York*, 2 (Oxford, 1892), p. 42; PRO, E101/54/2.

[27] See above pp. 59-60. for the supposition that there was a mutiny.

[28] Newhall, *Muster and Review*, p. 120.

[29] BN, MS Fr 25768/318; AN, K 64/1/34; BL, Ad Ch 11612; Ad MS 29315/2.

a commander in the royal army than as a captain of a private company. It seems that for most of the troops he retained he was but a distant, though no doubt awe-inspiring, figure. Only with a few garrison retinues, with whom he himself was resident, notably at Rouen in 1436-37, Rouen again and Harfleur in 1441-43, and lastly at Falaise in 1448-49, was he closely connected in a personal way. For the rest he relied heavily on his lieutenants to carry out his responsibilities and to look after his interests. The one retinue in which one can be certain that Talbot was acompanied by his *own* men was his personal retinue, constantly in attendance wherever he went. As we shall see below, this was more than just a fighting force; it was in addition his household and his military staff. Thus, our analysis concentrates only on the men employed by Talbot as his captains and lieutenants, and on the soldiers recruited to his personal retinue and to a handful of garrisons.

Captains and Lieutenants

Over the entire period of Talbot's service in Normandy, he is known to have subcontracted with some seventy captains of retinues in his company and lieutenants of garrisons in Normandy. The identity of all of them is not known. Those that are known came into his service from widely differing backgrounds and by several different routes. Only seven can be identified as men with whom he had probably had connections in England before they went with him to, or joined him in, Normandy. A similar number were from (or were to become part of) one or other of the magnate connections to which Talbot himself belonged. But the great majority would seem to have been employed by Talbot simply because they commended themselves to him as soldiers, or, in the case of recruiting in England, merely because he happened to be the man responsible for raising reinforcements.

When considering the few with whom Talbot may have had existing connections in England, it is important to bear in mind that he did not indulge in wholesale retaining at home. In his 1436 income tax return he claimed relief on only five fees and annuities, of which one, a payment of £100 a year to his wife, was by nature a family settlement; two were the fees of his chief administrative officers; another was a small payment to a mysterious Alice Redman, and only the fifth, £10 a year to Thomas Everingham, was the fee of an archetypical retainer.[30] This low level of expenditure on retaining is confirmed by the surviving records of his two largest estates the lordship of Blakemere in the 1430s and the lordship of Sheffield in the 1440s-

[30]PRO, E163/7/31.

where fees were paid almost exclusively to household and estate officials.[31] Talbot, like many peers, does not seem to have sought to bind large numbers of followers to him. Of course his affinity and connection is not to be understood merely in terms of formal contracts and annual cash payments. He also attracted well-wishers and servants from amongst his kin and neighbours in the districts where he had significant territorial power. In southern Yorkshire and, more especially, Shropshire the Talbot interest encompassed important figures among the local gentry.[32] But on the whole Talbot never was a powerful political figure commanding a large and influential following in England. His energies and time were too bound up in the defence of Lancastrian Normandy during the last twenty-five years of his life for him to have any larger connection in England than that which naturally accrued to a man of his standing and landed interest.

In the circumstances, it is not surprising that only a small proportion of Talbot's captains and lieutenants were drawn from his affinity in England. On the other hand, significant figures from that affinity did join him in Normandy. Most important of all was Thomas Everingham. Some difficulty surrounds the certain identification of Talbot's retainer. There were at least three Everingham families with estates in southern Yorkshire in the fifteenth century[33] and there were two Thomas Everinghams who were contemporaries of John Talbot. It is probable, however, that the retainer was the relatively humble Thomas Everingham of Stainbrough near Barnsley, a near neighbour of the lord of Sheffield who died at the end of 1453 and not the more distant and considerably more eminent Thomas Everingham of Newhall, Leicestershire, who fought at Agincourt and Verneuil, was twice M.P. for his county and died in 1461 or shortly after.[34] Thomas Everingham enjoyed a long and richly rewarded career with Talbot. He is first recorded in his employment in 1427, when for a short while he enjoyed a share of the fee of the office of janitor of Blakemere and

---

[31] Fees charged to the receiver of Blakemere in the accounting year ending michaelmas 1436 totalled £26 9s. 4d., the largest being £5 paid to the steward William Burley. Annuities and alms charged to the receiver of Sheffield in the accounting year ending michaelmas 1443 totalled £21 17s. 8d., the largest (£6 13s. 4d.) again being to the steward, Thomas Everingham. (Shropshire Record Office, Bridgewater Papers, 76/1435-6; *THAS*, 2, pp. 229-46).

[32] See Pollard, Ch 6 *passim*.

[33] The Everinghams of Stainbrough, the Everinghams of Birkin, and the Everinghams of Newhall, Leics., and Beverley.

[34] *Testamenta Eboracensia*, 2, ed. J. Raine (Surtees Society, 30, for 1855), p. 168. For Thomas Everingham of Newhall, see J.C. Wedgwood, *History of Parliament — Biographies of the Members of the House of Commons, 1439-1509* (London 1936), pp. 308-9.

was engaged in escorting the Irish chieftain, Donagh MacMurrough, Talbot's prisoner, from Goodrich to Chester. In 1428 he was promoted to the stewardship of Wexford in Ireland, a sinecure from which he probably made little profit since the lordship was largely in Irish hands. By 1436 he was enjoying the much more certain reward of £10 a year from the issues of the forest of Bradfield in Sheffield and by the early 1440s he was also steward of the lordship there, enjoying a fee of £6 13s. 4d. In addition, for an unknown period before 1443 he held the Talbot lordship of Painswick in Gloucestershire by way of gift, or more probably to use.[35] The stewardship of Sheffield was no sinecure. In April 1441 he was there to hold the 'Tourn of Hallamshire' and on 4 January 1443 he had to go to Rotherham to settle a dispute between Talbot tenants there. In September 1446 he was a witness to the will of Sir John Talbot, the earl's heir, also at Sheffield, and finally in September 1452 he was made an executor of the latter's own will.[36] Everingham spent a short time under Talbot's command as a man-at-arms in his personal retinue during the siege of Harfleur in the autumn of 1440 and became Talbot's lieutenant there after its recapture. By April 1441, however, he had returned to England.[37] In July and August of the same year a Thomas Everingham 'the younger', who was presumably his son, appeared as a man-at-arms in the personal retinue. It must have been Thomas the younger — although he is no longer specifically styled as such — who was in the personal retinue in June 1442 which returned to Normandy after Talbot's brief visit to England, and who was subsequently mustered before Dieppe in November 1442 and in the garrison of Harfleur in March 1443. Later in the year he succeeded to his father's post of lieutenant of Harfleur, where he stayed until he handed over the town to the French on 1 January 1450. Everingham, presumably again the younger man, later sailed to Bordeaux in the last fatal expedition to France and was a captain, or standard bearer, in the army with a place in Talbot's council of war. Although according to one account he advised against the attack at Castillon, he apparently led the charge and was shot dead as he planted his lord's banner on the French ramparts.[38] Talbot could not have asked for more from the Everingham family.

[35] Shropshire R. O., Bridgewater Papers, 76/1427; *Rotulorum Patentium et Clausorum Cancellariae Hiberniae Calendarium,* 1, Part 1 (Dublin, 1828), p. 241b; *THAS,* 2 pp. 74, 344-60; *CCR,* 1441-7, p. 155.

[36] T. W. Hall, *Sheffield Manorial Records* (Sheffield, 1926), p. 34; *THAS,* 2, p.242; *Testamenta Eboracensia,* 2, p. 253; Lambeth Palace Library, Register Stafford and Kemp, f 312b.

[37] AN, K 65/1/5; 66/1/33, 50.

[38] AN, K 67/1/34; PRO, E101/54/2; BN, MS Fr 25776/1596, 1623; *CPR,* 1441-6 p. 203; Stevenson, *Wars,* 2, p. 629; Basin, 2, pp. 195-6; Chartier, 3, p. 7. It is unlikely

Of the other English retainers who served Talbot in France the most prominent was John Green. A John Green of Blakemere, possibly his nephew,[39] was twice involved in riots on Talbot's behalf in 1423 and 1426, and he seems likely to have been the man who became lieutenant of Coutances in 1428 and held the place for Talbot until 1437. In 1437-38 he was in command, on Talbot's behalf, of troops in Ireland and in the later years of Talbot's life he enjoyed a fee charged to the manor of Middleton in Derbyshire which Talbot willed to be continued after his death.[40] He may possibly have been the John Green who was a 'serviteur' of the duke of Bedford, and who fought at Verneuil and received lands to the annual value of £120 1.t. for his services. And he was probably the same as the John Green who, on 30 October, just after he had vacated the lieutenancy of the garrison of Coutances, was given respite for taking the *prisée* of land in the bailliage of Cotentin and was again in July 1448 given respite for lands both in the Cotentin and Caen.[41]

Of the thirty-seven captains with whom Talbot subcontracted in the spring of 1442 for his army of reinforcements, only four can be identified as having a possible connection with him. They are John Chalouns of Archenfield, which was part of the Talbot lordship of Goodrich, Richard Cholmondley, perhaps the man who had been steward of the lordship of Blakemere in 1427-28, William Worsley, possibly a relation of Seth Worsley who received a small fee charged to Sheffield in the 1440s, and Richard Banaster of Hadnall, Shropshire, the head of a substantial gentry family. Worsley may have already seen service as a man-at-arms in his garrison at Coutances in 1431-34.[42] Banaster, the only one whose connection is certain, had served Talbot since the year 1433-34 at the latest, when he had been

that either Thomas Everingham senior or Thomas Everingham junior was the same as the Thomas Everingham who was Sir John Fastolf's marshal at Alençon in 1434 or the earl of Dorset's lieutenant there in 1437 (Marshall, 'English Captains', pp. 114-15).

[39] Green may have been a younger son of Sir Thomas Green and Talbot's sister Mary.

[40] *Rotuli Parliamentorum*, 4, p. 254a; *CPR, 1422-9*, p. 423; BN, MS Fr 25768/362; 25773/1127; Stevenson, *Wars*, 2, p. 541; *THAS*, 2, p. 235; Lambeth Palace Library, Register Stafford and Kemp, f312.

[41] D Len 21/275; 4/379, 405; 74/231. On the other hand, he was not the John Green who was a man-at-arms in the garrison of Rouen in 1429, nor the John Green who was a man-at-arms in the garrisons of Creil, Tancarville and St-Vigor in 1438 and 1439 (BL, Add Ch 6835; AN, K 64/23/14, 15, 19). I am grateful to Miss A. E. Curry for supplying this information on these men.

[42] PRO, E101/54/2; BN, MS Fr 25769/576; 25770/627, 696; BL, Add Ch 12089, *THAS*, 2, p. 358.

employed in the delivery of Talbot's ransom money to France, and was in France again in 1436, when for six months or more he served in the garrison of Caudebec. It was probably he who was in Edmund Beaufort's personal retinue in November 1440. In 1442 he and Hugh Banaster joined Talbot with a retinue of 20 archers. In the following year he was retained with another small company by John Beaufort, duke of Somerset and accompanied him on his disastrous expedition to France.[43] But four years later he was back in Talbot's service, for around Easter 1447 he became his receiver-general. In 1449, the same year as he represented his county in Parliament, he was also a foeffee to use for Talbot.[44] Fulk Eyton, a member of another Shropshire gentry family, whose elder brother was in fact Banaster's fellow M.P. in 1449, is the last of the English connection who served as a captain or lieutenant for Talbot. He was either Talbot's brother-in-law or his nephew. He was also a retainer of the earl of Arundel, being his constable of Oswestry castle in 1434 and serving in his company in France in 1433 and 1435. After Arundel's death in 1435, he became (in 1436) lieutenant for Talbot of the garrison of Caudebec. In 1437 he succeeded Talbot to the captaincy. After 1441 Eyton gravitated to the service of the duke of York and was active on the duke's behalf in England between 1450 and 1452. He died in 1454.[45]

In addition to being one of Talbot's English connection, Eyton was also one of those men who attached himself to the same magnate circle as Talbot. Another who went on to join York was William Minors. Minors began his career as one of Henry V's yeomen of the crown. He entered Bedford's household after the king's death and fought at Verneuil. He gave the duke a house in Harfleur in 1427 'pour les grands honneurs et profits que le duc et sa dame lui ont faits' and in 1428 was an usher in the duke's household. From 1424 at the latest he was captain of Harfleur and was still captain when the town fell to the peasants of the pays de Caux in December 1435. He was captain of a retinue under Talbot's command at the siege of Tancarville in 1437, becoming captain of the town after it was recaptured. He was still at

---

[43] Shropshire R.O., Bridgewater Papers 76/1433-4; BN, MS Fr 25772/1050; Marshall, 'English Captains', pp. 115-16. Banaster's father, Thomas, was in Talbot's retinue in 1421 (PRO, E101/50/1).

[44] THAS, 2, pp. 359-60; Wedgwood, Biographies, p. 38.

[45] Marshall, 'English Captains', pp. 287-90 gives full details of his career. He was the son of Thomas Eyton and Catherine Talbot, possibly Talbot's sister. See H. T. Weyman, 'Shropshire Members of Parliament, 1393-1584', Transactions of the Shropshire Archaeological Society, 4th series 9 (1, 1927), 20-1.

Tancarville in November 1438, but had moved to St Vigor by March 1439. Notwithstanding these independent commands, Minors became a man-at-arms in Talbot's personal retinue for the year 1440-41. After York's arrival in Normandy for his second tour of duty, Minors joined his household, becoming its controller in 1442. But eventually he left York for the dominant court party in England, being an usher of the royal chamber in 1450.[46]

Another discernible group of men who were Talbot's lieutenants were retainers of the earl of Warwick. Nicholas Burdet, the son of Warwick's retainer Sir Thomas Burdet, was Talbot's lieutenant in the castle of Rouen in 1436.[47] Sir Richard Curson, Warwick's chamberlain and retainer from December 1423, was Talbot's lieutenant at Château-Gaillard in 1435 and also in 1436 his lieutenant of the garrison in the town of Rouen. Early in 1438 he became captain of Château-Gaillard 'at the relation' of the earl of Warwick.[48] A third of Warwick's men who also served under Talbot was Sir William Peyto of Chesterton and Sowe, Warwickshire. He was a retainer of Warwick in 1423-24 and first went to France in 1432. In 1433 he was captain of Warwick's own castle of Aumale. Between 1434 and 1436 he was also Talbot's lieutenant of Neufchâtel, only a few miles away. After Warwick's death in 1439 he seems to have come more permanently into Talbot's service. In 1441-43 he was his lieutenant of the town and walls of Rouen and in 1442-43 was left in command at the siege of Dieppe, where he was captured. It was probably at this time that he was Talbot's lieutenant-general as marshal of France. However, by 1449 he was *maitre d'ostel* of the duke of Somerset, the husband of another of Warwick's daughters, in whose service he remained until at least 1453. He died in 1459 and was buried, at his own request, in the Beauchamp church of St Mary's, Warwick, so demonstrating in his death his devotion to his first lord and patron.[49]

In considering the careers of men like Eyton and Peyto one cannot emphasise too strongly that both Talbot and they were members of the same affinities. Eyton's eventual attachment to York and Peyto's

[46]ADSM, Tabellionnage, 20/491 (Dubuc, 'Calendar' no. 699); 21/153 (Dubuc, 'Calendar' no. 746); 30/7 (Dubuc, 'Calendar' no 1249); AN, K 64/23/14, 15; 67/1/34; BN, MS Fr 25775/1455; 25776/1510; NAF 8606/68; BL, Add Chs 137, 3603, 12158; Waurin, 4, p. 104; Stevenson, Wars, 2, pp. 394, 545; C. L. Kingsford, *English Historical Literature in the Fifteenth Century* (Oxford, 1905), p. 365.

[47]BN, MS Fr 2606/2897; 25773/1136; Marshall, 'English Captains', pp. 39-40.

[48]Marshall, 'English Captains', pp. 27-9, 32; C. L. Kingsford, *Chronicles of London* (Oxford, 1905), p. 140.

[49]BN, PO 2787, Talbot, 9; MS Fr 26062/3183; Marshall, 'English Captains', pp. 27, 32-4, 41.

eventual employment in Somerset's household should not therefore be interpreted as desertion of Talbot for a more powerful lord. Eyton's career is exactly matched by that of the lawyer William Burley of Broncroft, Salop, in England. Burley, too, began his career in the service of the earl of Arundel, in his case Earl Thomas who died in 1415. In 1418 he was one of Talbot's attorneys in England while Talbot was in Ireland and in 1427 he was one of the co-janitors of Blakemere with Thomas Everingham; by 1433 he was steward of Blakemere with an annual fee of £5. In the 1440s he too became attached to York, receiving in 1442-43 annuities worth a total of £73 6s.8d. And like Eyton, in the 1450s he was active in York's cause.[50] But neither Eyton the soldier nor Burley the lawyer was abandoning Talbot, for as we have seen Talbot was also a prominent retainer of York. Indeed, with annuities worth £200 a year he was without doubt York's most important retainer in the 1440s. In the late 1430s and 1440s, from his headquarters in Ludlow, York came to dominate the landed society of Shropshire, and Talbot, like Burley and Eyton, was part of his powerful connection there.

Whereas Talbot's ties with York were territorial and financial, his links with Warwick and Edmund Beaufort were marital. The second Lady Talbot was Warwick's eldest daughter, Margaret. Her sister, Eleanor, was the wife of Edmund Beaufort. Talbot, as we have seen, was to remain closely associated in England as well as in France with both Warwick and Somerset. He is undoubtedly to be counted as part of Warwick's affinity until his death in 1439 and a close friend of Somerset, especially after 1448. Thus, Talbot's occasional retaining of men like Burdet, Curson and Peyto should also be seen in the light of this wider context of his own personal connection. This tendency is demonstrated just as clearly in the careers of some of the men who rose from the ranks. John Clay is first recorded as a man-at-arms in the garrison of Rouen in 1421. By 1429 he had risen to his own independent command of the garrison of St Katherine's, Rouen. In 1437 he was Talbot's lieutenant in the castle at Rouen and in 1442 he returned to Normandy with Talbot, accompanied by a retinue of nine men-at-arms and over a hundred archers. But by 1443-44 he was treasurer of York's household and in 1445 holding captaincies for York in his possessions in Normandy.[51] Andrew Trollope first went to Normandy in 1425 and served as a man-at-arms under several captains before becoming lieutenant of Fresnay for Sir Richard

---

[50] J. S. Roskell, 'William Burley of Broncroft', *Transactions of the Shropshire Archaeological Society* 56, (3, 1960), 263-72 *passim*, but also *CPR, 1416-22*, p. 153 and Shropshire R. O., Bridgewater Papers, 85/1424-5, 75/1427, 1427-8, 1433-4 for the Talbot connection.

[51] BN, MS Fr 25774/1260; PRO, E101/54/2; Marshall 'English Captains' p. 69.

Woodville in 1441 and succeeding to his first independent command as captain of Gavray in 1447. At the very end of the war he was serving as captain of a company of soldiers under Talbot at Falaise and was responsible for surrendering the town to the French on his behalf. Subsequently he moved to the garrison of Calais, where he became master porter under the duke of Somerset.[52] In the complex web of clientage in fifteenth-century England it is neither surprising that Talbot should be retaining men in France whom he knew from his connections with prominent magnates nor exceptional that these and other men, risen from the ranks, should, like himself, develop their primary attachment to such magnates. Somerset and York had a naturally magnetic pull for all the veteran 'officers' in France after 1441 because of the patronage at their disposal as governors of Normandy. Talbot, with a close relationship with each of them yet without their authority and resources, never pretended to be a rival attraction.

Less need be said of the large majority of captains and lieutenants with whom Talbot had no identifiable connection. Most of the captains who raised troops for him in England in 1442 did so because he represented the crown or because, as in the case of Sir Henry Clifford, they were ordered in person by the crown to go to France. The captains with whom he contracted for an army to recover Tancarville in 1437 were established soldiers whose sole connection with Talbot would seem to be professional. Talbot knew of them as soldiers and they happened to be available at that time.[53] The same would seem to be true of several of the lieutenants of his garrison: men like Sir William Breton, lieutenant of the castle of Rouen in 1441, Sir Thomas Hoo, lieutenant of the garrison of Gisors in 1436 and 1437, and Sir Henry Norbury, lieutenant of the garrison guarding the bridge of Rouen in 1441-43.[54] Finally, one or two of Talbot's lieutenants were men who rose from the ranks in his service. One such was Richard Bolt, lieutenant of Saint-Germain-en-Laye during 1435, who in the summer of 1434 had been a man-at-arms in his garrison at Neufchâtel. Unfortunately, Bolt lost Saint-Germain to the French in January 1436 and was demoted to serve as a man-at-arms in the garrison of Gisors in October 1436 and March 1437 and in Rouen castle in July 1437.[55] Richard Good, another man-at-arms in the

[52] Marshall, 'English Captains', pp. 301-4.

[53] They were Sir Philip D'Arcy, Sir Robert Griffin. Sir Thomas Griffith, Sir Robert James, Thomas Ashton, Robert Brid, Richard Hasteseld and William Minors. But see Minors above pp. 79-80. Their retinues are mustered in BL, Add Ch 131.

[54] BN, MS Fr 25776/1546; Clair 201/8457/59; MS Fr 25776/1552.

[55] BN MS Fr 25771/859; 25772/946; NAF 1482/142; BL, Add Ch 11871; Clair 201 8457/59; ADSM, Fonds Danquin, 11/83.

Rouen garrison, had moved to Falaise by 1439, though still as a man-at-arms, but he had been promoted by Talbot to be his lieutenant at Lisieux by 1440 and at michaelmas 1441 he was transferred by him to the lieutenancy of the more strategically important Château-Gaillard. In 1446 and 1447 he served as York's lieutenant at Falaise and stayed on under Talbot again in 1448 and 1449, by which time he had acquired a coat of arms and lands in Normandy.[56]

It is not surprising that most of Talbot's captains and lieutenants were professional soldiers whose only discernible connection with him was that they were fellow officers in the army. Neither did he maintain a large enough affinity in England from which to draw any but a handful of his lieutenants, nor did he have the political and financial weight to attract large numbers of them into his service. This means that he recruited most of his officers from amongst those resident in Normandy who were making their careers in the war and that they stayed with him only so long as the military situation demanded it or Talbot himself had need of them. The relationship between captain and lieutenant was primarily professional.

The Personal Retinue

The personal retinue was Talbot's élite corps. The men in it were his closest companions in arms. The surviving muster rolls make it possible to examine in detail the changing composition of the personal retinue, and, on the basis of this analysis, offer some necessarily tentative conclusions on the way they were recruited, the way in which they were organized, and the role they played in Talbot's service.

On 11 June 1421 Talbot arrived at Sandwich for muster with eighteen men-at-arms and sixty-six archers ready to embark for France.[57] Fourteen of the men-at-arms are known to have seen service with him before or to have had some other connection with him. Five had been in his company in Ireland in the years 1414-18. And of these one, William Savill, had been in his retinue in 1412 and had been severely wounded in a fight with a group of outlaws whom Talbot had been arresting at Broughall on the family estate of Blakemere in Shropshire; another, Richard Lokkay, had been in the retinue with which Talbot had garrisoned Montgomery during Owain Glyn Dŵr's

[56]*Ibid.*, AN, K 65/1/33; BN, MS Fr 26068/4243; 25776/1550; D Len 74/255; Marshall, 'English Captains', p. 250.

[57]PRO, E101/70/50/1.

revolt as far back as 1405.[58] Eight others had possible connections with the Talbot family estates. Surprisingly only one, John Kersford, can be linked with John Talbot's own lordship of Sheffield,[59] whilst seven can be linked with Shropshire, of whom four might have come from the lordship of Blakemere which at that time was in the possession of Talbot's widowed sister-in-law.[60] The Blakemere link is reinforced by the presence of at least four tenants of the lordship amongst the archers and by the evidence from the receiver's account for this same year that arrows were provided from the estate for this retinue.[61] Indeed we know that Talbot was in Shropshire in April 1421[62] and one may safely conclude that he was in the county partly to recruit to this retinue. The fourteenth of the possible personal connections was Richard Talbot, either an Irish cousin from the Malahide family or, possibly, an illegitimate brother. A clear picture of this retinue thus emerges. Its core was a group of men who had been in Talbot's personal retinue in Ireland and had presumably also been with him in France in 1420. This core was augmented by men recruited in the spring of 1421 from the Talbot family following, especially in Shropshire. But when one turns to the next surviving muster, that of December 1428, a stark contrast appears. Seven years later only one man, William Sutton, who had also been in Ireland, remained. Two other recently recruited men-at-arms were possibly drawn from the Blakemere household but that is all.[63] However, if one looks further forward, one finds that no fewer than

[58] John Kirkham, captain-general of county Kildare, 1415, and messenger from Talbot to the king and Bedford in 1417 (*Rot. Pat. Claus. Hib.*, p. 211; BL, Cotton MS, Titus B.XI, ff31,6). Lokkay, Savill, William Sutton and James White all received grants of land or office in Ireland (*Rot. Pat. Claus. Hib.*, pp. 204b, 205b, 206, 216b). For Lokkay at Montgomery, see PRO, E101/44/6. For Savill in 1412, see E. Kimball, *The Shropshire Peace Roll* (Shrewsbury, 1959), p. 105; in 1427-8 he received a grant of land in Blakemere (Shropshire R. O., Bridgewater Papers, 76/1427-8).

[59] In 1441-2 he was described as Talbot's councillor and in 1446 was a witness to Sir John Talbot's will (*THAS*, p. 242; *Testamenta Eboracensia*, 2, p. 253).

[60] The Shropshire men were Thomas Banaster of Hadnall, John Husee of Balderstone and Bryan de Sandford of Whixall. The Blakemere men were John Camvill, steward of the household, 1414-15 (Shropshire R. O., Bridgewater Papers, 75/1414-15); Thomas Mayre, 'servant' in 1417-18 (*ibid.*, 85/1417-18); William Walsh, perhaps a relation of John Walsh of Allerton, steward of the lordship in 1417-18 (*ibid.*, 85/1417-18), and Hugh Overton, perhaps a relation of Richard Overton, receiver in Blakemere in 1400-1 (*ibid.*, 75/1400-01).

[61] Edmund Leighton, William Stuych, Edmund Bowland and Walter Ferrour were the tenants. For the arrows, see *ibid.*, 75/1420-1.

[62] *CCR, 1419-22*, p. 196.

[63] BN, MS Fr 25768/318. Richard Emond was a household official at Blakemere in 1420-1 and 1424-5 (Shropshire R. O. Bridgewater Papers, 25/1420-1; 1424-5) and William Wenlock, perhaps a relation of John Wenlock, the receiver of the lordship from 1427 to 1436 (see below p. 89).

eight of the twenty-three men-at-arms mustered in 1428 were to be employed in Talbot's retinues after 1436. By 1428 a break had been made with his earlier career and Talbot was already relying far less on his English connections. He had, one may suggest, already begun to recruit in Normandy itself, a practice which is clearly revealed by the much more numerous surviving musters for the years 1436-42.

Sixteen muster rolls of the personal retinue for the years 1436-42 and three muster rolls of the auxiliary personal retinue in the summer of 1435 have been traced. Of these, no fewer than ten fall in the two years from michaelmas 1439 to August 1441.[64] This series of musters, spread over two years, provides the basis for the following analysis. Although no indenture has survived, one may assume that the retinues mustered between 1439 and 1441 were raised under the terms of two contracts: one in the autumn of 1439 and the other in the autumn of 1440. The renewal of Talbot's contract every michaelmas presumably also provided the occasion for the renewal of the contracts between himself and his men and for a change in personnel. The extent of the change in personnel in 1440 can be shown by an analysis of the men-at-arms named in a group of musters that were held in October and November. The last muster of the 1439-40 retinue was taken before Harfleur on 8 October. The next extant muster was taken at Pont-Audemer on 27 November, followed on 29 November by another at the same place.[65] There are marked differences in the composition of the retinue on these three dates. On 8 October it was, with two exceptions, the same as had been mustered, in two parts, at the beginning of the siege of Harfleur in late July and early August. On 27 November it contained only ten of these men out of the total of nineteen. But two days later all nine of the replacements and one of the nine survivors had left. The gaps were filled by the return of four who had been mustered in October and August and by the recruitment of seven newcomers.

The muster rolls themselves do not explain these comings and goings, but if one takes into account Talbot's military operations at this time an explanation can be found. Harfleur did not fall until the end of October, after the expiry of the indentures, and it is likely that Talbot's men were released immediately after the end of the operations. Some of those who left the personal retinue before 27 November may well have gone into the new English garrison of Harfleur, of which Talbot was made captain. Thomas Everingham became lieutenant and could have taken with him at this time John Hensacre, who was controller of

---

[64] See below Appendix 1.

[65] AN, K66/1/50; BN, MS Fr 25775/1451, 55.

the garrison early in 1442, Watkin Bailly and Richard Bannes, who were men-at-arms with him at the same time, and Jean Gracieu dit Guy who was in the garrison in 1443.[66] A month after the fall of Harfleur Talbot was at Pont-Audemer gathering an army for the projected relief of Louviers and Conches which was mustered on 29 November. Sometime between the fall of Harfleur and this date Talbot's indenture with the crown must eventually have been renewed, but unfortunately we have no knowledge of exactly when. Nevertheless, it is reasonable to assume that there was a delay and that during this time Talbot continued to maintain a personal retinue on a strictly temporary basis.[67] It would make sense if this was the body of men mustered on 27 November just before it was disbanded and replaced by the new 'official' retinue for the year 1440-1, mustered two days later. If this construction is allowed, the comparison between the permanent retinue of one year and the next should be between the companies mustered on 8 October and 29 November. And this shows that twelve of the retinue of 1439-40 elected to continue in Talbot's service for the following year and that seven new men-at-arms were recruited.

When one examines the composition of the retinue *within* a contracted year, one finds that the turnover in personnel could be as great from one quarter to the next, or even from month to month, as it was from year to year. Eight new men-at-arms joined the personal retinue between 7 November 1439 and 7 February 1440. Four joined between 29 November 1440 and 26 March 1441. And between 13 July and 20 August 1441 Talbot had to find three replacements.[68] On the basis of the surviving musters, it appears likely that only eight men could have served throughout 1439-40 and thirteen throughout 1440-41. On average, therefore, only half of the men-at-arms could have served throughout one year. Taking the two years as a whole, only six, or but a third of the men-at-arms, are to be found in all the surviving musters.[69] These figures alone could give an exaggerated view of the impermanence of Talbot's personal retinue. For one thing, Talbot

[66]BN, MS Fr 25776/1554, 1623; ADSM, Fonds Danquin, 3/3/17.

[67]In the summer of 1437 the council ordered that retinues be kept in existence month by month after the expiry of their indentures.

[68]BN, Clair 201/8466/68; AN, K 65/1/5; BN, MS Fr 25775/1455, 25776/1510; BN, NAF 8606/68, 71; AN, K 67/1/34; BN, MS Fr 25776/1533. It would appear that there were monthly musters during the summer of 1441. These rates of turnover can be compared with Lord Fauconberg's personal retinue in the summer of 1442, when he had to find eight new men-at-arms between April and June and a further eight between June and August (AN, K 67/12/12, 38, 52; BN, NAF 8606/86).

[69]But in Fauconberg's retinue only two could possibly have seen continuous service with him between July 1439 and July 1441.

himself could well have sent certain individuals elsewhere. Thus, four of the men missing in February 1440 were back again in July and stayed with Talbot until October. And as we have seen above, at the end of October 1440 Talbot could well have placed some of his men in the garrison of Harfleur. Secondly, one should not forget that this was after all a fighting force and casualties must have occurred. The replacements of 20 August 1441 could well have been of men lost during operations in defence of Pontoise. However, it still remains the case that at this stage of the war, after five years' service in France, there was a constant turnover of men in Talbot's personal retinue. On the other hand, it appears as if the majority of the men-at-arms who served Talbot during these two years formed a loosely defined group, somewhat larger than the numbers required at any one time, from which the major part of the personal retinue was always drawn. In 1439-40 he called on no more than twenty-six men-at-arms during the whole year. In 1440-41, he called on twenty-eight. Over the two years together he called on forty-six.[70] Fifteen of these were mustered only once, five in the temporary retinue mustered on 27 November 1440. The remaining thirty-one seem to have formed a kind of pool of men-at-arms who were known to Talbot and were available for service under him from time to time. No fewer than twenty-one of these are known to have served in the personal retinue, or in a garrison retinue, or in a *creu* in 1436-7 or earlier. Of the remaining ten who cannot be traced in Talbot's service before 1439, five are known to have continued in his service after 1441. This pool of men-at-arms was in no way a formal body. It was merely a collection of men, some connected very closely, some quite casually, with their captain, the composition of which was constantly changing. Some had a record of long and almost continuous service, others a record of only short and intermittent active service with him. Prominent amongst them was a group of five — Thomas Dowe, John Le Prince, Rimon Mannessier, Ralph Rainford and Robert Stafford — who did see more or less continuous active service in Talbot's retinues from 1436 until the loss of Normandy. This was the nucleus of his personal retinue. Another sixteen served Talbot less regularly but over a comparable length of time, some of them — Richard Bannes, Edmund Cantock, Jean Gracieu dit Guy and John Montfort, for instance — from as early as 1428 until the 1440s. A last identifiable group is formed by the five — André Chabannes, Henry Doudeley, Griffith Gwyn, Geoffrey Hore and Jenkin Woodford — who came into the personal retinue between 1437 and 1439 and served regularly for two years and then never

---

[70]This compares with at least fifty-seven men-at-arms over an eighteen-month period from February 1436 to September 1437 (AN, K 64/1/32, 34; BN, NAF 8602/23; BN, MS Fr 25774/214; BL, Add MS 29315/2).

again. These men may well have replaced a similar number who were in the personal retinue in 1436-37 and were in their turn replaced by a similar group in 1442.

How the men of the pool available in 1439-41 first came to be there is largely unknown. A large number of men-at-arms are first noticed in garrison retinues before appearing in the personal retinue, including eight of the pool of 1439-41. Particularly noticeable is the fact that six of these were at Caudebec in the first months of 1436.[71] Nine men in the auxiliary retinue of 1435 subsequently served in the personal retinue itself, two of them being in the pool after 1439.[72] Others have been traced first of all in a *creu*. At least three of the men-at-arms in the personal retinue in 1442, for instance, were in the *creu* which was raised for the recovery of Louviers and Conches over the winter of 1440-41.[73] Interestingly, four of the nucleus of five are known to have come into Talbot's service by one or other of these routes. Thomas Dowe's first traceable service in Talbot's pay is in 1436 in the garrison of Gisors, where the lieutenant was Thomas Hoo. John Le Prince was in the garrison of Caudebec at the same time. Rimon Mannessier was in a *creu* which took part in the siege of Orléans. And Robert Stafford was in the auxiliary personal retinue in 1435.[74] These men were veterans. Dowe had been a man-at-arms at Rouen since 1422 at the latest and had served under several captains. He had taken part in the siege of Orléans as part of a detachment from the Rouen garrison and had actually been with Talbot at Meung on 10 May 1429 and Beaugency on 5 June and had thus almost certainly fought under his command at Patay. But he appears to have escaped from the field, for he was back in the garrison at Rouen in December of the same year and served other captains, including Warwick, before joining Talbot in 1436. He served in the garrisons at Gisors in 1436-37 and Vernon in 1438, finally joining the personal retinue in 1439.[75] Robert Stafford first came into contact with Talbot in quite different circumstances. He had been in Normandy since at least 1419 in the service of Henry V, Bedford, Clarence and Salisbury, and had enjoyed independent command. His promising career had been

---

[71] The eight from the pool were Thomas Dowe (Gisors, January 1436 — November 1437, BN MS Fr 25772/1052; BN, NAF 1482/142; AN K 64/12/17), Gerrard Lencedit, John Sterky, elder and younger, John Le Prince, Baudwyn Wake, Jenkin Woodford (Caudebec, January — June 1436, BN, MS Fr 25772/1050, 25773/1102), William Massy (St-Germain-en-Laye, 1435, BN, MS Fr 25772/972).

[72] Robert Stafford and Richard Conningston were in the pool after 1439.

[73] Thomas Dalton, Mathew Bieta and John of Ynde (BL, Add Ch 6949).

[74] BN, MS Fr 25772/1052; BL, Add Ch 11612; BN, MS Fr 25772/944, 954 bis, 963.

[75] ADSM, Fonds Danquin, 11/74; BL Add Ch 110; BN, MS Fr 25768/363, 85, 94, 99, 437; 25768/43; 25770/709; 25771/802, 44; Jarry, *L'armée Anglaise*, pp. 181-3.

ruined, however, when he lost La Ferté Bernard in Maine on 1 March 1427. Having been adjudged by Bedford as having offered insufficient resistance, all his lands and possessions in Normandy were confiscated and granted to Talbot. But Stafford appealed and, after a long suit before the parlement of Paris, recovered his property in 1434.[76] Thereafter he entered Talbot's service.

On the other hand, few of the men-at-arms in the pool had English connections with their captain. Apart from Thomas Everingham, father and son, who have been discussed above, the only other possibilities are Simon Baudwyn, a man-at-arms in the summer of 1441 who may be the same as the Baudwyn who was on occasion employed on Talbot's business in England in the 1420s, and Robert Stafford (noted above) who may have been related to Henry Stafford, rector of Treeton and receiver of Sheffield in the late-1440s.[77] It was a body of soldiers recruited from the ranks of the established veterans resident in Normandy. The extent to which this was so is well illustrated by the personal retinue with which Talbot returned to Normandy in the summer of 1442 after a brief visit to England. How many of his personal retinue he took with him to England on this occasion is not known, but he was certainly accompanied by Richard Bannes and five other men-at-arms from the garrison of Harfleur.[78] When he landed again at Harfleur in June he was accompanied by a personal retinue containing thirty men-at-arms. Amongst them were Bannes and nine others from the pool of 1439-41 and ten more who had served recently in his retinues in Normandy. Of the remaining third, Richard Talbot, himself a veteran, can be assumed to be a relation, John de la Mare was his nephew and John Wenlock was the receiver of his lordship of Blakemere.[79] By 1442, it is clear, there was no need for Talbot himself to be recruiting extensively in England for his personal retinue.

Replacements for the personal retinue who were not in the pool came from several quarters. In the temporary retinue mustered on 27 November 1439 three men joined Talbot for the month or so who had

[76]D Len 4/114, 74/285; AN, XI[a] 68, ff149v-150v; 1481, f80v; 4797; ff103v, 107v, 109v, 124v; R. Charles, 'L'Invasion anglaise dans le Maine de 1417 à 1428 *Revue historique et archéologique du Maine* 25 (1889), 57-8, 92-8; *English suits before the Parlement of Paris*, ed C.T. Allmand and C.A.J. Armstrong (Camden Fourth Series, 26, 1982) pp. 220-30.

[77]Shropshire R. O., Bridgewater Papers, 76/1427-8. Baudwyn went to Ireland on Talbot's behalf in May 1428.

[78]ADSM, Fonds Danquin, 3/3/17.

[79]PRO, E101/54/2. For Wenlock, see Pollard, pp. 301-4. He is not to be confused with John Wenlock of the Someries, for whom see J. S. Roskell, 'John Wenlock of the Someries', *Publications of the Bedfordshire Historical Record Society* 38 (1958), 12-48.

served him between 1435 and 1437, but had subsequently dropped into the background. One of these had been in the personal retinue of these years, two in various garrisons.[80] Some vacancies occurring during the campaigning of 1440-41 were filled by men coming from the *creu* at that time under Talbot's command. John de la Brosse and Mathew Bieta, who had both been in the *creu* in May 1441, were mustered for the first time in the personal retinue in August.[81] Other replacements were found from among the archers. In August 1441 a third newly mustered man-at-arms was Duvant le Vavassour, who had campaigned throughout the year as an archer.[82] *Creus* and the archers proved useful sources of recruitment to the greatly enlarged retinue in 1442. Two new men-at-arms, Thomas Dalton and John of Ynde, had both served in a *creu* in 1441.[83] And as many as five men who had served as archers in the years 1439-41 were mustered as men-at-arms in 1442.[84] Rimon Mannessier, who by the early 1440s was one of the nucleus of the personal retinue, had himself been first mustered under Talbot as an archer.[85] But only a handful of the archers were ever promoted. The archers as a whole were a far less regular body of men than the men-at-arms. Only half of those mustered on 29 November 1440 were still in the personal retinue in the following March. And only one-third (twenty men) who were archers in November 1439 were still in the retinue in August 1441. Just six of these had seen service in 1437 or before. Whether these archers were attached to Talbot himself or to individual men-at-arms is impossible to tell, but the relatively high turnover was presumably one reason why more were not promoted. Another, more important, reason was that few could afford the more expensive equipment or harness of a man-at-arms.[86]

How men of the pool occupied themselves when not on active service in their captain's personal retinue is as difficult to determine as

[80] Alan Stewart had been in the personal retinue from February 1436 to September 1437 (AN, K 64/1/34; BN, NAF 8602/23; BL, Add MS 29315/2; BN, MS Fr 25774/1214). William Corournaille and John Monyn had been in a Rouen garrison in 1436 (AN, K 64/10/1) and Thomas Young had been in Rouen in 1436 and Neufchâtel in 1437 (AN, K 64/1/31, 10/1; BN, Clair 201/8459/63).

[81] BL, Add Ch 6949.

[82] BN, MS Fr 25775/1455; 25776/1510, 1518; AN, K 67/1/34.

[83] BL, Add Ch 6949.

[84] Edward Clyn, Lawrence Furness, Edward Spring, William Trumpet and Thomas Warbretton (BN, MS Fr 25776/1596).

[85] BL, Add Ch 11612.

[86] See P. Contamine, *Guerre, état et société à la fin du moyen âge* (Paris, 1972), Annexe XII, pp. 655-63.

is the means by which they first came to his notice. Garrison duty was one obvious alternative employment. Eight have been traced in garrison retinues between spells in the personal retinue. Cantock, Bannes and Montfort, all of whom had been in the personal retinue in 1428, were in the garrison of Rouen castle in the early months of 1436. By March 1437 Cantock had moved to Gisors, and between April and December 1437 Montfort was in the garrison of Neufchâtel. Richard Conningston, who was at Neufchâtel with Montfort in April, was in the personal retinue in September and back at Neufchâtel in December.[87] Rouen and Gisors were special cases in 1436-7. Early in 1436 Rouen was under threat and the garrisons there were much strengthened by Talbot, who undertook the personal command of its defence. Gisors had actually fallen for a short while to the French in the spring of 1436 and, after recapturing it, Talbot's retinue, under the command of his lieutenant Sir Thomas Hoo, was maintained not only for the defence of the town, but also for service in the field. This might explain why these particular garrisons, like Caudebec, not only had men from the pool of 1439-41 but also men who served during the same period in the personal retinue. The only other garrison to have more than the occasional man from the personal retinue was that of Harfleur after its recapture in 1440. For three years there was some considerable interchange between this garrison and the personal retinue. Over the winter of 1441-42, for instance, it is known that at least seven men from the pool spent some time in the garrison.[88] But for the most part garrisons were kept quite separate from the personal retinue. As many as eleven musters of the garrison of Coutances between September 1428 and August 1436 have survived. Of the thirty-one men-at-arms known to have served in the garrison over the entire eight years, only one, William Worsley, served Talbot elsewhere and that was not in the personal retinue. In fact, an analysis of the men-at-arms in this garrison, which grew in size from eight to twenty over the period, shows that a significant number were in fact resident. Four of the eight lances mustered in November 1428 were still in the garrison in August 1436. A year later, after a change of captain, seven of the twenty men-at-arms had stayed on, six of whom had been mustered in a garrison of twelve in 1432, and three of whom

[87] AN, K 64/1/31, 10/1, 12/1; BN, Clair 201/8459/63, NAF 1482/142.

[88] BN, MS Fr 25776/1623, 1554; ADSM, Fonds Danquin, 3/3/17. This can be compared with Lord Fauconberg's garrisons in Évreux and Verneuil between 1437 and 1439 which contained about half-a-dozen men-at-arms in each who served earlier or later in his personal retinue. A similar pattern has been discerned in the relationship between Lord Scale's personal retinue and his garrisons in Domfront and Vire. I am grateful to Miss A. E. Curry for this information.

were veterans of 1428.[89] At Avranches there was a similar continuity of service between 1430 and 1446 and at Château-Gaillard, regardless of changes of captain, a third to a half of the men continued in the garrison between 1436 and 1441.[90]

If they were not in the garrison, it is possible that men-at-arms who left the personal retinue joined the ranks of those men who did not take royal wages and lived off the land. We have seen that several men initially joined the retinue from this background. One or two also reverted to this way of life. William Doule, a Norman, who had been in Talbot's garrison retinues at Neufchâtel and Rouen in 1437, was living off the land in May 1441 when he enrolled in a *creu* and subsequently joined the personal retinue in 1442. John de la Brosse is a more interesting case. He was living off the land without wages in September 1440, when he was recruited by Talbot into a *creu* during the siege of Harfleur. On 29 November, after the end of the siege, he joined the personal retinue. He was still in it in March 1441 but left shortly after, for he was again living off the land without wages in May when he was recruited for a second time into a *creu*. In August he was back in the personal retinue. At michaelmas he joined Talbot's garrison in the 'palais' at Rouen, but he left his post on 30 October for reasons unknown. However, he was back once again in Talbot's personal retinue in October and November 1442.[91] There were probably other apparently property-less men like de la Brosse who drifted into the life of a freebooter between periods in the personal retinue, but by the very nature of their existence no record of their activities has survived. When not on active service some of Talbot's men-at-arms may well have turned aside from war to the enjoyment of the estates and property they had acquired in Normandy. It has recently been established beyond doubt that the English came to Normandy to settle as well as to conquer. The crown made a large number of grants to Englishmen of land confiscated from Normans who remained loyal to the Valois. The chief beneficiaries were among the senior ranks of the army and administration, but as the war continued and more land became available, especially after 1435-36, and as a flourishing land market developed, possession of property in

[89]See Appendix 1 and BN, MS Fr 25774/1291.

[90]Marshall, 'English Captains', p. 120; Appendix 1 and BN, MS Fr 25774/1303; 25776/1550.

[91]AN, K 64/12/1; BL, Add Ch 191, 192, 6949 for Doule: BN, Clair 202/8474/2; MS Fr 25775/1455, 1510; BL, Add Ch 6949; AN, K 67/1/34; ADSM, Fonds Danquin, 11/89; BN, MS Fr 25776/1591, 6 for de la Brosse. On 19 March 1442 Fauconberg recruited a *creu* which included two men-at-arms who had previously seen service in his personal retinue (BN, MS Fr 25776/1528, 66; Clair 185/57/6878).

Normandy was extended widely to men of quite humble rank. Several towns, Harfleur, Cherbourg and Caen in particular, attracted large English colonies and in the countryside as a whole an English petty nobility and gentry established itself. The opportunity to acquire land in Normandy was conceivably a principal inducement to the rank and file in the English army to volunteer for service abroad.[92] Talbot himself became a substantial French landowner. Most of the men who served as his captains and lieutenants, men like William Minors and John Green, are known to have acquired estates,[93] and so also did his men-at-arms. Robert Stafford, although ruined in 1427, did well enough subsequently under Talbot to acquire by 1443 new lands in the *bailliage* of Alençon to the value of 300 livre tournois *per annum*. By 1448 two brothers John le Prince had been granted lands to the same value in the *bailliage* of Rouen. One or other of the brothers also acquired Bascaille in the *bailliage* of Gisors, lands in the *chatellenie* of Andelys and a house in Rouen, all in the 1440s. John Montfort had acquired the lands of Chesnebrun and Courteilles in the *bailliage* of Alençon by May 1439 and in 1445 he sold a windmill at Verneuil to one John de Sercy. Thomas Dalton, who only came into Talbot's personal retinue in 1442, held lands in the *bailliage* of Rouen and at Pont-Audemer in 1446.[94] There were almost certainly others from Talbot's personal retinue who likewise possessed property in Normandy. Although the evidence is patchy, it is sufficient to suggest that these men-at-arms were in the process of establishing themselves in the ranks of the Norman gentry. The men of the pool of 1439-41 were men of obscure origin in England. Montfort may have been related to the family of Coleshill in Warwickshire, but there were at least two other families of the same name in the English gentry and at least one yeoman.[95] Ralph Rainford could have been connected with Henry Rainford of Rainford, Lancs, and William Massy may have been the William Massy of Rixton in the same county.[96] But it is well nigh impossible to trace with any certainty their English origins. One can perhaps justifiably conclude, therefore, that they were for the

[92]C. T. Allmand, 'The Lancastrian Land Settlement in Normandy, 1417-50', *EconHR* 2nd Ser. xxi, 3 (1968) *passim*.

[93]For Talbot see below p. 106, for his lieutenants see above pp. 78-80, 83.

[94]ADSM, Tabellionage, 30/162v (Dubuc, 'Calendar', no 1279); D Len 4/1651, 181, 187, 323; 74/239, 47; BL, Add Ch 14501.

[95]There were also the Mountfords of Hackforth, in the North Riding of Yorkshire, Montforts of Wiltshire and a John Montfort of Stinsford who received a royal pardon in 1446 (*CPR, 1441-6*, p. 439).

[96]See J. S. Roskell, *The Knights of the Shire of Lancaster*, (Chetham Society, new series 96, (1937), pp. 193-4.

most part men of humble birth who had come to seek their fortune in the conquest of France. Amongst those who settled, some may have been granted fees and annuities by Talbot from his French estates. No direct evidence has survived concerning this, but there are signs that Talbot's connections with one or two of his men extended beyond merely military service. In the late 1420s Talbot acted as a feoffee in France for his man-at-arms John Montfort in the settlement of certain lands. Thomas Dalton, the brothers John le Prince, Nicholas Overton and John Hensacre, men-at-arms with varying lengths of service in the personal retinue, were all on occasion referred to as Talbot's servants in grants to them by the crown.[97] The word servant implies a personal tie beyond, and separate from, employment in his retinue. It is thus conceivable that Talbot built up in Normandy a network of clientage amongst those who had come to settle and that in the manning of his personal retinue he came to draw, in part at least, on this network.

The practice of manning personal retinues from a pool of men-at-arms was not unique to Talbot. Lords Fauconberg and Scales, his fellow commanders, enjoyed the backing of similar, if smaller and apparently less reliable, reserves.[98] So also did François de Surienne, the Aragonese soldier of fortune who served the English for most of the war.[99] The reason why these experienced and successful commanders adopted this system is probably to be found in the peculiarly individualistic organisation of the army and the prevailing attitude to discipline. One should probably not look upon the men-at-arms who served in the army as full-time, regular soldiers. Many had other interests, and some had estates, which they wished to enjoy. Despite the imposition of a rigid central control of the army, it still remained in essence a collection of privately recruited companies. Neither the central administration nor the individual captains had powers to make soldiers stay at their posts. It was an army, as R. A. Newhall observed, 'oblivious to real military authority and efficiency'.[100] There was nothing apart from the stopping of his pay to prevent a soldier packing up his harness and going home whenever he liked.

[97]AN, JJ 175/67; BL, Add Ch 14501; D Len 74/231, 247; *CPR, 1452-61*, p. 37.

[98]An analysis of fifteen musters of Fauconberg's personal retinue between 1436 and 1442 suggests that he could call on some twenty-five men-at-arms from time to time, but that the service of all but a handful of these was infrequent and that he had to rely to a greater extent than Talbot on men with whom he had no apparent lasting connection. I am grateful to Miss A. E. Curry for this information.

[99]A. Bossuat, *Perrinet Gressart et François de Surienne, Agents de l'Angleterre* (Paris, 1936), pp. 290-1.

[100]Newhall, *Muster and Review,* p. 53.

Thus, absenteeism and desertion were commonplace. In these circumstances the development of a pool of reserves from which to fill the gaps in the ranks as and when they occurred was a natural response. Thus it was, for example, that during the abortive winter campaign of 1440-41 Talbot was able to keep his personal retinue up to full strength while the army he commanded, and of which this retinue was a part, dwindled from 1,600 to 900 men in three months.[101]

The maintenance of Talbot's retinues at full strength clearly required careful and time-consuming attention. But recruiting was not the only administrative problem. All the retinues had to be equipped, provisioned and paid. And on top of this Talbot had his responsibilities as a senior field commander, as a member of the ducal council, and as marshal of France. Inevitably much of the routine work was delegated. Sir William Peyto was for a while his deputy as marshal of France. In the summer of 1434, whilst he himself was campaigning in the Île de France, his councillors or servants in Rouen were left with the task of completing his indentures for the captaincies of Gisors and Neufchâtel (16 May) and of finding the men who took up their posts on 24 June and 1 July respectively.[102] Who it was he employed then we do not know, but later in the more routine matters concerned with the administration of his retinues he came to employ men from the regular nucleus of his personal retinue. And for those aspects in which he came into contact with the central administration – the paying and mustering of troops – ample documentation has survived. One of the more important officers was the paymaster, who handled the receipt and distribution of wages. His identity is revealed by his signature on the official receipts or acquittances given to the receiver-general of Normandy when wages were handed over. Talbot very rarely signed these himself[103] and they were almost invariably signed by his own deputy. In 1436, when he was captain of Rouen and resident there, the names of two of his men-at-arms in the garrison, John Pasquier and Richard Conningston, are found on acquittances.[104] In February 1437, Conningston was superseded by Robert Stafford, at that time also a member of the Rouen garrison, whose signature thereafter is found on the great majority of acquittances until the end of Talbot's fighting career in Normandy in 1449. Stafford had enjoyed positions of responsibility in Talbot's retinues before he became his paymaster. In January 1436 he had been master porter of the garrison of

[101] See above pp. 53-4.

[102] BN, PO 2787, Talbot, 9-12; MS Fr 25771/894.

[103] He did so at the height of the attempt to save Pontoise in 1441 (see BN, PO 2787, Talbot, 41; MS Fr 26068/4363).

[104] AN, K 64/10/9, 15; BN, PO 2787, Talbot, 16, 19; BL, Add Chs 7980-83.

Caudebec, a position which seems to have made him second in command to the lieutenant. From March 1436 he had been in the garrison of Rouen, where he was quarternier of the Porte Cauchoise. He remained in Rouen as long as Talbot was captain, but he had left by the end of 1437 when Warwick was captain. One may guess that he joined the personal retinue at about this time, for he was in it by November 1439[105] and is to be found in every surviving muster except one until the end of the war. The first surviving acquittance signed by him is dated 7 February 1437. From this date he appears to have had charge of Talbot's seal[106] and all moneys, including Talbot's personal salary and the wages of armies in the field, paid to Talbot by the receivers-general of Normandy probably passed through his hands. While still in Rouen, for instance, on 10 August 1437 he travelled to Jumièges to deliver the first month's wages of the army laying siege to Tancarville.[107] During the 1440s he was assisted occasionally by Rimon Mannessier, another of Talbot's long-serving companions, especially during the periods of March-May 1441, September 1442 and May 1445. When both Stafford and Mannessier were in England in 1442 a third of Talbot's regular companions, John Le Prince, deputised for them.[108] The last surviving acquittance for Talbot's wages was signed by Stafford on 1 February 1449.[109]

The office of paymaster was quite distinct from that of captain's clerk. The clerk was responsible for the recruiting, supplying, provisioning and day-to-day deployment of his captain's retinues.[110] In 1449 John le Prince the younger, who had been in the personal retinue since October 1440 or earlier, was Talbot's clerk. It was he who took care of all the practical details concerned with Talbot's share in the taking of Fougères. He provided artillery and powder for its defence; he personally took the artillery from Falaise to Fougères; he arranged for powder to be brought down from Rouen; and he persuaded the reluctant carrier to transport it from Falaise to

[105] BN, MS Fr 25772/1050; BL Add Ch 6911; BN, MS Fr 25774/1241, 5; Clair 201/8466/68.

[106] BN, Clair 201/8463/66. All acquittances were both signed and sealed. The Clairambault collection in the Bibliothèque Nationale has several with the seal attached.

[107] BN, PO 2787, Talbot, 23. It is worth noting that between 1435 and the end of 1437 Talbot's paymaster was permanently based in Rouen. Thereafter he was a member of his personal retinue.

[108] See, for example, BN, MS Fr 26068/2489; Clair 201/8849/51, 8451/52, 8453/55; PO 2787, Talbot, 44.

[109] AN, K 68/29/2.

[110] See Newhall, *Muster and Review*, pp. 53ff.

Fougères.[111] Paymaster and clerk were frequently employed as musterers. As marshal of France, Talbot was responsible for mustering armies in the field. This was another task delegated to his most trusted subordinates. Between 1439 and 1442, in particular, Stafford, Mannessier and Le Prince mustered many contingents serving in the field under their captain. One can take as an example the mustering of the duke of York's army in the summer of 1441. On 24 May Talbot was commissioned to take the muster of this force after its landing in Normandy. On 13 and 14 July at Juziers these musters, and those of the army already with Talbot, were duly taken by Stafford, Mannessier and Le Prince. The same three mustered the garrison of Pontoise in September 1441 and the contingent left to garrison Conches a year later.[112] In addition to this delegation of routine matters to the key men in his personal retinue, whom one might term his staff officers, it also appears that Talbot found it necessary or desirable to delegate the command of the personal retinue itself to a lieutenant or adjutant whilst he was in general command of an army in the field. This is nowhere made specific, but can be deduced from the muster rolls themselves. From 1436 the muster roll is almost invariably headed by a knight banneret or bachelor, or an esquire of distinctly higher rank than the remainder of the men-at-arms, who, in all but one case, had had considerable experience in the war and had exercised independent command. It was a position never occupied for more than a year by any one man. They were Sir William Bishopton in 1436, a retainer of Warwick who had been captain of Château-Gaillard in 1427-29; Sir Thomas Griffith, an old retainer of Bedford, in November 1439; Thomas Everingham, Talbot's own retainer from England, in February and August 1440; William Minors in November 1440, March and September 1441; Sir John Ripley in September and November 1442; and Sir Here John in July and December 1448.[113] Ripley had probably been with the retinue since michaelmas 1441 and appears to have taken over command of part of the retinue when Talbot was in England in the early months of 1442 and again before Dieppe from December 1442 until he was captured in August 1443.[114] These men are clearly distinct from the rest of the men-at-arms by both rank and term of service and the most plausible explanation is

---

[111]'Evidence before Juvenal des Ursins' in *Histoires des regnes de Charles VII et de Louis XI par Thomas Basin,* ed. J. Quicherat, 4, (Paris, 1859), pp. 307, 311, 315-17.

[112]*CPR, 1436-41,* p. 571; AN, K67/1/23-7, 40, 41, 12/71-4; BN, MS Fr 25776/1533.

[113]Both Griffith and Minors had served as captains under Talbot at the siege of Tancarville. Minors had been captain of Tancarville and St- Vigor in 1438-39 and went on to join the household of the duke of York. See above pp. 79-80.

[114]See above pp. 59-60. Ripley had also served with Sir William Chamberlain in Talbot's garrison at Meaux in 1439 (Waurin, 4, p. 256).

that they fulfilled within the personal retinue a similar function to that of a lieutenant of a garrison.

Finally, there is evidence to suggest that Talbot's personal retinue, or at least the nucleus of it, was looked upon as part of his household in Normandy. That he had a domestic establishment in the duchy goes without saying, its existence being suggested obliquely by the presence of his wife in Normandy on occasion in the early 1440s. In April 1441 Lord and Lady Talbot together received an indult to have a portable altar and to celebrate mass in places under interdict. Later, early in 1445, the countess of Shrewsbury was in France with her husband and was a participant in the homecoming of Queen Margaret.[115] Other pieces of evidence link members of the personal retinue with Talbot's household. In the year following michaelmas 1437 Gerrard Lensedit, at that time Talbot's standard-bearer and a man-at-arms in the personal retinue from time to time between 1437 and 1443, was resident for a period in Talbot's household in the monastery of St Ouen in Rouen. In 1441-42 Thomas 'Douve', probably Thomas Dowe from the nucleus of Talbot's personal retinue since 1439, was his *maître d'hotel*.[116] The brothers John Le Prince in 1446 and in 1448 Nicholas Overton, another man-at-arms in the personal retinue in the early 1440s, were all styled Talbot's 'familiers domestiques' in royal grants to them.[117] And, finally, Robert Stafford's responsibilities clearly extended into Talbot's household. In 1440 he was Talbot's attorney for receiving property granted to him by the crown, and after the fall of Rouen in 1449 he was specifically associated with his master in terms imposed on him to secure repayment of loans made by the citizens of Rouen.[118] A similar role appears to have been played in earlier years by Thomas Clerc, a member of the personal retinue in 1428 and in 1436 but not thereafter; the captive Talbot appointed him on 1 September 1429 as his attorney and special messenger, with power to plead his causes and to attend to his rights and business.[119] It seems probable, therefore, that no distinct line was drawn between the personal retinue and the household, and that in this period of constant warfare Talbot's closest companions in arms were not only his staff officers but also his household officials.

[115]*Calendar of Papal Registers, Papal letters,* 9, p. 239; Ramsay, *Lancaster and York,* 2, pp. 58-60; Beaucourt, *Charles VII,* 4, p. 92.

[116]ADSM, Série G, 158, 257.

[117]D Len, 74/221, 247.

[118]ADSM, Tabellionnage, 20/272 (Dubuc, 'Calendar', no 277); AN, J 1038/9.

[119]AN, K 64/1/32, 4; BN, MS Fr 25768/318, 26052/1162.

All but one of the team of staff and household officials whom Talbot had gathered round himself stayed with him until the loss of Normandy. By 1448, the year of the last surviving musters of the personal retinue, Mannessier had either retired or was dead, but Stafford, Le Prince, and Dowe were still in his company. In fact, a total of seven of the thirteen men-at-arms who in 1448 formed the inner personal retinue actually in his company in these last years were veterans from before 1442, including Richard Bannes, Thomas Cooks and Ralph Rainford. We know also that another veteran, John Hensacre, had returned to the garrison of Harfleur of which he was again controller.[120] What happened after 1450 we do not know, but one can assume that many of these men remained in his service. Robert Stafford and Richard Bannes survived their master's death to enter the service of his eldest son, the second earl of Shrewsbury.[121] Other veterans from Talbot's service in France, including John Montfort and John Sterky, were in the force which seized Berkeley castle for the Countess Margaret in September 1451.[122] Who and how many sailed with Talbot on the last fateful expedition to Gascony in 1452 we have no way of knowing. John Hensacre did, for he received a grant of land there. So also did Thomas Everingham, who was killed at Castillon.[123] Was this a fate shared by Hensacre, Thomas Dowe, John Le Prince, by Montfort and by Sterky? It may well have been that some of these men, who had been with Talbot for almost twenty years, met their death at his side in the last stand at Castillon.

Talbot's captains and lieutenants and the men-at-arms in his personal retinue were drawn primarily from the ranks of the veteran soldiers who had made their careers in Normandy under the Lancastrian kings. Some men, more noticeably amongst the lieutenants and captains, came into his service from his own or the English connections of his baronial associates, but the majority of his troops were men not previously connected with him whose principal qualification was that they, like him, were professional soldiers. Talbot's own élite corps in his personal retinue was drawn from a pool of such veterans. The ties he had with them away from the field of battle remain shadowy, but several had lands of their own and several were his servants, even those not frequently on active service in his retinue. It may be that they became members of a Norman affinity with whom he had independent contractual or financial links. By

---

[120]AN, K 68/29/6; BN, NAF 8606/102.

[121]PRO, C139/179.

[122]PRO, KB 27/763/42. See also below pp. 131-3.

[123]*CPR, 1452-61*, p. 37; Basin, 2, pp. 195-6.

1436, when our sources become full enough, the men from Talbot's English affinity have dwindled to a minute fraction. A distinct contrast is revealed between 1421, when Talbot's company drew heavily on his Irish and English connections, and 1448, when his company was made up almost entirely of Norman veterans recruited since 1435. This is not a surprising development. From 1427 to 1450, including the years of his captivity, Talbot was chiefly resident in France. Not only was he the longest serving and most respected commander in the English army; he was also a Norman noble in his own right. Thus, for the war and for his private affairs in Normandy he came to recruit his personal following from among men like himself – veteran Anglo-Norman soldiers and settlers.

From these veterans he selected a band of men to staff his household and carry out the manifold day-to-day duties and responsibilities he acquired as marshal of France and a senior field commander in the English army. The personnel of this headquarters staff, as one may style it, which emerged in the years between 1436 and 1440 remained largely unchanged until the end of the war. The structure of his household-cum-personal retinue was almost a replica in miniature of the household of the governor of the duchy, except that its personnel was of more humble status and more obscure origin. Like the household followers of York and Somerset, they returned with Talbot to England after 1450. On the other hand, there is no evidence that the numbers of people dependent on Talbot were swollen as a result of the war. Of all the thousands of soldiers who at one time or another took his pay in France, only the members of his personal retinue in 1448-50, and perhaps only the closest members at that, stayed in his service. The rest, their hopes and ambitions in Normandy destroyed, were left to sink or swim. Many returned destitute to England and disappeared into the obscurity from which they had sprung when Henry V first launched his conquest.[124] Thus, although the composition of Talbot's personal following was transformed by the experience of war, its size remained much the same. Indeed, when in 1452 Talbot came to recruit again for his expedition to Gascony there are signs that Norman veterans were less willing to serve and that he had to resort, for probably the first time, to large-scale recruitment from amongst his own tenants for the greater part of his army. Sheffield, Whitchurch and probably Painswick were called upon to supply men in large numbers to make up the rank and file.[125] This hardly suggests that,

---

[124] See Marshall, 'English Captains', Ch 7 *passim*.

[125] Local legend at both Whitchurch and Sheffield has it that the lordships provided large numbers for the Gascon expedition. (J. Hunter, *Hallamshire: The History of Sheffield* (Sheffield, 1819), p. 45 and the memorial plaque in the porch at St

over and above his immediate household, Talbot brought home in his train from Normandy hordes of restless soldiers with nothing to do but brawl and bully. This is not the place to continue the discussion concerning the possible links between defeat in France and the outbreak of civil disorder in England, but if Talbot is typical of peers other than the royal dukes, his case suggests that the war and its aftermath had little to do with the so-called evils of bastard feudalism. In his case, it neither intensified the practice of retaining nor led to an expansion in the numbers of armed followers. Rather could it be said that by giving this particularly violent and quarrelsome nobleman a foreign enemy on whom to work out his aggression for so many years the war, while it lasted, helped to lessen the extent of domestic disorder and violence.

Alkmund's, Whitchurch, commemorating the dead of Castillon). Unfortunately, there is no surviving record evidence against which to test these legends. A manorial court held at Painswick at the end of Talbot's life recorded the fact that sixteen tenants had served abroad in his wars (S. Rudder, *A New History of Gloucestershire* (Cirencester, 1779), pp. 593-4).

6

SOLDIER OF FORTUNE: JOHN TALBOT AND THE PROFITS OF WAR

Men did not go to war in the fifteenth century solely to serve their prince dutifully in his just causes; they also went to seek personal enrichment. In this John Talbot was no exception. Devoted and tireless servant of Lancastrian dynastic ambitions in France as he was – indeed none more so – he was nevertheless also seeking to augment his wealth through war. As K.B. McFarlane frequently reiterated, soldiers of all ranks in the fifteenth century looked upon war as a speculative business in which huge fortunes could be won. Whether or not the English in France in the fifteenth century were successful in this has been, and indeed remains, a matter of dispute. McFarlane was convinced that while 'England' was beaten the English were enriched.[1] And of all the English, he asserted, it was the nobility, especially the great landed families, who benefited most.

> It is not my intention to minimize the part played by needy adventurers of obscure birth and no inherited property; scores of them made notable fortunes. But it is the unbroken service of the greater baronage from Crecy to Castillon that is in danger of being taken for granted and ignored. There is no truth in the theory that the aristocracy started the war and left the professional mercenaries to finish it off. The names of the captains from Bohun, Fitzalan and Stafford to Beauchamp, Montagu, Mowbray, and Talbot, would be recognized for what they are by any English schoolboy.[2]

But this has long been a view from which M.M. Postan has dissented. Not only has he argued that the wars of the fifteenth century were economically and financially unprofitable for the English, but he has also maintained that the nobility and great landed families were not the chief beneficiaries. Against the great wealth and high status won by a number of men of relatively modest origins one has to balance the fact that some great fortunes were extinguished and some fortunes and families, among them those of famous captains such as John Talbot, may not have been ruined by the war but merely failed to benefit from it.[3] Although here we are not concerned with the wider

---

[1] K.B. McFarlane, *The Nobility of Late Medieval England* (Oxford, 1973), p. 21.

[2] *Ibid.*, p. 40.

[3] M. M. Postan, 'The Costs of the Hundred Years' War', *Past and Present* 27 (1964), 51.

problem of the economic and financial impact of the Hundred Years' War on the English, the profitability of Talbot's war is of some significance in that he was the head of a great landed family and has been specifically cited in support of both sides of the argument. Unfortunately, the evidence by which a conclusion might be reached is not all that it might be. Precise and final figures cannot be deduced for any of the items on the balance sheet. There is nothing of the order of information about Talbot which has enabled historians to chart precisely Sir John Fastolf's entrepreneurial successes.[4] Nevertheless, sufficient evidence has survived to make the attempt worthwhile and to enable a tentative conclusion to be offered as to whether Talbot was a major profiteer or a mere survivor in the business of war.

Profits of war came from four principal sources: wages, prisoners, plunder and the income from land and office. As the army was professional, royal wages provided the first opportunity for profit. Talbot received from the crown his personal wages, a supplementary salary for his maintenance as a field commander and the wages of his soldiers. As a baron he received the personal wage of four shillings a day, which was increased in 1442 to six shillings and eight pence after his promotion to an earldom. On occasion, as in 1434, he received an extra 100 marks a quarter as a customery 'regard' for every thirty men-at-arms in his retinue. In view of the fact that he was frequently a captain of several retinues, care was taken, as surviving indentures and acquittances show, to see that he was paid his personal wage with only one of his retinues at any one time.[5] One may assume, therefore, that his personal wages came to at least £73 *per annum* before 1442 and £121 13s. 4d. thereafter. Talbot's service in the field as lieutenant-general from 1434 and marshal from 1436 entitled him to a salary or 'pension pour son estat', which fluctuated from year to year but was worth approximately £500 *per annum* between 1434 and 1444.[6] On his return to active service in Normandy in 1448 the 'pension' was settled at £220 *per annum*; the reduction might have been because in the interim Talbot's wages as marshal had been

[4]K.B. McFarlane, 'The Investment of Sir John Fastolf's Profits of War', *TRHS* 5th series 7 (1957), 91-116 *passim*.

[5]PRO, E404/50/159; McFarlane, *Nobility,* pp. 23-4; R.A. Newhall, *Muster and Review* (Harvard, 1940), p. 21.

[6]See the following acquittances: BN, PO 2787, Talbot, 14; Clair 201/8436/67, 8467/72, 8445/45, 8453/54; BL, Add Ch 1264 (a monthly instalment?). The payments were in *livres tournois*. I have everywhere converted *livres tournois* to pounds sterling on the basis of William Worcester's rate of exchange of nine livres tournois to one pound sterling, as followed by K.B. McFarlane, 'England and the Hundred Years' War', *Past and Present* 22 (1962), 13, n.18.

doubled. The last quarterly instalment was paid on 1 August 1449.[7] In addition to this generous salary, he was paid from time to time a kind of bonus to cover his expenses. This was described as being 'for the support of his retinue', or 'in recompence for his expenses' or once, in 1440, more fully in order 'to assist him in maintaining his position more honourably and to aid him in supporting the charges which he must necessarily incur by the occasion of the same'.[8] He is known to have received at least eight such payments over the years 1434-44 totalling £1,000.[9] In all, between 1434 and 1444 Talbot was receiving at least £700 *per annum* from the crown in wages, salary and expenses, a sum which was approximately 50% of his declared income from land and annuities in England in 1436. How much of this he retained as net profit we cannot tell. A considerable amount was no doubt expended on household and related domestic and military costs. No doubt Talbot did incur large expenses in royal service. But his payment was generous and we should not assume that a fifteenth-century baron was any less alive than a twentieth-century business man to the supplementary income that could be drawn from expenses. In addition, Talbot was entrusted with far greater sums for distribution to his soldiers. This may have offered opportunity for further gain, but as we shall see below, it is more likely that here Talbot ended out of pocket.

Indentures and general treatises on war make it abundantly clear that a soldier was not expected to make a living merely on his wages. Of the various gains of war, prisoners and the ransoms received for them were the most important. Distressingly little is known about prisoners taken by John Talbot. No really prominent men fell into his hands until 1452, when he reserved the important prisoners taken at Bordeaux to himself. These were left in the possession of his family at his death in 1453.[10] How many others there were one cannot say, but there was doubtless a succession bringing in a steady stream of

---

[7] BL, Add MS 11, 509, f39v and below p. 108. It is clear from the entry in this account of the receiver-general of France and Normandy for 1448-49 that the 'pension' (renewed on 1 April 1448) was granted only when he was on active service in France. Talbot received payment for three quarters in equal parts on 1 February, 2 May and 1 August 1449.

[8] Stevenson, *Wars*, 2, pp. 317-19.

[9] AN, K 66/1/2; BN, MS Fr 26065/3758; Clair 201/8469/74, 202/8475/37; PO 2787, Talbot, 37; BL, Add Ch 579, 11883; Stevenson, *Wars*, 2, pp. 317-19.

[10] William Gougeul alias Rouville, Olivier de Coetivy and others, prisoners of Margaret, countess of Shrewsbury, received safe conducts to travel to France during 1455 to obtain their ransoms. 'Calendar of French Rolls' in *The Forty-eighth Report of the Deputy Keeper of the Public Records* (1887), pp. 404, 406. See also P. Marchegay, 'La rançon d'Olivier de Coëtivy, seigneur de Taillebourg, sénéchal de Guyenne, 1451-77', *Bibliothèque de l'Ecole des Chartes* 38 (1877), 9-10.

ransom money. In 1434 Talbot returned to Paris after a summer campaign with 'great riches and fatte prisoners'. As captain of Rouen he would have received his share of the profit from the prisoners taken in the skirmish at Ry in February 1436. Monstrelet recorded that his armies returned to Normandy with many prisoners after successful raids into Burgundian territory in 1437 and 1440. And prisoners were also taken during the relief of Meaux in August 1439.[11] Little more can be gleaned about plunder. In 1428, during his successful campaign in Maine, Talbot had some rich pickings. When he took Le Mans the French fled, 'Levyng behind therin all their apparel, horses, armure and riches'. He also took Laval, in which he found 'moult de richesses' and in addition he picked up £3,000 as part of the surrender terms imposed on the garrison of the castle.[12] Other incidents followed after 1433. At the rescue of Gisors in 1436 'there was moch good gotyn therein'. At the spectacular capture of Pontoise in 1437, the fleeing French garrison left practically all their harness and belongings behind. And late in 1437 the duke of Burgundy abandoned a rich stock of personal property and military supplies when he broke off the siege of Le Crotoy. In the Santerre raid early in 1439, Folville and Lihons paid handsome rachats to their captors and the rich and comparatively unspoiled countryside was plundered. During the campaign to save Pontoise in 1441 Talbot is reported to have seized much of King Charles's personal property.[13] Although it is impossible to quantify the level of profit from prisoners and plunder, one can justifiably assume that Talbot's penchant for surprise and sudden descent on an unsuspecting enemy brought him definite financial as well as military advantage. That Talbot had a keen eye for every opportunity that presented itself for personal gain, and that such opportunities existed right up to the end of the war, is demonstrated by his actions following the seizure of Fougères in March 1449. Talbot, from Falaise, took over the responsibility for securing the town's defence and arranged for a thousand tons of gunpowder to be transported there from Rouen. On the return journey the carriers took away four bales of the finest cloth, seized by Talbot's men; one was delivered to Falaise, the remainder being taken on to Rouen to be delivered to his agents for disposal.[14] Plunder, like ransom money,

[11] See above pp. 19, 23, 49, 52-3; Monstrelet, 5, pp. 316, 409.

[12] E. Hall, *The Union of the Noble and Illustre Famelies of Lancastre and Yorke* (1809), p. 143: *Chronique de la Pucelle ou chronique de Cousinot,* ed. M. Vallet de Viriville (Paris, 1839), p. 254.

[13] Monstrelet, 5, pp. 316, 407; C. L. Kingsford, *Chronicles of London* (Oxford, 1905), pp. 140, 141, 144-5; Bourgeois, pp. 329-30.

[14] 'Evidence before Juvenal des Ursins on the taking of Fougères' in T. Basin, *Histoire des regnes de Charles VII et Louis XI,* ed. J. Quicherat, 4 (Paris, 1859), pp. 306-18.

continued to supply Talbot with a substantial income until the end of the war.

Talbot would not have pocketed the gross income from ransoms and plunder. The king himself had a right to a third of all proceeds and in the case of ransoms it has been suggested that no more than a third of agreed sums eventually reached the captor.[15] This was partly made up by Talbot's own rights as captain to a third of the gains of war of his own men in garrisons and his personal retinue, as well as his rights as marshal after 1436 to a share of plunder throughout the whole army.[16] One piece of surviving evidence makes it clear that Talbot could make a substantial profit from these rights. On the counter-roll for his garrison at Château-Gaillard for the period from 29 September to 5 December 1436, at which date Talbot was discharged from the captaincy, the controller noted that no fewer that thirty-two prisoners had been taken by men of the garrison and of the garrison of Longempré on 24 August 1435 and later. At the foot of the roll he recorded the information that the captain's share of their gains of war was £123 18s. 11d. (just under £14 sterling).[17] This may be an exceptional case: other counter-rolls do not reveal information about Talbot's share of the gains made by his troops. But this particular document does illustrate how on occasion he could and did enhance his income handsomely from the winnings of his men.

The remaining important profit was the income from land and office. From 1428 Talbot held extensive property in Normandy and the Île de France. This included the county of Clermont, the lordships of Graville-Sainte-Honorine, Heugueville, Thouars, Longempré and Bretteville sur Laize, lands in Romilly, Escorchebeuf and La Motte Fontaines and lands and houses in Harfleur and Honfleur. The value of all these estates, even in peacetime, is not known, although Heugeville had a nominal gross annual value of approximately £195 in 1400; certain lands once belonging to Jean Morelet which Talbot was granted in 1438 had been worth £20 *per annum* in 1410; and one house in Honfleur produced an annual income of £3 6s. 8d. in 1410.[18] Nor is it certain that Talbot ever took

[15] See M. M. Postan, *Past and Present* 27 (1964) 49-50.

[16] D. Hay, 'The Divisions of the Spoils of War' *TRHS* 5th Ser 4 (1954), esp. 109.

[17] Archives Departementales de l'Eure, Série 11 F/4069. I am grateful to Miss A. E. Curry for drawing my attention to this document.

[18] AN, JJ 174/45/108, 47/112; JJ 175/318; Archives du Calvados, E443 (I am grateful to Dr C. T. Allmand for this reference); D Len 4/277, 26/187; Lambeth Palace Library, Register Stafford and Kemp, f311b; *Calendar of Papal Registers, Papal Letters,* 9, p. 269; Stevenson, *Wars,* 2, p. 620.

possession of Clermont. But even with the difficulties of wartime, and taking into account the known waste of much of the Norman countryside after 1435, one can assume that like Sir John Fastolf he continued to enjoy a substantial income from these lands even late in the occupation.[19] The captaincy of a town also involved a property right, for it was partly a military command, partly a grant. In 1440, for example, he was made a special payment by the Norman council because 'for a certain time past he has not had from us any charge as a captain ... and that at this present time he has none from us except Lisieux and the custody of that of Harfleur and Montivilliers which have been delivered to him of late ... to hold until he shall have some other higher and more ample provision'.[20] One assumes that six captaincies in 1436 and 1438 had proved to be financially rewarding. Rouen was one town at least which paid an annual tribute (approximately £110) to its English captain. And it was no doubt because of its financial value that Talbot refused to hand over St-Germain-en-Laye to a new captain, François de Surienne, early in 1439 until he had been given compensation of some £75.[21]

The governorships of Auge, Orbec and Pont-Audemer which he held in 1438, would have brought in an additional income, as would the office of master investigator and general reformer of the waters and woods of Normandy which was granted to him in 1447.[22] But of all the offices he held, that of marshal of France was potentially the most rewarding. A marshalcy of France not only carried a wage of £220 *per annum*, but, according to a statement in 1447, it also produced a profit from fees for mustering, fees paid in the marshal's court and other emoluments totalling £800-900 a year.[23] Talbot did not enjoy all of this huge profit continuously from 1436, for he became involved in a costly dispute with the duke of Gloucester. In 1440, or thereabouts, Gloucester claimed to exercise the sole rights of the marshalcy in Normandy as lord of Orichier. As a result, the rights in Normandy were removed from Talbot and placed in commission. Talbot successfully appealed and had his rights restored. He enjoyed these for a while until in 1444 or early 1445 he was removed again by York, and his counsellors and officers were arrested. To resolve the

[19] McFarlane, *TRHS* 5th Series 7 (1957), 105-6. Fastolf's holdings in Normandy and Maine, producing over £675 *per annum* in 1435, were still rendering £410 in 1444-5.

[20] Stevenson, *Wars*, 2, pp. 317-19.

[21] BN, PO 2787, Talbot, 24; A. Bossuat, *Perrinet Gressart et François de Surienne, Agents de l'Angleterre* (Paris, 1936), p. 271.

[22] BL, Add Ch 12005; D Len 74/219.

[23] D Len 4/153.

dispute Talbot was now persuaded to purchase the lordship from Gloucester. This opened the way for the king to issue new letters to Talbot in July 1445 confirming his possession of the marshalcy with full rights in Normandy, and henceforward he enjoyed the wages and profits without hindrance.[24] In March 1447, immediately after Gloucester's death, the king created Talbot sole marshal of France, partly in consideration of the fact that during the quarrel with Gloucester he had received none of the profits. Now he was to have a wage of £440 *per annum* and those profits which in the past had been shared by two marshals.[25] It is to be doubted whether the actual income was in practice as high as this implies. Nevertheless, and in spite of the costly dispute with Gloucester, from 1436 Talbot may still have received a substantial income from the office of marshal.

Every action, command and responsibility in the war offered an opportunity for financial gain. As we have seen, Talbot was taking advantage of the opportunities right up to the very end of the occupation. During these last years the gains of war were no longer as spectacular as earlier, and the income to be derived from land was substantially reduced. But even so, Talbot was still earning a handsome income every year. It is impossible to quantify it, but Talbot's actual annual *gross* income from all the profits of war — wages, ransoms, plunder, estates and offices — could well have brought in a sum comparable with that from his estates and lands in England; that is, it doubled his income. But was there a net profit from the war? Was this income larger than the costs Talbot faced as a result of the war?

The principal costs of war lay in wages and expenses unpaid by the crown, the maintenance of household and military establishments and, above all in Talbot's case, ransoms paid out to the French. In addition to their personal wages, all captains were responsible for paying the men in their retinue. The more senior the command and the more captaincies held, the greater were the sums which the crown contracted to pay to an individual captain. This gave opportunities for personal enrichment at the expense of either crown or soldiers, but at the same time created the risk of loss if the crown failed to honour its

---

[24]College of Arms Library, WH, ff312-14. Orichier, in the pays de Caux, had belonged to Sir John Fastolf in 1434. It was presumably one of those properties sold by him after 1435. It would seem likely that the purchaser, Gloucester, challenged Talbot's rights as marshal soon after acquiring the title (ADSM, Tabellionnage, 25/158v: Dubuc, 'Calendar', no. 931; McFarlane, *TRHS* 5th Series 7 (1957), 106.

[25]D Len 4/153. The wage of £440 *per annum* was confirmed in the grant of a 'pension' over and above this sum on 1 April 1448 (BL, Add MS 11, 509, f39v and above p. 104).

obligations.[26] The annual wages' bill for Talbot's retinues was frequently over £10,000 and sometimes as high as £15,000. The crown's system of mustering was designed to make sure that its troops were regularly paid and to keep an eye on captains who were tempted to claim the pay of soldiers no longer in their company. It was an efficient system, but cunning men still managed to defraud the crown of wages for non-existent soldiers and embezzle part of the wages of those they did retain. One must not assume that Talbot was above such pilfering. That he cheated the crown from time to time is suggested by the case of the Caudebec wages in 1436. In 1438 he claimed that among other sums he had not received any payment at all for the garrison he kept in Caudebec in the first three-quarters of 1436. His claim was accepted and arrangements made to pay off the arrears. Yet acquittances for £333 of these wages, signed by Robert Stafford as received in 1436, have survived.[27] Unless the acquittances were for assignments on revenue and not cash itself, which is not stated to be the case, one can only conclude that Talbot on this occasion was deceiving the treasurer-general. Such fraud, if such it was, may well have been considered fair gain in circumstances in which the crown did indeed frequently default on payment of wages, leaving a captain to pay his soldiers out of his own pocket. In June 1438 Talbot claimed a total of £3,800 in arrears of wages accumulated in France since 1435. A sympathetic crown agreed only to pay them in instalments.[28] Record of only four such payments has survived, the last in April 1439, totalling £1,419 3s. 4d.[29] By August 1443, when Talbot negotiated a second settlement, the unpaid arrears, 'verily ascertained for truth' by royal accountants, had climbed to £4,627 10s. 6½d.[30] But this total, built up over nine years, has to be put in perspective. First of all, it is a trifling amount compared with the sums he must have received. It can have been no more than five per cent of the total due to him since 1434, the rest of which he presumably was paid. Secondly,

[26]McFarlane emphasised the opportunity for profit (e.g. *Nobility,* p.27); Postan has stressed the risk of loss (e.g. *Past and Present* 27 (1964), 43).

[27]BL, Add Chs 439, 7983; BN, PO 2787, Talbot, 22, 26, 27.

[28]BL, Add Chs 439; BN, PO 2787, Talbot, 26-7. *Inter alia* Talbot had not been paid the wages for his garrison of Gisors from 29 September to 10 November 1436, for Neufchâtel for the half-year ending 28 December 1437 and for his garrisons in Rouen for the quarter ending 28 June 1437.

[29]BN, Clair 202/8483/17; PO 2787/32; MS Fr 26065/3628, 3760. It may be significant that the payment of arrears, from Norman sources, was authorised by relation of the earl of Warwick, that the last known payment was made three days before Warwick's death, and that no evidence has survived of payments made subsequently.

[30]Stevenson, *Wars,* 1, pp. 434-6.

the sum was small compared with the £38,666 owed to Richard, duke of York three years later or even the £19,000 owed to Humphrey, duke of Buckingham for his wages as captain of Calais.[31] It would thus seem likely that what Talbot lost between 1434 and 1443 on the swings of unpaid wages he made up for on the roundabouts of fraud and embezzlement.

Before 1443, when Talbot was paid almost entirely from French sources, he was not significantly out of pocket.[32] But after 1443, for the last ten years of his life, he was far more dependent on payment from less reliable English sources. At first he was well satisfied. In February 1444, when he was retained in England to continue to serve in France for a further six months with a personal retinue of 100 men-at-arms and 300 archers, knowing the uncertainty of receiving payment from the exchequer, he secured an undertaking that 2,000 marks from the settlement of 1443 would be paid in cash rather than assignments on future revenue. And on 20 February his attorneys, Richard Legett and Geoffrey Halford received on his behalf not only the first quarter's wages, but also £1,000 towards the 2,000 marks. The remaining £333 6s. 8d. was paid three months later.[33] In the spring of 1445, when Talbot was appointed lieutenant of Ireland for seven years, the crown committed itself to pay larger sums. At first the annual salary was fixed at 4,000 marks.[34] But Talbot seems to have had difficulty securing any form of advance payment and this was probably the reason why he did not go to Ireland until eighteen months after his appointment. It was only after the parliamentary grant of taxation in April 1446 that the exchequer was in a position to meet his demand. The terms were then renegotiated: Talbot accepted a reduction in his annual salary to £2,000 in exchange for a down payment of £3,666 13s. 4d. (apparently including back-pay) which he received on 1 July.[35] Accordingly, by 18 August Talbot could be described as being in all haste to go to Ireland when he was granted a further 2,000 marks to help pay the wages of his retinue.[36] He sailed to Ireland in September and returned to England the following July: in December 1447 he was replaced by Richard of York. Talbot's early

[31] R. L. Storey, *The End of the House of Lancaster* (1966), p. 75; T. B. Pugh, *The Marcher Lordship of South Wales, 1415-1536* (University of Wales, 1963), p. 178, n. 3.

[32] On the occasion in 1435 when Talbot was paid from the English exchequer for six months wages he received speedy settlement (PRO, E403/720, m 6, 12, 14).

[33] PRO, E404/60/130; E403/751, m 5, 6.

[34] PRO, E403/762, m 5.

[35] *Ibid.*

[36] PRO, E404/62/231; E403/762 m 13. The exchequer was instructed to pay 'redy money'; Talbot's attorney accepted assignment on future revenue.

return was almost certainly occasioned by his quickly running out of money, for later it was accepted by the crown that it owed him as much as £3,527 6s. 8d. for his period of office.[37] Indeed, when in March 1448 the king and council entreated Talbot to return once more to France in the service of the duke of Somerset he agreed to do so only on condition that this sum was paid. On 10 March, therefore, letters patent were issued granting him half of the debt (£1,763 13s. 4d.) from the income of the recent parliamentary grant, to be paid in November, and the rest to be paid from the first moneys received from any future clerical aid.[38] The first half was in fact paid, but the second had not materialised by June 1451 when Talbot sought once more to recover his recent debts. These now included not only the £1,763. 13s. 4d. outstanding from his Irish expedition, but also a further £1,500 in bad tallies which had been passed on to him by Richard of York in settlement of sums owed for service in Normandy in 1444-45.[39] By the king's 'special grace' he secured fresh assignment of both sums, but by now it was becoming virtually impossible to squeeze money out of the exchequer and neither debt was settled before his death.

The difficulties faced by Talbot during these last years are clearly revealed by the history of the £1,500 originally owed to him by York. York himself was owed a total of almost £40,000 for his years as governor of Normandy in the early 1440s, and Talbot had always depended on York's debts being settled before he could recover his own. On 20 and 21 July 1446 the crown assigned over £14,000 to York in an attempt to honour part of its obligation.[40] Included in these assignments were seven tallies raised on the customs at Boston and Chichester for £1,500 which York delivered to Talbot. These proved worthless. Talbot therefore petitioned the king for alternative assignment who 'signed a bill with our owne handes' whereby the debt was assigned to the revenues from the estates of the late duchess of Warwick (Talbot's kinswoman) then in the king's hands.[41] These, too, proved valueless as they had already been ear-marked to meet the expenses of the royal household. By June 1451 Talbot had 'as yet hath no paiement ne noon can gete' and so the debt was once more re-assigned.[42] Still not paid by July 1452 because 'the places upon the whiche the saide tailles been smyten out ben overcharged in other

[37] PRO, E404/67/172; CPR, 1446-52, p. 146.

[38] Ibid.

[39] PRO, E404/67/172.

[40] A.B. Steel, The Receipt of the Exchequer, 1377-1485 (Cambridge, 1954), p. 226.

[41] PRO, E404/67/172.

[42] Ibid.

wyses', the tallies were exchanged again.[43] Even so, another year later, in the two weeks before Talbot's death at Castillon, his attorneys were yet again seeking alternative settlement. This time the whole £1,500 was assigned to the revenue from recent parliamentary taxation.[44] It is almost certain that his executors failed to collect it.[45]

Between 1443 and 1453 Talbot showed himself to be a hard **bargainer with the crown and a tenacious pursuer of his wages. He** exploited to the utmost his favour at court and the crown's need for his services overseas. But by the early 1450s the finances of the crown were in such disarray that it proved no longer possible for him to secure his payments. Indeed the exchequer was unable to pay wages in cash to Talbot's army in July 1452 and he was probably owed a new and considerable debt for his last year's service.[46] Nevertheless the fact that the new debts for his services between 1443 and his departure for Gascony in 1452 were restricted to two items totalling £3,263 13s. 4d. is perhaps indicative of the success with which he and his councillors protected his financial interests until the eleventh hour.

Far less can be said about the second of the principal costs – those involved in maintaining Talbot's private establishment in France. Lady Talbot and her attendants were in France with him on at least two occasions, in 1441 and again in 1444 when they accompanied Queen Margaret to England.[47] The costs involved in managing his Norman estates and in retaining followers and servants in the duchy are completely unknown. These estates had to be defended at his own private charge as well. In the summer of 1446 his secretary, Jean le Fevre, was granted arms for his distinguished service in the defence of the castle of Longempré, which was one of Talbot's own possessions.[48] What size of garrison Talbot maintained in Longempré

[43] PRO, E404/68/156.

[44] PRO, E404/69/177, 183; E401/831 20 July and 24 July.

[45] There is no record of the collectors of the subsidies in the relevant counties having handed over these sums (PRO, E369/31).

[46] Steel, *Receipt of the Exchequer,* pp. 238, 272-3; M. G. A. Vale, 'The Last Years of English Gascony, 1451-1453'. *TRHS* 5th Series 19 (1969), 135; and *English Gascony, 1399-1453* (Oxford, 1970) pp. 146-53. I have been unable to trace any reference to the payment of Talbot's wages from the exchequer for his expedition to Normandy in 1448. He was paid from Norman sources for his wages from michaelmas 1448 (BL, Add MS 11.509, f39v; and above p. 104). It may be assumed, since he himself made no subsequent claim, that he received satisfaction for the six months from Easter to michaelmas 1448.

[47] *Cal. Pap. Reg. Letters,* 9, p. 239; Lady Margaret had also been in France in 1431-2 in her father's household (H. A. Cronne and R. H. Hilton, 'The Beauchamp Household Book', *University of Birmingham Historical Journal* 2 (1950), 208-18).

[48] ADSM, Série G9195. In 1428 Talbot paid for a horse bought in Rouen out of the revenues of Blakemere (Shropshire Record Office, Bridgewater Papers, 76/1427-8).

and his other places, and how much it cost him, we just do not know. The amount cannot have been insignificant. Above and beyond these regular costs, and overshadowing everything else, was the burden of Talbot's ransom. When Talbot was taken prisoner at the battle of Patay in 1429 he was set to ransom at a sum considered to be exorbitant. Custom, if not the laws of war, demanded that a ransom should not exceed the means of the prisoner or threaten his financial ruin. As Christine de Pisan wrote:

> But of ryght wryton he (the captor) ought to be myldefull unto hym (the captive), so that in takying of his prysoner reanson whyche is permytted in ryghte of armes, by especyall of one natyon ayenst another whan they doo werre togyder, as englysshe men and Frenshe men and other in lyke wyse, ought to be taken heed that the reanson be not so cruell that the man be not undoo thereby, and his wiffe & children distroied and brought to poverty. Other wise it is tirannye ayenst conscience & aienst al ryght of armes. For it appateyneth not that a gentylman shulde begge hys bredde after the payement made for his reanson, but ought to be lefte hum wherof he may lyve, kepyng his astate.[49]

The reaction in England in 1429 including the establishment of something like a public subscription and petition by the commons on Talbot's behalf in view of the 'unreasonable and importable raunceon',[50] suggests most strongly that convention had been broken by the demand for a sum way beyond his means. What this sum was we do not know. It was probably not only well in excess of the 12,500 *reaux* paid by Charles VII to Poton de Xaintrailles in March 1431,[51] but also considerably more than the £3,000 paid by Sir Walter Hungerford, who was also captured by the French at Patay. It could even have been more than the £20,000 demanded of the earl of Suffolk, who was also taken prisoner in 1429.[52] A sum of £25,000 would have required Talbot to sell practically all his inheritance and would have left his

---

[49] *The Book of Fayttes of Armes and of Chivalrye*, ed. A. T. P. Byles, Early English Text Society (1937), p. 223.

[50] *Rotuli Parliamentorum*, 4, p. 338b.

[51] AN, Chartrier de Thouars, 1 AP 175/27. If *reaux* are taken to be worth approximately 3s. 4d each, this gives a sum of just over £2,000 sterling (Spufford, *Camb. Econ. Hist*, 3, p. 2), which is clearly much lower than Talbot's worth. Mr Roger Little has suggested to me that this sum may represent either the difference between what Xaintrailles had already received for Talbot and the minimum figure which the king was obliged to pay to gain possession of his prisoner, or simply the sum Xaintrailles was content to receive.

[52] McFarlane, *Nobility*, p. 128; C. L. Kingsford, *Prejudice and Promise in Fifteenth-Century England* (Oxford, 1925), p. 148.

family financially ruined. The demand was, presumably, something of this order. Fortunately for Talbot, he was not left to pay it all himself. As early as 1429, twenty-seven burgesses of Coventry, with which town Talbot had no apparent connection, contributed twenty marks towards his ransom. Coventry was perhaps not alone in subscribing. Other persons and institutions may have contributed to the 250 marks which were presented to Talbot's retainers, Richard Legett, Hugh Burgh and Henry Perpoynt, in November 1429 for delivery to France.[53] After the failure of the plan to effect an exchange with Barbazan, the crown granted to Talbot a sum of £9,000 towards his ransom, to be paid from the income of the *gabelle* raised in Normandy and France.[54]

The agreement with Charles VII whereby Talbot was eventually released in 1433, partly in exchange for Poton de Xaintrailles, still left him with a substantial sum of money to find. The royal gift of £9,000 was never withdrawn, although, as we shall see below, Talbot found great difficulty in making it good. In addition he also received a gift from the duke of Brittany, specifically in aid of his ransom, of 2,000 mewes of salt, which in July 1432 he was licensed to export from France and import into England free of customs duty. He was still shipping this salt to England in 1439.[55] Again we do not know the nature of Talbot's obligations to Warwick, but it may be significant that in 1434 he began to set in motion the series of conveyances by which he sought to transfer a substantial part of his inheritance, concentrated in Shropshire and Gloucestershire, to his family and descendants by his second wife, Margaret Beauchamp.[56] This may well have been the price he paid for Warwick's support.

The cost of a ransom did not lie solely in the capital sum. The prisoner was also required to pay for his maintenance and the expenses involved in negotiating his release. These additional costs could be high. In 1453 Lord Moleyns, captured at Castillon, was ransomed for £6,000. The extra payments came to over £3,800.[57] It was presumably to meet the costs of maintenance, as well as any early instalment of his ransom, that Talbot was granted permission to take

[53]*CCR, 1429-35*, p. 27; J. Hunter, *Hallamshire: the History of Sheffield* (1879), p. 45.

[54]*Rot. Parl*, 4. p. 338b; J. H. Ramsay, *Lancaster and York*, 1 (Oxford, 1892), p. 414; Stevenson, *Wars*, 1, pp. 434-6; see also below pp. 117-18.

[55]*CPR. 1429-36*, p. 211: *Chancery Proceedings, Elizabeth I*, 1, p xl.

[56]PRO C139/154, 179.

[57]McFarlane, *Nobility*, p. 126.

up to 8,000 marks (£5,332 13s.4d.) out of England in January 1430 and that he sold his lordship of Douville sometime before January 1432.[58] There can be little doubt that when he was released in 1433, in spite of the generous support he had received from fellow Englishmen, Warwick, the crown and even England's allies to save him from ruin, he was still substantially out of pocket. In February 1434 the Council agreed to pay the sum of £1,000 to him in settlement of certain sums due to him, presumably as arrears of wages, in recognition of the service he had rendered to Henry V without wages and in consideration of the great necessity in which he then found himself. Talbot accepted the settlement and promised to present no further demands for these debts.[59] The great necessity that Talbot was said to be in could only have been the consequence of his recent captivity and the costs incurred in securing his release.

The cost of ransoms did not end with Talbot's own personal burden. Before 1438 he had had to pay 'grans sommes des deniers' to ransom a son, though which one, legitimate or illegitimate, we do not know. In 1443 another son, Henry, undoubtedly illegitimate, was taken when the bastille before Dieppe fell to the French counter-attack. He too was ransomed.[60] Talbot may also have contributed to the ransoms of members of his personal retinue, including John Hensacre and Robert Stafford, who fell into French hands in 1443. That Talbot involved himself in the release of men-at-arms is shown by the influence he exerted on behalf of one Guillaume Quesnel, a member of the garrison of Caudebec who was taken by the French in 1443 and who was subsequently exchanged for a prisoner of the archbishop of Rouen.[61] Although the sums involved in these transactions could only have been paltry in comparison with the burden Talbot himself carried, they cannot be ignored in the final balance.

---

[58] Stevenson, *Wars*, 1, pp. 422-3; P. Le Cacheux, *Actes de la chancellerie d'Henri VI concernant la Normandie sous la domination anglaise* 2, Société de l'histoire de Normandie, (1908), pp. 371-2.

[59] PRO, E404/50/164; *Issues of the Exchequer,* 3, ed. F. Devon (1837), p. 423; *Proc. Priv. Council,* 4, p. 202. Talbot was said to have served Henry V in France for eighteen months without taking wages. This had also been recited in 1429 (*Rot. Parl.,* 4, p. 338b). It is known, however, that he was mustered for wages from June 1421 until he returned to England in 1422 (PRO E101/70/5/706; 10/110, 116; 15/111, 114). He could have been in France from the late summer of 1419 until February 1421, but for the first six months of this period (until February 1420) he was still being paid as lieutenant of Ireland. Professor Postan was exaggerating when he claimed that in 1434 Talbot was in great necessity ' after nearly a lifetime of campaigning in France and despite the high commands and offices he had held' *Past and Present* 27 (1964), 51-2).

[60] BL, Add Ch 439; Waurin, 4, pp. 381-2.

[61] *Ibid.*, ADSM, Tabellionnage, 30/162v (Dubuc, 'Calendar', no. 1279, p. 248); série G, 1889.

Talbot, it has been argued, received a handsome annual income from the wars. But he also bore substantial costs. Was the balance in the black or in the red? His own claims, revealed in a series of documents dating from the last twenty years of his life, present a picture of hardship, indebtedness and near-bankruptcy. In 1434, following his release from captivity, he was in considerable difficulties. In 1438 he complained that to meet his obligations he had 'expended all his money, pledged his plate and jewels and borrowed where he could'.[62] In 1446, when he was in Ireland, his receiver-general wrote from Naas to the receiver of Sheffield commanding him to repay a debt of £100 to the London goldsmith, John Wynne, to pay 'all the remnant of your good that lieth in your charge' to another creditor, Henry Kent, and to send back the bearer of the letter with £5, 'for I have but skant of money'. In fact almost all the clear profit of Sheffield in this financial year (£219) was assigned to creditors.[63] In June 1451, after his last compaign in Normandy, Talbot presented another petition concerning his arrears of wages before 1448. In the preamble to the warrant for issue to the exchequer to make restitution the crown recognized,

> the great destresses, hurte and charge also that our saide cousin hath had and borne nowe of late as well by emprisonment amonge our enemys as of loss of his goodes other wyse and howe there is owyng unto him for the tyme that he was in Fraunce and Normandie right good sommes of money wherin he as yit woll not attempte us for any payement thereof consideryng our grete charge ne nought wolde of the sumes above specified ne were his greet hurt and losse abovesaid to him overchargeable.[64]

Talbot's affairs looked no better a year later. In his will, drawn up in 1452, he instructed his executors to

> sue unto the kynge our soverayn lorde and other lordes of his counsell for such dettis as ben due unto me by oure saide soverayn lord consideryng the grete coste and impertie of my person that y have had in his service, that my wife and myn executours may have my said dettis in performyng my wille without which may not be don.

At the same time, he willed that the proceeds of the sale of his moveable goods and the revenue from certain estates in the hands of his feoffees should also be used to pay off his debts.[65] His executors

---

[62] BL, Add Ch 439. York used almost exactly the same formula to describe his financial plight in 1452 (Storey, *House of Lancaster*, p. 75).

[63] *THAS*, 2, pp. 359-60.

[64] PRO, E404/67/172.

[65] Lambeth Palace Library, Register Stafford and Kemp, ff 312, 312b.

did as they were bid and sued to parliament in 1454 for payment of the crown's debts, presenting a petition, apparently composed before Talbot's death, which asserted that he 'continueth daily in the kynges service, to his right grete and sumptuous charge, costes and expenses'. The sum claimed was £6,797 18s. 2½d.[66] This tale of deepening financial distress cannot, however, be taken at face value. Claims against the crown for arrears were not all that they appeared to be. It is to be noted that at each stage in his negotiations, despite his moving pleas, Talbot was willing to make substantial concessions. In 1434 he settled for £1,000 and agreed to drop his claim to other, unspecified sums. In 1443 he settled for £2,426 0s. 4d.: which was just over half of the sum of arrears which he claimed and was acknowledged by the crown. He took £1,000 in cash and accepted the rest in assignments on future royal revenues. Added to this modest total was the sum of £9,000 promised to Talbot many years earlier from French sources to help with his ransom, none of which had yet been realized. Thus, the crown granted a total of £10,426. 0s. 4½d. in assignments.[67] Not surprisingly these assignments proved difficult to make good. From the beginning Talbot had accepted that Cardinal Beaufort would have priority over him. Nevertheless various payments were at first secured. In 1444 he received £1,333 6s. 8d. in cash and from time to time thereafter he was able to convert other assignments back into cash, as for instance on 18 May 1446 when £66 13s. 4d. was paid.[68] More typical was the dishonouring of thirteen tallies, worth £1,827 6s. 8d., on 1 July of the same year.[69] The sum owed by the crown was reduced but assignments were finally stopped by the Act of Resumption in 1450, leaving the £6,797 18s. 2½d. which his executors claimed following his death.[70] They too were prepared to compromise, agreeing to drop their claim to two-thirds of the sum in exchange for £2,000 to be paid indirectly through relief of customs paid by them on the export of wool. Whether this last device proved more successful than earlier assignments is not known.[71]

It transpires, therefore, that over the years Talbot and his executors waived just over £7,000 and recovered only £4,628 2s.

[66]*Rot. Parl.*, 5, p. 263b.

[67]*Proc. Priv. Council*, 4, p. 202; Stevenson, *Wars*, 1, pp. 434-6; *CPR, 1441-6*, pp. 277-8.

[68]PRO, E403/7762, m 2.

[69]Steel, *Receipt of the Exchequer*, p. 226.

[70]*Rot. Parl.*, 5, p. 263b.

[71]*Ibid., CPR, 1452-61*, p. 116. I have not been able to trace the ports through which Talbot's executors traded.

2*d.* of their acknowledged crown debts. In 1454 there was still outstanding a further £3,500 assigned to parliamentary subsidies and to customs relief.[72] They had almost certainly been prepared to sacrifice almost one-half of the recognized debts amounting to over £15,000 so as to make certain of payment of at least a part of the whole. Richard of York had done the same. One can be reasonably certain that neither he nor Talbot would have made these concessions unless they could have afforded to. Many of the nobility of England had personal experience of the crown's inability to pay its debts; they were, largely against their will, substantial creditors of the monarchy. Finally, in Talbot's case it is to be remembered that the greater part of the sum which his executors claimed he was owed at his death was the outstanding amount from the gift which the crown had made to help with his ransom. The slate was almost clean as far as the arrears of wages were concerned. The actual words of Talbot's will seem to imply a recognition of this fact when he ordered his executors 'to sue unto the kynge our soveraygn lorde... consideryng the grete coste and *impertie of my person'*: surely a reference to the sum owed for his ransom. The position at Talbot's death was therefore somewhat more complex than at first appears. That he was much in debt and short of cash cannot be denied. Magnate finances in the later middle ages were characterized by confusion, indebtedness and 'cash-flow' problems.[73] This in itself is not evidence of bankruptcy. In fact, Talbot seems to have had during his last years one important asset or collateral — the promised gift from the crown. In effect, his finances were underwritten by this grant. We will never know the exact state of Talbot's finances at the end of his life — in all probability neither did he. But it would seem that the oft-repeated claims of hardship and distress, as well as being the customary language of petitions, contained a large measure of special pleading. It is worth remembering, too, that even Sir John Fastolf, whose profits of war are not in doubt, could rake up claims worth £11,000 against the crown in his later years.[74]

Another way of looking at the balance is through investment . Here again the evidence is not all it might be. The standard investment was in land. And Talbot did in his later years purchase some property, mainly in Shropshire. These purchases, of some eight manors in the south of the county and properties in Shrewsbury and Ludlow, he made for his younger sons. It is to be doubted, however, whether he

[72] See above p. 112.

[73] For example, Talbot's own father-in-law, Richard Beauchamp. See C. D. Ross, 'The Estates and Finances of Richard Beauchamp, Earl of Warwick,' *Dugdale Society Occasional Papers* 12 (1956), 17-18.

[74] McFarlane, *TRHS* 5th Series 7 (1957), 93.

paid much over £1,000 for them.[75] Nor does he seem to have undertaken any large-scale building projects or religious foundations. A tower at Sheffield was rebuilt in 1446-47, but this seems to have been a necessary repair and the cost was met out of the regular income of the lordship. There are remains of improvements at Goodrich castle in the fifteenth century, but these were not extensive, nor can they be definitely attributed to his lifetime.[76] More significantly, perhaps, Leland, that great recorder of English castles built from the profits of the wars in France, had nothing to say in this respect about any of the Talbot possessions. Talbot's favourite residence, the manor house at Blakemere, would surely have been transformed if he had had large sums at his disposal, but all Leland had to say was that it was 'a fair place or loge'.[77] Moreover, Talbot made provision for a college to be established at Whitchurch, next to Blakemere, but nothing came of this, perhaps because his executors could not collect sufficient of his royal debts, without which, as he recognised, his will could not be fully performed.[78] It is possible that Talbot broke with tradition and invested more heavily in trade than most of his peers. He was, it would appear, a merchant on a fairly large scale, owning several ships and trading in salt, wool and cloth. Four of his ships were disposed of in his will: the 'Christopher', the 'Margaret', the 'Carwell' and the 'Tregoe'. A fifth, the 'Magdalen Lisle', returned from Bordeaux after his death in 1453, loaded on his command with merchandise, and was handed over to his widow.[79] His captains occasionally ran into trouble on the high seas. On 16 February 1440 orders were issued for the arrest of Thomas Williamson, master of one of Talbot's ballingers, and his crew for the capture and robbing of a Hanse ship. Two years later another act of piracy was committed by one of Talbot's ballingers when six packs of cloth were taken from a Hanse ship near Queenborough.[80] These activities should perhaps be considered as part of his profits of war and it is unfortunate that, apart from recording that he traded in the salt granted to him by Brittany and goods from Bordeaux in 1453, and was apparently a large scale exporter of wool at the time of his death, we cannot assess the scope of

[75] Lambeth Palace Library, Register Stafford and Kemp, f311b; PRO, C139/179; *Calendar of Inquisitions, Henry VIII*, 1, pp. 428-9.

[76] Royal Commission of Historical Monuments, England, *An Inventory of the Historical Monuments in Herefordshire*, 1, pp. 74ff; *THAS*, 2, pp. 352-6.

[77] *The Itinerary of John Leland*, ed. L. Toulmin Smith, 4 (1909) p. 2 cf. McFarlane, *Nobility*, pp. 22-3.

[78] Lambeth Palace Library, Register Stafford and Kemp, ff312 312b. See above p. 116.

[79] *Ibid.*, f312; *CPR, 1452-61*, p. 166.

[80] *CPR, 1435-41*, p. 408; *1441-6*, p. 108.

his commercial activities. There remains, too, the point that a net profit from the war need not have been invested at all, but may have been consumed in extravagant living. But this cannot detract from the conclusion that Talbot appears not to have had vast sums at his disposal for investment.

Lastly, one may cast a brief glance at the fortunes of his family after his death. It is perhaps important to note that his executors, who could afford to be realistic, were prepared to surrender their claim to the greater part of the sum still owed for Talbot's ransom. His eldest son and heir, the second earl of Shrewsbury, treasurer of England in 1456-58, was able to lend the crown at least £3,295, a circumstance which suggests that his family was not left completely devoid of liquid capital. The second earl was also able to purchase, for something approaching £1,000, the manors of Windfield and Crich in Derbyshire from the executors of Ralph, Lord Cromwell.[81] But this purchase may well have been made out of the profits of his own office. Even so, it is clear that Talbot's son was not one of the impoverished peers of the mid-fifteenth century.

The indications are that, in spite of the burden of his ransom, Talbot was perhaps able to make a slight profit out of the war. It would appear that he enjoyed a substantial income from his wages, prisoners, plunder, lands and offices in France after 1433. He was not substantially out of pocket in the payment of his and his soldiers' wages; the sums which the crown owed him on this score were relatively small and almost all of those which he did not waive were eventually paid. In the final analysis even his ransom was perhaps not as crippling as it might appear. He received considerable help in meeting it, and if not all of the promised assistance was forthcoming, the promise by the crown itself effectively underwrote the confused and complicated personal finances of his last years. Only a small amount of the profit was invested; more may have been conspicuously consumed. His family was certainly not impoverished after his death. In the strictly material sense one can conclude that Talbot was certainly not a major profiteer; he was in the end something more akin to a mere survivor.[82] But in a broader sense his profit was more

---

[81] Steel, *The Receipt of the Exchequer*, p. 330; Historical Manuscripts Commission, *Report on the Manuscripts of Lord de Lisle and Dudley* 1 (1925), pp 207-8, 212.

[82] Thomas, Lord Scales, who served alongside Talbot from 1428 to 1450, may not have done so well. He was captured at Patay, ransomed, and was back in the war making a steady profit in the 1430s. But in 1442 he lost Granville 'and the substance of all the goodes that my lord had in that land whas therein' (Kingsford, *Chronicles*, p. 151). He was captured again in 1450 and had to find another ransom to secure his liberty.

substantial. During the years of fighting after 1433 his honour was much enhanced. He raised himself and his family from the baronage to an earldom, and with the earldom went not only prestige, but also office and future favour at court. In the long run, through the wars, he established a line which, having carefully survived the snares of the 'Wars of the Roses', flourished under the Tudors. Honour and fame thus eventually ensured for his descendants the substantial material gain he failed to make for himself.

7

MAN OF HONOUR: JOHN TALBOT AND CHIVALRY

There were different ways of approaching war in the later Middle Ages. One, as we have just seen, was to treat it as a business enterprise. The more idealistic way was to view it as an opportunity for the pursuit of honour and renown through the execution of valiant deeds on the field of battle. Yet, it was more than this. For warfare was held to be the proper occupation, even the divinely appointed social purpose, of the nobility. Thus, the profession of arms was idealised through the code of chivalry as the most honourable and truly noble way of life open to a layman.[1] There is no reason to suppose that John Talbot as well as being concerned with lining his own pocket, was not also imbued with these chivalric values.

Unfortunately, we have little direct knowledge of Talbot's views and beliefs, but there is plentiful indirect evidence to suggest that he took contemporary attitudes towards chivalry very seriously. We do not know of his taking part in tournaments — perhaps he was always too busy engaged in the real thing. But he had relations who were renowned in the joust. His father-in-law, the earl of Warwick, had in his youth been an international star of tournaments, and his second son, Sir Christopher Talbot, clearly enjoyed a high reputation in the early 1440s.[2] In his own household Talbot employed the customary team of heralds, part of whose role it was 'to honowre chivalry and to desyre to be present in all actes off warre;. . . . . .to shewe ffeythefully and trewly bysynes bytwene enemyse'.[3] Talbot's herald Shrewsbury had served his master for over forty years when he had to perform the

[1] See M.H. Keen, 'Chilvalry, Nobility, and the Man-at-Arms', in *War, Literature and Politics in the Later Middle Ages,* ed. C.T. Allmand (Liverpool, 1976), pp. 32-45 *passim;* C.T. Allmand, *Society at War: The Experience of England and France during the Hundred Years' War* (Edinburgh, 1973), pp. 21-30, 185-6; and A.R. Bridbury, 'The Hundred Years' War: Costs and Profits' in *Trade, Government and Economy in Pre-Industrial England,* ed. D.C. Coleman and A.H. John (1976), pp. 82-3.

[2] *The Pageant of the Birth, Life and Death of Richard Beauchamp, Earl of Warwick,* ed. Viscount Dillon and W.H. St John Hope (1914) *passim;* A.B. Ferguson, *The Indian Summer of English Chivalry* (North Carolina, 1960), p. 45; *The Paston Letters,* ed. J. Gairdner, 2 (1904), p. 47. Robert Repps wrote to John Paston in November 1440 that a Spanish knight had arrived in England who would 'renne a cours wyth a sharpe spere for his soveregn lady sake; quom other Sir Richard Wodvyle or Sir Christofere Talbot shall delyver, to the Wyrchip of Englond and hemselff, be Goddes grace'.

[3] *The Essential Portions of Nicholas Upton's De Studio Militari,* ed. F.P. Barnard (Oxford, 1931) p. 2.

unpleasant duty of identifying his master's body on the morrow of Castillon.[4] Talbot was also a knight of the Garter. He was elected in 1424.[5] To be a member of the select Order of the Garter was in itself a sign of honour and distinction. But the Order was also a society of mutual help and a brotherhood dedicated to the application of chivalrous ideals in the service of the king of England. That Talbot took its ideals seriously is suggested by his long standing quarrel with Sir John Fastolf, whom he accused of conduct unbecoming a knight in his flight from Patay. For a time Fastolf was stripped of his Garter and the case was still being heard before the king and peers in the early-1440s.[6] Talbot's dispute with Fastolf may have been tinged by a belief that he himself would not have been faced with his huge ransom if Fastolf had stayed and fought, but it is likely that his deeper feeling was that Fastolf had dishonoured the Order to which they both belonged. A clearer insight into Talbot's mind is provided by the books he possessed, or at least those with which he was familiar. In 1445 he presented a superbly produced volume to Queen Margaret as a welcoming gift to England. This book is a compilation of fourteen works on chivalry — chansons de geste, prose romances, chronicles, treatises on war and the statutes of the Order of the Garter. The treatises include Christine de Pisan's *Book of feats of arms and chivalry* and Honoré Bonet's *Tree of Battles*.[7] We do not know whether Talbot believed these works to be the recipient's preferred reading. But it is reasonable to assume that Talbot himself possessed copies of them, from which this presentation volume was made up, and that he was familiar with their contents. Moreover, the illustrations depicting Talbot himself amidst all the panoply of heraldry in humble submission to his king and queen seem to suggest that Talbot saw himself, and indeed was even then seen by others, as the very embodiment of chivalry in England.[8] And in fact a royal grant of

[4]M d'Escouchy, *Chronique*, ed. du Fresne de Beaucourt 2, Société de l'Histoire de France (1864), pp. 42-3. The badly disfigured body was only recognised by the absence of a molar tooth on the left side, which seems to have been a congenital trait of the Talbot family. See also M.A. Rushton, 'The Teeth of Anne Mowbray', *British Dental Journal* (19 October 1965), 355-6 and W.H. Egerton, 'Talbot's Tomb', *Transactions of the Shropshire Archaeological Society* 8, 413-40. A glimpse of Talbot's herald and his poursuivant, Furnival, in more routine work is provided in the 'Enquiry before Juvenal des Ursins on the taking of Fougères' in T. Basin, *Histoire des règnes de Charles VII et Louis XI*, ed. J. Quicherat, pp. 307, 312, 316, 319.

[5]*Order of the Garter, Register*, 1 (1724), p. 90; *C.P.*, 11, p. 700.

[6]Waurin, 3, p. 306; K.B. McFarlane, 'William Worcester: A Preliminary Survey', in *Studies Presented to Sir Hilary Jenkinson*, ed. J. Conway Davies (Oxford, 1957), p. 200, citing Magdalen College, Oxford, Fastolf Papers 72m 8.

[7]BL, Royal MS 15 E VI and *Catalogue of Royal and Kings Manuscripts* 2 (1921), pp. 177-9.

[8]BL, Royal MS 15 E VI, illustrations 1 and 142. See frontispiece.

1448 recited in its preamble that it was made in consideration of the 'faits de ses guerres en France en telle prowesse et si grant valliance de sa personne comme il est notoire à un chacun'.[9]

There is a further dimension to chivalry which is relevant to this discussion. In the minds of many, devotion to the ideals of chivalry brought not only honour in this world but also salvation in the next. To be a true knight was to join an order in the same sense as a monk of the cloister. Chivalry was, or could be, 'an order, the highest and hardest among those that God had instituted and by means of which a man might save his soul'.[10] It is quite possible that Talbot shared this elevated view of knighthood and the profession of arms. He had papal licence to have a portable altar and to have masses said wherever he was residing. Accounts of the battle of Castillon stress how he had mass said before he unfurled his banners and advanced on his enemies. He maintained priests and chaplains in his household, at least one accompanying him when he was a hostage of the French during the winter of 1449-50. For a while in the late 1430s he resided in the monastery of St Ouen in Rouen. In 1450 he spent six months on pilgrimage to Rome in the year of the Jubilee, during which one may surmise that he had an audience of the Pope. And in 1452 he willed that a chapel dedicated to Our Lady and St George be founded in his home church of St Alkmund's, Whitchurch, where masses for his soul might be celebrated.[11] This religious devotion is explicitly linked to chivalric ideals in at least one instance. Talbot donated to the church of the Sepulchre in Rouen ornaments for the altar decorated with the emblem of the Garter ('ornements et parements d'autel semes de jartiers pers') specifically for use in services celebrating the feast of St George.[12] It may well be, therefore, that Talbot would have agreed with his contemporary Jean de Bueil, who commented in Le Jouvencel, 'If God is willing we soldiers will win our salvation by the exercise of arms just as well as we could by living a life of contemplation on a diet of roots'.[13]

---

[9] D. Len 74/219.

[10] Keen, War, Literature and Politics, passim, esp. p. 36.

[11] Calendar of Papal Registers, Letters, 9, p. 239; R Jouet, La résistance à l'occupation anglaise en Basse Normandie (1418-1450), Cahiers des annales de Normandie 5 (Caen. 1969), p. 59, citing AN, JJ 191/33/16r; ADSM, série G, 158; Stevenson, Wars, 2, p. 738; Lambeth Palace Library. Register Stafford and Kemp, f312.

[12] ADSM, série G, 9336.

[13] Jean de Bueil, Le Jouvencel, ed. L. Lecestre 2, Société de l'histoire de France (1889), p. 21, translated and cited by Keen, War, Literature and Politics, p. 36. See also Allmand, Society at War, p. 28.

Yet the chivalric ideal was shot through with apparent contradictions. How did a man reconcile plundering and looting with true knighthood? It has been suggested that a social distinction existed between those of humble birth seeking to establish themselves in the world who fought for financial gain and the more blue-blooded who were indifferent to the material prospects.[14] As we have seen, this was certainly not the case with Talbot. He was as hardheaded in the pursuit of profit as any soldier of fortune. Personal enrichment at the expense of enemies was in fact justified by the ethics of chivalry. Provided the knight believed that he was engaged in a just war — and this was a legalistic concept, not a moral position — all gains were conceived as part of the honour won amid the glorious hazards of battle. In theory, little distinction was drawn between personal honour and material gain. Plunder and loot taken in the honour of chivalry were thus sanctified.[15] There were other considerations. As Sir John Fastolf made clear in his memorandum on the conduct of the war in 1435, rebels and traitors — by which he meant the Burgundians — placed themselves beyond the normal restraints and should be punished by sharp and cruel war.[16] Great plundering raids, such as that undertaken in the Santerre in 1440, were thus additionally justified. Moreover, chivalry was essentially a code which respected only the rights and privileges of its own members. Honour could exist only between nobles. The peasant, the urban labourer, the artisan were of little account. Despite the appeals and blandishments of Honoré Bonet and Christine de Pisan, their goods and their lives were not protected. Thus, an elaborate code of practice had been evolved to deal with ransoms, which were agreements between knights, as men of honour, whilst the knight faced only moral restraint in his dealings with the 'hedge born swain'.[17]

Similar considerations apply to the question of brutality and terror. Talbot's brutality made a particular impression on French commentators. Chartier wrote in an obituary comment, 'Ce fameux et

[14] Allmand, *Society at War*, pp. 8, 186.

[15] Keen, *War, Literature and Politics*, p. 41.

[16] Stevenson, *Wars*, 2.2, p. 580; M.G.A. Vale, 'Sir John Fastolf's Report of 1435; A new Interpretation Reconsidered', *Nottingham Medieval Studies* 17 (1973), 80-2.

[17] Christine de Pisan recognised that in a just war the poor labourers wre bound to suffer, but, she added; 'it is true that the valyaunt and gentlyman of armes ought to kepe hem self as moche as they can that they dystroye not the goode, symple folke' (*The Book of Fayttes of Armes and of Chivalrye*, ed. A.T.P. Byles (1937), p. 225). Honoré Bonet was more forthright but equally unheeded: 'in these days all wars are directed against the poor labouring people and against their goods and chattels. I do not call that war, but it seems to me to be pillage and robbery. Further, that way of warfare does not follow the ordinances of worthy chivalry ...' (*The Tree of Battles of Honoré Bonet*, ed. and trans. G.W. Coopland (Liverpool, 1949), p. 189).

renommé chef anglois qui depuis si longtemps passoit pour l'un des fleaux le plus reformidable et plus jurez ennemis de la France dont il avoit paru estre l'effroy et la terreur'.[18] Basin more philosophically wrote of his death: 'Il fut jugé sans miséricorde, lui qui n'avait pas fait miséricorde aux autres, et, selon la parole du Sauveur, il périt par l'épée, lui qui en avait frappé beaucoup par l'épée. Il avait été, en effet, extrêment dur et cruel pour les Français, qui, à la fin, lui rendirent la pareill.'[19] These judgements are borne out by reports of individual acts. After taking Laval in 1428 he is supposed to have had sixty-five men, including priests, executed as traitors. In 1434 he hanged the men of the garrisons of Jouy and Crépy after he had taken those places. At Gisors in 1436 he hanged some of the citizens for their part in handing over the town to the French. During the raid into the Santerre in 1440 he was responsible for the massacre of men, women and children who had taken refuge in the church at Lihons. The church was set alight and, as Monstrelet wrote, 'si y furent mors et brulé très piteusement bien trois cens personnes ou plus, tant hommes, femmes, commes enfants, et très peu en eschapa de ceulx qui estoient en ladicte église.' On another occasion, during the siege of Pontoise in 1441, Basin tells us that he struck down a helpless French prisoner with his own hand.[20] This story may be fanciful, but the fact that Talbot was believed to be capable of such acts is in itself revealing. There can, therefore, be little doubt that Talbot was vicious. But there is nothing to suggest that any act committed by him infringed the laws of war. Garrisons and the citizens of towns who refused to surrender faced the risk of retribution. Traitors and rebels risked summary punishment. What would be judged by a modern tribunal as most heinous war crimes were condoned by medieval laws of war. For the laws provided a code of honourable conduct, not a guarantee of human rights. Provided the right forms and procedures had been adhered to there was nothing dishonourable about hanging sixty-five rebel burghers and priests.[21] There were critical voices raised against the excesses permitted by the code of chivalry.[22] And perhaps in the fifteenth century more notice was being paid to these. It could be that Talbot picked up such a fearful reputation in France not because what he did was in itself exceptional, but because values were changing and more

[18]Chartier, 3, p. 7.

[19]Basin, 2, p. 199.

[20]E. Hall, *The Union of the Noble and Illustre Famelies of Lancastre and Yorke* (1809), p. 143; Monstrelet, 5, pp. 91, 231, 406; Waurin, 4, p. 45; Basin, 1, p. 274.

[21]M.H. Keen, *The Laws of War in the Later Middle Ages* (1965) esp. pp. 120-2.

[22]Especially Honoré Bonet. See above n. 17 and below p. 127 and C.T. Allmand, *Society at War*, pp. 37-40.

people were coming to see that nothing could justify the wholesale destruction and murder perpetrated under the cloak of chivalry. Thomas Basin, who witnessed the final years of the war in Normandy, seems to have been under no illusions. And even Monstrelet appears to have been shocked by the massacre at Lihons in 1439. By this time some men were beginning to see chivalric warfare for what it really was. But it is to be doubted that Talbot ever saw beyond the confines of the ideals of the Order to which he belonged, or was ever conscious of any contradictions between his beliefs and his behaviour.

This is not to suggest that Talbot did not think about chivalry and its role. In one respect he may well have shared contemporary opinion. Chivalry was essentially anarchic. It was looked upon as an international order. Knights, in theory, did not belong to any particular nation. They sought out honour and fame in any battlefield wherever that might be. And knights seeking honour, fame and fortune spread mayhem wherever they went. It has recently been suggested that Honoré Bonet wrote his *Tree of Battles* in the late-fourteenth century as a reforming tract to try to bring some discipline into knightly society and so curb the worst excesses associated with the free-lance companies spawned by the Anglo-French conflict. Bonet deplored senseless and immoderate individual heroism, wanton murder and indiscriminate destruction. War itself was not evil: what was needed, he concluded, was more discipline, in particular more princely discipline. War, he argued, should only be fought by princes in a just cause, and knights and soldiers should submit themselves to discipline imposed by their prince. This would have been very much in tune with the fifteenth century. It is one possible reason for the popularity of the *Tree* among military leaders 'who were attempting to create disciplined national chivalries in a world where chivalry had traditionally accepted neither discipline nor nationalism as virtues'.[23] Talbot was apparently familiar with the *Tree* and certain aspects of his career lend weight to the suggestion that Bonet's ideas were put into practice during his lifetime. The English army of occupation in Normandy was in itself a disciplined national chivalry. Talbot as marshal of France after 1436 played an important role in maintaining, or at last in seeking to maintain, the discipline which was one of the hallmarks of this army. Indeed, one of the reasons given for his appointment was his success in keeping good order, justice 'et discipline de chevalerie'.[24] There can be little doubt that personally he saw himself as a knight in the service of his prince. His loyalty to Henry V and Henry VI was never

[23]N.A.R. Wright, 'The *Tree of Battles* of Honoré Bouvet and the Laws of War' in *War, Literature and Politics,* ed. Allmand, esp pp. 18-19, 31.

[24]D. Len, 26/1931.

questioned. In royal letters the king and his councillors constantly praised his 'high and notable desire to do the best he can for you against your said enemies' and 'his strenuous probity even to old age in the wars'.[25] A sense of Talbot's own feelings emerges in the dedicatory verses in the book he presented to Margaret of Anjou in 1445. In an *envoi* written in verse so execrable that one cannot help feeling that he composed it himself, he wrote:

> Mon seul desir
> au Roy et vous
> et bien servir
> jusqua au mourir
> ce sachant tous
> mon seul desir
> au Roy et vous[26]

That Talbot identified himself — and was identified by others — with a specifically English cause needs no special emphasis.[27] Indeed, it is arguable that this proto-nationalist dimension coloured his reputation in both France and England. It is plausible therefore that Talbot looked upon chivalry in this subtly transformed way. He was devoted not to the invisible international order of earlier generations but to the plainly visible service of his prince. His renown was won not just by his personal prowess, but by the dedication of that prowess to the service of the Lancastrian dynasty. Like his father-in-law, he won lasting fame as the model knight labouring in the service of prince and nation.[28]

This attitude perhaps helped resolve another of the contradictions inherent in chivalry, for, as it has been said, chivalrous behaviour tended to detract from the efficient conduct of war. In theory at least the emphasis of chivalry was on the manner of the accomplishment rather than on the achievement itself, on glory rather than results.[29] In Talbot's war career there was perhaps one fatal moment when chivalric honour and pride may have outweighed tactical consider-

---

[25] Stevenson, *Wars*, 2, p. 60; *CPR, 1441-6*, p. 448.

[26] BL, Royal MS 15 E VI, f1.

[27] Talbot's will was written in English. In 1452 wills in the vernacular were still comparatively rare. It is possible that Talbot employed English as a nationalistic gesture, reminiscent of Henry V's encouragement of the vernacular. See K.B. McFarlane, *Lancastrian Kings and Lollard Knights* (Oxford, 1972), pp. 119, 209, and M.G.A. Vale, *Piety Charity and Literacy among the Yorkshire Gentry, 1370-1480*. Borthwick Paper 50 (1976), p. 5.

[28] Ferguson, *Indian Summer*, p. 45.

[29] K. A. Fowler, *The Age of Plantaganet and Valois* (1967), p. 149.

ations. This was at the battle of Castillon, where it is possible that, acting on incorrect information, Talbot unfurled his banner and opened the battle before he discovered that he was launching his men against an impregnable position. To have retreated then would have brought lasting dishonour.[30] During the rest of his long career it is difficult to find him seeking personal glory at the expense of tangible results. In the long drawn-out campaigning in the defence of Normandy after 1435 Talbot seems to have constantly subordinated notions of chivalric heroism to the overall strategic and tactical requirements of siege and counter-siege, surprise assault and plundering raid. It was a manner of fighting noticeable for the eschewing of unnecessary personal risk. But if it did not live up to the ideals expressed in the *chansons* which he apparently knew, it nevertheless matched more recent notions of selfless service in the just cause of his prince. A deep and genuine commitment to the code of chivalry as he understood it offers the most convincing key to Talbot's character and career. It perhaps provides the underlying reason why Talbot soldiered on 'jusqua au mourir' when most of his peers had lost interest in, and commitment to, the Lancastrian cause in France. It is quite possible that material considerations reinforced his natural inclination. But at bottom it is likely that we have here a man who simply loved the soldier's life and all that it entailed. Jean de Bueil may have shared his sentiments when he wrote in a famous passage:

> What a gratifying thing war is, for many are the splendid things heard and seen in the course of it, and many are the good lessons to be learnt from it. . . . When one feels that one's cause is just, and one's blood is ready for the fight, tears come to the eye. A warm feeling of loyalty and pity comes into the heart on seeing one's friend expose his body with such courage to carry out and to accomplish the will of our Creator; and one makes up one's mind to go and die or live with him, and, out of love, not to abandon him. No man who has not experienced it knows how to speak of the satisfaction that comes from this sort of action.[31]

It is difficult for the modern mind to comprehend, let alone sympathise with, John Talbot and his world. What one must not do is automatically assume that there was an underlying cynicism towards the values which dominated his life. It is more probable that he had a sincere conviction of the morality of what he did and saw no contradiction

---

[30] See the account of the battle by M. d'Escouchy, *Chronique,* 2, pp. 36-41. Basin, on the other hand, puts Talbot's action down to his usual impetuosity (2, pp. 195-6). See also A.H. Burne, *The Agincourt War,* pp. 333-42.

[31] Jean de Bueil, *Le Jouvencel,* 2, pp. 20-1 translated by C.T. Allmand in *Society at War,* pp. 27-8.

between the elevated ideals and the acquisitive and brutal reality. It is only in more recent times that the bright side of chivalry has been romanticised and the dark side of it condemned. But the two went together. Thus it is that Talbot may well have been a fitting subject for a late chivalric legend and a suitable model for commentators like Worcester and Caxton who still believed that social and moral reform could be achieved through a revival of its ethic. Shakespeare understood this attitude. The result was that his play about Talbot, although it has little respect for the 'facts' of his career, skilfully captures its spirit.

8

'LE ROI TALBOT': THE LAST YEARS, 1450-53

On 20 December 1450 John Talbot returned to England from his pilgrimage to Rome. The London chronicler who noted his return commented that he was 'fierce in fight and most dred of all other in France in war'.[1] But with Normandy lost and Gascony on the point of falling, Talbot could well have believed that his fighting days were over. Now well over sixty he could perhaps have expected an honourable retirement. This was not to be. After spending twenty-one months in England., he set sail once again to reconquer and defend Gascony, where he was killed nine months later.

Talbot's short stay in England was dominated by the suppression of popular revolt, the pursuit of his own feud with Lord Berkeley, and the rivalry between Somerset and York. Although Cade's revolt had been crushed well before December 1450, Kent was still in ferment. It is perhaps not surprising that Talbot, with his fearful reputation, was almost immediately employed on a judicial visitation designed to restore order in that county. On 27 January 1451 he was appointed to a commission of oyer and terminer under the duke of Somerset. The government clearly attached great importance to this commission, for the king himself presided over the tour of Rochester, Canterbury and Faversham which saw the execution of at least thirty convicted persons and the submission of many more erstwhile rebels. Nevertheless, unrest continued. There was a further rising under Henry Hasildene in April which involved Sussex as well as Kent. In May the commission was renewed, its jurisdiction being extended to include Sussex, Surrey, Hampshire and Wiltshire. And in June, again with the king present, it made a further progress through the south-eastern counties, sitting at Tonbridge from 26 to 30 June.[2] This second judicial visitation seems to have completed the work of repression and Talbot's services appear to have been no longer required in the home counties. He could now turn his attention to his own pressing private affairs.

The Talbot-Berkeley feud arose from the claim to the lordship of Berkeley inherited by the countess of Shrewsbury from her mother. It

[1] C. L. Kingsford, *English Historical Literature in the Fifteenth Century* (Oxford, 1913), p. 372.

[2] *CPR, 1446-52*, pp. 435, 42-4, 75, 77; Kingsford, *English Historical Literature*, p. 372; R. Virgoe, 'Some Ancient Indictments in King's Bench Referring to Kent, 1450-52', *Kent Archaeological Society Record Publications* 18 (1964), 216-18, 243-56.

first flared up after the earl of Warwick's death in 1439 and was in essence a revival of the late earl's own earlier attempt to gain control of the lordship.[3] The countess of Shrewsbury was only one of three co-heiresses to her mother's claim, but she and her husband were particularly anxious to make it good as their eldest son, John, soon to become Lord Lisle, was not the heir to the main Talbot inheritance. Behind the Talbot feud with Berkeley lay the desire of the earl and countess of Shrewsbury to create a patrimony for their son that would match that to be enjoyed by the earl's eldest son by his first wife, Sir John Talbot. Indeed, so anxious was Talbot to provide for Lisle, that he went so far as to attempt the partial disinheritance of the future earl in his favour.[4] The importance Talbot attached to the claim is indicated by his threat in 1440, early in the legal wrangles over the fate of Berkeley, to withdraw from the siege of Harfleur unless he had his way.[5] Frustrated by the slowness and uncertainty of due legal process, in 1442 the countess eventually took the law into her own hands and seized the manors of Wotton under Edge, Cowley and Simondshall which were part of the lordship.[6] Thereafter, negotiations continued until, on 5 April 1448, shortly before Talbot returned to Normandy for his last tour of duty, a compromise was reached whereby the Talbots kept these manors for life.[7] But in the summer of 1450, taking advantage of the crisis created by Cade's revolt and the absence of Lord, now Viscount, Lisle from Gloucestershire in the king's army at Blackheath, Lord Berkeley ransacked the manor house at Wotton.[8] An open war now ensued which the crown was powerless to prevent. In the summer of 1451 Talbot was at last free to throw his weight into the quarrel.

Isabel, Lady Berkeley wrote from London on 15 June 1451 to her husband at Berkeley castle:

> The Earle of Shroesbury lieth right nye unto you, and shapeth all the wyles that hee can to distrusse you and yours, for hee will not meddle with you openly noe manner of wyse, but it bee with great falsdome that he can bring about to beguile you, or else that hee

---

[3]For the feud see J. Smyth, *The Lives of the Berkeleys*, ed. J. McLean, 2 (Gloucester, 1885), pp. 34-113 and Pollard, pp. 39-51.

[4]See Pollard, pp. 51-62.

[5]*CCR, 1435-41*, p. 325.

[6]Smyth, *Berkeleys*, 2 p. 59.

[7]*Ibid.*, p. 61.

[8]Kingsford, *English Historical Literature*, p. 366; *Six Town Chronicles*, ed. R. Flenley (Oxford, 1911), p. 130; *A Calendar of Proceedings in Chancery in the Reign of Queen Elizabeth*, ed. J. Bayley, 1 (1827), lxxviii.

caused yee have so fewe peopull about you, then will hee set on you, for he saith hee will never come to the king againe till hee have done you an ill turne.[9]

Her information may have been well founded, for during 1451 Talbot himself remained carefully in the background while Lisle prosecuted the war with Berkeley. At the same time Talbot did indeed recruit most of the local gentry into his service, thus effectively isolating Berkeley.[10] And on 6 September Lord Lisle did in fact 'set on' Lord Berkeley, for that night he succeeded in seizing Berkeley and his castle. It appears that Berkeley had sent a band of men to raid the house of Richard Andrews, a blind tenant of the Talbots. But Lisle had been forewarned, came to the rescue and overwhelmed Berkeley's men. Their leader was Ryse Tewe, who under threat of death was marched back to Berkeley castle and made to persuade the unsuspecting guard to open the gates. Lord Berkeley and his sons were surprised and taken in their beds.[11] Among the men who took Berkeley castle were several veterans from Talbot's personal retinue who had seen service with him in Normandy.[12] Having thus done Berkeley the threatened 'ill turne', Talbot was summoned back to court, for in September he was in attendance at Coventry and Kenilworth with a 'grete felaship' where the king was preparing to deal with the Bonville-Devon conflict that was concurrently disrupting Somerset and Devon.[13] It was left to his countess and Viscount Lisle to convert their military victory into a hoped-for lasting legal settlement.

During the summer of 1451 Talbot ruthlessly and shamelessly exploited his own high renown and position of favour at court, as well as the general powerlessness of the crown in the face of popular unrest and baronial feuding, to further his own private ambitions. Behind the public image of England's champion[14] lay a grasping and self-seeking baron, whose propensity for creating domestic disturbance was undiminished by decades of fighting against the French. At the same time Talbot was not prepared to throw himself into the principal feud undermining the Lancastian monarchy — that between York and Somerset. There was nothing altruistic or statesmanlike in this — merely another calculation of self-interest. Talbot was placed in

---

[9]Smyth, *Berkeleys*, 2, p. 63.

[10]See Pollard, pp. 235-8.

[11]*Proceedings in Chancery, Elizabeth*, 1, 1xxvi ff.

[12]PRO, KB 27/763/42.

[13]PRO, E 404/68/99; R. L. Storey, *The End of the House of Lancaster* (1966) p. 91.

[14]See above p. 66.

a potential dilemma by the conflict between York and Somerset, for he was closely attached to both.[15] But York, by his actions in the autumn of 1450 and his subsequent withdrawal to the marches of Wales, had done nothing to diminish the suspicion with which he was regarded at court.[16] Somerset, on the other hand, was high in favour. There was no reason for Talbot to break off his connections with Somerset and the court. His standing was entirely undamaged by his activities during the summer; indeed, he and Lisle were granted the custody of Porchester castle and the governorship of Portsmouth in November 1451.[17] But at the same time Talbot managed to maintain his position of trust with York, for with the bishop of Hereford, at York's request he visited Ludlow late in December. To them, York later wrote, he offered to swear his loyalty on the sacraments and begged them to report this offer to the king.[18] York clearly valued Talbot as an intermediary and potential friend at court. But, when in February 1452 York ended his self-imposed exile and made an attempt to oust Somerset from favour by force, Talbot stood firmly by the king — and Somerset. He was with the king's army (perhaps in *de facto* command) when it moved to Northampton to face York and still there, with 'a grete and notable nombre of persones', at the final confrontation at Dartford on 3 March.[19] He was not one of those chosen then to act as a mediator between the parties, but he probably was at hand during the negotiations between the two dukes at Westminster, for on 13 March he was one of the arbitrators appointed to find a permanent settlement.[20]

Early in 1452 there were other matters to attend to beside the political crisis at home. Having conquered Gascony in 1451, Charles VII was preparing to attack Calais, the last remaining English foothold on the continent.[21] If in disagreement in all else, Somerset and York probably both approved of Talbot's appointment on 14 March to the command of a fleet for the defence of Calais and the

[15] See above pp. 40-1, 63, 81-2.

[16] For York's actions in 1450 see R. A. Griffiths, 'Duke Richard of York's Intentions in 1450'. *Journal of Medieval History* 1(1975), 187-209 *passim*.

[17] *CPR, 1446-52*, p. 569.

[18] *The Paston Letters*, ed. J. A. Gairdner, 1 (1904), p. 96.

[19] PRO, E404/68/69; Kingsford, *English Historical Literature*, p. 373.

[20] *CCR, 1447-54*, p. 327. For York's attempted coup in 1452 see Storey, *House of Lancaster*, Ch 6 *passim*, pp. 93-104.

[21] G. du Fresne de Beaucourt, *Histoire de Charles VII*, 5 (1890), p. 364; *Proceedings and Ordinances of the Privy Council of England*, 6 (1834), p. 119; Stevenson, *Wars*, 2, p. 477.

coast of England. In the spring steps were taken to gather together ships and men for this fleet, but the immediate danger passed when Charles VII abandoned his threatened campaign.[22] In the meantime fresh disturbance took place in Kent. There is evidence to suggest that York, or his supporters, who had been disappointed not to receive popular support from Kent in March, were involved in the short-lived rising under John Wilkins that took place on 6 May. The response of the government was immediate. Talbot was appointed on 11 May to a commission of oyer and terminer to punish the rebels. During the assize John Wilkins and twenty-eight Kentishmen were executed and their heads were displayed on London Bridge.[23] This internal threat having been promptly countered, the king and his council could turn their attention once more to France.

The initial intentions behind renewed English military preparations in the summer of 1452 remain unknown. When Edward Hull and Gervase Clifton were retained on 20 June for a period from 17 July to 16 October their commission was described as service 'on sea as well as for the safe-keeping of our land', which suggests that the council still feared a French attack and was merely extending the commissions of March. But by 6 July, Talbot, who had been retained on 27 June for a similar period of service, was described as being in command of an 'army for the keeping of the sea in which journey he must perform great good', which hints at a more aggressive intention.[24] It may have been planned at this stage to employ the army, which had a nominal strength of 5,000, in an attack on Normandy, where the French took elaborate precautions to resist invasion.[25] But during the summer, a group of Gascon exiles, who were in communication with a handful of prominent dissidents in Bordeaux, appears to have persuaded the council to send the army to Gascony.[26] To this end Talbot was appointed lieutenant of Guyenne on 2 September.[27] The expedition set sail later in the month. Because the French had expected a descent on Normandy, they were completely unprepared for Talbot's sudden appearance in the Gironde on 17 October. With the help of the collaborators who opened the Beyssac gate to the invaders, Bordeaux

---

[22] *Proceedings of Privy Council*, 6, pp. 120-25; Stevenson, *Wars*, 2, pp. 477-8.

[23] Kingsford, *English Historical Literature*, p. 368; *CPR, 1446-52*, p. 577; Virgoe, *Kent Arch. Soc. Rec. Publns.* 18 (1964), 218-19.

[24] PRO, E 404/68/ 144, 45, 49, 56.

[25] M.G.A. Vale, 'The Last Years of English Gascony, 1451-53', *TRHS* 5th Ser. 19 (1969), 124-5.

[26] *Ibid.*, pp. 126-31 and also M. G. A. Vale, *English Gascony, 1399-1453* (Oxford, 1970), pp. 142-5.

[27] *CPR, 1452-60*, p. 55.

fell to Talbot's surprise attack on the night of 22-23 October.[28] Within the next two months Talbot was able to establish English control over the Bordelais, Médoc and Entre-deux-Mers, where Saint-Makeris, Ryons, Langon, Mark, Libourne, Saint-Emilion and Castillon had all been occupied by 25 December.[29] The dramatic and almost bloodless success of the enterprise was the result, it has recently been demonstrated, not of the unwillingness of the Gascons to accept French rule after centuries of English sovereignty, but of a skilfully executed conspiracy.[30] That the English came as conquerors not liberators is further indicated by the pillaging and looting indulged in by the English soldiers, the unprecedentedly high level of taxation immediately imposed by Talbot to pay his troops, and the very size of the army he brought with him to control Bordeaux and its hinterland. Gascony, it has been suggested, came nearer to experiencing an occupation then ever before.[31]

Bordeaux and its district having been won so easily in the autumn, the real test for Talbot was whether he could defend it against the full force of the French army in the summer of 1453. In the spring Talbot received reinforcements from England under the command of his son, Viscount Lisle. These men, recruited in England in the early months of 1453, and mustered at Dartmouth and Plymouth on 5 March, numbered 2,325. By the beginning of the campaigning season Talbot had about 7,000 men with whom to face the French attack.[32] As in Normandy in 1449, Charles VII advanced on several fronts. The count of Clermont, Gaston de Foix and Jean Bureau were given command of three separate armies converging from the north and west on Bordeaux. Talbot, however, was first in the field and took Fronsac, but as the French armies closed in he fell back on Bordeaux. By June, Clermont had reduced St Sever and entered the Médoc. Here he was joined by Gaston de Foix. On 21 June Talbot sent a verbal challenge to the French commanders and advanced from Bordeaux to confront them at Martignas. But neither side was prepared to launch an attack. And Talbot, having assessed the strength of the enemy,

[28] Fresne de Beaucourt, *Charles VII*, 5, pp. 265-7. For fuller accounts of the events of 1452-3 see H. Ribadieu, *Historie de la conquète de la Guyenne* (Bordeaux, 1866), pp. 260 ff., and C. Higounet, in *Bordeaux sous les rois d'Angleterre*, Histoire de Bordeaux, 3 (Bordeaux, 1965), pp. 512-21.

[29] *CPR, 1452-61*, pp 78, 108.

[30] Vale, *TRHS* 19 (1969), 126-31, 136-8.

[31] *Ibid.*, pp. 131-2.

[32] Stevenson, *Wars*, 2, pp. 479-80; Vale, *English Gascony*, p. 146. For English administrative and financial difficulties in raising these and later reinforcements see *ibid*, pp. 146-52.

withdrew.[33] Outnumbered by the enemy, he may have been hoping for the arrival of yet more reinforcements from England. Be that as it may, he waited for two more weeks in Bordeaux, allowing the French to continue their advance unmolested. On 8 July, Bureau's army, moving down the Dordogne, laid siege to Castillon. The garrison wrote desperately for aid. Talbot mustered his army once more and dashed to the garrison's assistance. One chronicler, Matthieu d'Escouchy, suggested that he would not have gone had not the Anglophile citizens of Bordeaux accused him openly of bad faith and cowardice for remaining inactive for so long. But the more favourably inclined, and perhaps more militarily aware, de Bueil reported that he planned to take on and defeat Bureau's smaller army before turning on the stronger forces of Clermont and Foix.[34] This would certainly have been the sound strategy to be followed by a commander operating on short lines of communications against a stronger but divided enemy. But Talbot had first to defeat Bureau.

The campaign to relieve Castillon was launched with Talbot's customary speed and vigour. Setting off at dawn on 16 July, he reached Castillon by a day and night march at dawn on 17 July. The mounted vanguard under his command, which had outstripped the greater part of the army on foot, fell on and captured the French outpost in the priory of St Laurent, a little to the north of the town. A reconnaissance party found that the main French force was encamped in an artillery park, defended by a strong rampart, half a mile to the west of the town. It would appear that Talbot's first decision was to wait for the main party of his army to come up before launching an attack. But while he was celebrating mass during this break in the action, messengers from the town brought news that the French could be seen riding off from their camp in a great cloud of dust. Fearing that the enemy was about to escape him, and in spite of more cautious advice from one or more of his captains, Talbot promptly ordered his men to fall in and advance on the artillery park. When they arrived before it they found the full French army waiting behind their massed cannon. It might still have been possible to delay and to await the arrival of his footmen, but Talbot took the fateful decision of launching his attack immediately. As the battle raged, units of the main English army came up and were thrown in. But the odds were hopeless and after less than two hours the English had broken and

[33] Fresne de Beaucourt, *Charles VII*, 5, pp. 268-70.

[34] Matthieu d'Escouchy, *Chroniques*, ed. G. du Fresne de Beaucourt, 2 (1864) 2, pp. 34-5; Jean de Bueil, *Le Jouvencel*, ed. L. Lecestre, 2, Société de l'Histoire de France (Paris, 1889), p. 296.

fled, leaving Talbot, his son, his principal captains and the pick of his troops dead on the field.[35] Talbot's body, badly disfigured and trampled, was found and identified by his herald on the following day.[36] It was at first buried on the field, but forty years later was brought back by his son, Sir Gilbert Talbot, to be reburied in the parish church at Whitchurch. So high was the respect in which he was held by his enemies that the victorious commanders established in his memory a chapel on the spot where he died; it was dedicated to the Virgin Mary and was known as Nôtre Dame de Talbot.[37] As well as delivering a fatal blow to English morale by the overthrow of their renowned commander, the battle of Castillon destroyed the only English army capable of putting up resistance to the French in the field. Bordeaux and one or two other places were able to hold out against the French until October, but in the absence of any further reinforcements from England, their fate had been sealed on 17 July. Gascony was effectively lost to the English at Castillon.[38]

Although his contemporaries could not have foreseen it, Talbot's defeat and death at Castillon brought to an end the long conflict between the Plantagenets and Valois for possession of the throne of France. Talbot himself won lasting fame and honour, in France as well as in England, by his tireless efforts to stave off the final English defeat. As a military commander he remains enigmatic. He seems to have been a born leader of men; he was perhaps what one might describe as 'a soldier's soldier', who in innumerable small actions from the capture of Laval in 1428 to the assault on Bordeaux in 1452

[35] The earliest account of the battle is the official history by the herald Berry (Gilles le Bouvier dit Heraut), *Les Cronicques du feu Roy Charles septiesme du nom*, ed. D. Godefroy (Paris, 1661), p. 469, written within one year. Chartier, 3, p. 7 and d'Escouchy, *Chroniques*, 2, pp. 36-41 were written within a few years. Basin, 2, pp. 195-6, written twenty-four years after the event, tells of the advice to delay giving battle. For detailed, modern reconstructions of the battle see A. H. Burne, *The Agincourt War* (1956), pp. 333-42; and Fresne de Beaucourt, *Charles VII*, 5, pp. 273-6.

[36] The acounts of how Talbot was killed vary. Berry and Chartier say that having been wounded and unhorsed his throat was cut; d'Escouchy reports that he received a blow on the head. The evidence of Talbot's skeleton, when disinterred in 1884, seemed to endorse d'Escouchy, for there was a fracture measuring 2¾ x ⅝ inches in the skull (W. Egerton, 'Talbot's Tomb', *Transactions of the Shropshire Archaeological Society* 8 (1874), 425). The herald identified the body by the absence of a molar tooth on the left hand side of the jaw. It so happens that Talbot's grand-daughter, Anne Mowbray, whose body was uncovered at the Minorites in 1965, was found to have 'a congenital absence of the upper and lower permanent second molars on the left', (M. A. Rushton, 'The Teeth of Anne Mowbray', *British Dental Journal* (19 October 1965), 355-6). In 1874 Talbot's skull too was found to have missing molars. It seems likely, therefore, that Talbot and his grand-daughter shared the same abnormality.

[37] Burne, *Agincourt War*, pp. 341-2.

[38] For the reasons given, I cannot agree with Dr Vale's judgement ('Last Years' *TRHS* 19(1969), 133) that Castillon 'solved little'.

could, with the cry of 'A Talbot, A St. George', inspire his men to daring feats of arms. It is not true that he was an irresponsible and reckless commander. Basin was incorrect when he wrote that he was 'normally impelled to drive the enemy into flight by impetuous daring rather than by deliberate assault'.[39] Talbot's surprise attacks on unsuspecting enemy positions seem usually to have been carefully calculated. On several occasions during his long career he refused to be drawn into open combat when the odds appeared to be against him — during the closing stages of the siege of Orléans, at Beaugency a few weeks later in 1429, during the siege of Pontoise in 1441, at Harcourt in July 1449 and again at Martignas in June 1453. He shared with all his contemporaries on both sides during the later stages of the war an unwillingness to be drawn into open, pitched battle. Throughout most of his career Talbot led his troops astutely, with the minimum of risk and with a high rate of success. Yet he suffered two major defeats. At Patay he seems to have misjudged the strategic position and was operating too far in advance with too small an army. Withdrawing too late, he was himself caught by surprise. At Castillon he seems for once to have been reckless. There is an air of desperation about his decision to attack the French artillery encampment. We do not know why he ordered that last, fatal attack, but it may be that pride and honour were at stake for he had already ordered his men to battle when he discovered the strength of the French position. Perhaps in the last resort Talbot's weakness as a commander was not that he was reckless, but that merely, at critical moments, he was wanting in judgement.

As a man, Talbot can hardly appeal to the modern reader. He was without doubt hard, cruel and self-seeking — as the people of Wales, Ireland, France and even England itself discovered during his long life. Paradoxically, he combined years of devoted and loyal service abroad (albeit underwritten by a sharp eye for his own personal interest) with a naked self-aggrandisement at home. While he did his best to prop up the crumbling Lancastrian régime in France, his actions in England contributed to the collapse of the dynasty at home. Although he exemplified all those chivalric qualities which Worcester, Caxton and Malory believed could restore social and political harmony to England in the later fifteenth century, his very actions in England reveal that the type of person they most admired could cause the greatest havoc. If John Talbot was the last of an old breed, it was probably as well for his countrymen that this was so.

[39] Basin, 2, p. 196.

APPENDIX: MUSTERS AND COUNTER-ROLLS
OF TALBOT'S RETINUES

A = muster of auxiliary retinue
C = counter-roll
F = muster of garrison contingent serving in the field

Personal

11 June	1421	PRO, E101/50/1
Dec	1428	Ms Fr 25768/318
A 31 Jan	1429	Add Ch 11612
A 12 May	1435	Ms Fr 25772/944
A 20 June	1435	Ms Fr 25772/954 bis
A 20 July	1435	Ms Fr 25772/963
8 Feb	1436	AN K 64/1/32
28 Feb	1436	AN K 64/1/34
16 Mar	1436	NAF 8602/23
23 Mar	1437	Add Ms 29315/2
8 Sept	1437	Ms Fr 25774/214
7 Nov	1439	Clair 201/846/68
7 Feb	1440	AN K 65/1/5
22 July	1440	NAF 8606/64
10 Aug	1440	AN K 66/1/32
8 Oct	1440	AN K 66/1/50
27 Nov	1440	Ms Fr 25775/1451
29 Nov	1440	Ms Fr 25775/1455
26 Mar	1441	Ms Fr 25776/1510
10 May	1441	Ms Fr 25776/1518
13 July	1441	NAF 8606/68
18 July	1441	NAF 8606/71
20 Aug	1441	AN K 67/1/34
6 Sept	1441	Ms Fr 25776/1533
15 June	1442	PRO, E101/54/2
27 Oct	1442	Ms Fr 25776/1591
28 Nov	1442	Ms Fr 25776/1596
2 July	1448	AN K 68/29/6

21 Sept	1448	NAF 8606/102
27 Dec	1448	Ms Fr 25778/1830

Caudebec

4 Jan	1436	Ms Fr 25772/1050
12 June	1436	Ms Fr 25773/1102

Coutances

24 Sept	1428	Ms Fr 25768/296
4 Nov	1428	Ms Fr 25768/310
19 Mar	1429	Ms Fr 25768/362
C Sept-Dec	1429	Ms Fr 25769/451
6 Mar	1431	Ms Fr 25769/576
18 Sept	1431	Ms Fr 25770/627
25 Apr	1432	Ms Fr 25770/696
23 Sept	1433	Rouen, Bib. Mun. Martainville 199/11(1)
C Dec 33-Mar	1434	Ms Fr 25771/809
8 Sept	1435	Ms Fr 25772/991
16 Aug	1436	Ms Fr 25773/1127
n.d.		Add Ch 12089

Creil

22 Aug	1439	AN K 65/1/32
C May-Aug	1439	AN K 65/1/30
25 Aug	1439	NAF 8606/60
C Aug-Sept	1439	AN K 65/1/35

Falaise

29 Dec	1428	AN K 63/1/10
8 July	1429	AN K 63/7/7
15 Sept	1429	AN K 63/7/12
15 Dec	1429	Ms Fr 25768/419
4 Sept	1439	AN K 65/1/33
F 13 April	1441	AN K 66/1/12

Château – Gaillard

A	1 Feb	1436	Add Ch 6894
	1 Feb	1436	Add Ch 6875
C	Sept-Dec	1436	Archives Départmentales de l'Eure, sérié II, F/4069.
	27 Dec	1441	Ms Fr 25776/1550

St-Germain-en-Laye and Poissy

	28 May	1435	Ms Fr 25772/946
	10 Aug	1435	Add Ch 11871
A	10 Aug	1435	Ms Fr 25772/972
F	18 Aug	1435	Ms Fr 25772/979
A	16 Nov	1435	Ms Fr 25772/1023
	16 Nov	1435	Ms Fr 25772/1022

Gisors

C	June-Sept	1434	Ms Fr 25771/894
F	early	1435	Ms Fr 25772/923
	31 July	1435	Ms Fr 25772/966
	24 Jan	1436	Ms Fr 25772/1051
	28 Jan	1436	Ms Fr 25772/1052
	18 Oct	1436	Clair 201/8457/59
	23 Mar	1437	NAF 1482/142
	1 Nov	1437	AN K 64/12/17

Harfleur

C	Oct-Dec	1441	Ms Fr 25776/1554
C	Jan-Mar	1442	ADSM, Fonds Danquin 3/3/17
	27 Mar	1443	Ms Fr 25776/1623
C	Dec 45-Mar	1446	Ms Fr 25777/1726

Montivilliers

	26 Mar	1442	Ms Fr 25776/1561
	24 Sept	1442	Ms Fr 25776/1582
	27 Mar	1443	Ms Fr 25776/1622

Neufchâtel

	1 July	1434	Ms Fr 25771/859
	14 Apr	1437	AN K 64/12/1
	28 Dec	1437	Clair 201/8459/63
F	1 Dec	1437	Ms Fr 25774/1276
F	17/19 June	1438	Ms Fr 25774/1330

Rouen : Castle

7 Jan	1436	AN K 64/1/31
24 Apr	1436	AN K 64/10/1
11 Sept	1436	Ms Fr 25773/1136
5 Jan	1437	AN K 64/10/17
27 July	1437	ADSM, Fonds Danquin 11/83
Aug	1437	Add Ch 191
Oct	1437	Add Ch 137
1 Nov	1437	Ms Fr 25774/1260
28 Dec	1437	Bib. Mun. Rouen, Martainville 198/11 (17)
26 Oct	1441	Ms Fr 25766/734
28 Dec	1441	Ms Fr 25776/1546
12 Feb	1441	Ms Fr 25776/1556

Rouen : Palais

C Oct-Dec	1441	ADSM, Fonds Danquin 11/89
C Dec 41-Mar	1442	ADSM, Fonds Danquin 11/90

Rouen : Town, walls and gates

C Mar-June	1436	Add Ch 6911
18 Aug	1436	ADSM, Fonds Danquin 11/80
20 Nov	1436	Ms Fr 25773/1150
C June-Sept	1437	Ms Fr 25774/1245
23 Sept	1437	Ms Fr 25774/1241

F Sept	1437	Add Ch 137
C Sept-Dec	1437	Ms Fr 25774/1252
C Dec 41-Mar	1442	Ms Fr 25776/1559
28 Dec	1442	Ms Fr 25776/1605
June	1443	Add Ch 12184

Rouen : bridge

A 27 June	1436	NAF 8606/51
27 Dec	1441	AN K 67/1/60
C Dec 41-Mar	1442	Ms Fr 25776/1552
C June-Sept	1442	ADSM, Fonds Danquin 11/91

Vernon

F 6 May	1438	Ms Fr 25774/1322

Creu (field)

28 June	1440	NAF 15543/143
25 Sept	1440	Clair 202/8474/2
3 Jan	1441	Ms Fr 25775/1490
10 May	1441	Add Ch 6949

BIBLIOGRAPHY

I: PRINCIPAL PRIMARY SOURCES USED

MANUSCRIPT SOURCES

Archives Nationales, Paris
Trésor des Chartes, Layettes (J)
Registres (JJ)
Monuments Historiques (K 60-68)
Collection Dom Lenoir

Archives de la Seine Maritime, Rouen
Fonds Danquin
Sérié Tabellionnage, 1418-1444 (Unpublished Calendar of acts concerning the period of the English occupation, compiled by M. Andrè Dubuc)
Sérié G: Archives Ecclésiastiques, Clergé séculier

Arundel Castle Archive
G2/69

Bibliothèque Municipale, Rouen
Fonds Martainville

Bibliothèque Nationale, Paris
Coll. Clairambault, 201/02, Talbot
Montres, Charles VI et VII, vols 3-15, Manuscrits Français 25766-78
Nouvelles Acquisitions Françaises, vols 8602-06, 1482 and 1543
Pièces Originales, 2787, Talbot
Quittances et Pièces Diverses, Charles VI et VII, vols 53-90; Manuscrits Français 26044-81,

British Library, London
Additional Charters
Additional Manuscripts
Royal Manuscripts

College of Arms Library, London
R26
WH

Lambeth Palace Library, London
Register Stafford and Kemp

Public Record Office, London
Chancery, Inquisitions Post Mortem, Henry VI and Edward IV

(C139-40)
Exchequer King's Remembrancer, Accounts Various (E101)
Exchequer, Receipts Rolls (E401)
Exchequer, Issue Rolls (E403),
Exchequer, Warrants for Issue (E404)
King's Bench, *Coram Rege* Rolls (KB27)

Shropshire Record Office, Shrewsbury
Bridgewater Papers, Blakemere Receivers' Accounts, Henry IV to
VI, (75-6)
   Blakemere Bailiffs' Accounts, Henry IV to VI, (81-2)
   Blakemere Household Accounts, Henry V and VI (85)

PRINTED SOURCES

Basin, Thomas, *Histoire de Charles VII,* ed. C. Samaran, 2 vols,
Paris, 1933-44, Les Classiques de l'histoire de France au Moyen
Age, nos 15 & 21
de Beaurepaire, F. 'Les sources de l'histoire du moyen âge à la
bibliothèque de Rouen', *Cahiers Léopold Delisle,* 14, fasc. 2
(1965): *Répertoire périodique de Documentation Normande,*
no. 2
Berry (Gilles le Bouvier, dit Heraut), *Les Cronicques du feu Roy
Charles septiesme du nom,* ed. D. Godefroy, Paris, 1661
Blake, N.F., *Caxton's Own Prose,* 1973
The Boke of Noblesse, ed. J.G. Nichols, Roxburghe Club, London,
1860
Calendar of Close Rolls
Calendar of Fine Rolls
Calendar of Inquisitions Post Mortem, Edward I-Edward IV, 4 vols,
1806
Calendar of Papal Registers
Calendar of Patent Rolls
Catalogue des Rolles, Normans et François, ed. T. Carte, 2 vols,
1743
Chartier, Jean, *Chronique de Charles VII,* ed. M. Vallet de Viriville,
3 vols, Paris, 1858
Chronicles of London, ed. C.L. Kingsford, Oxford, 1905
La Chronique d'Enguerran de Monstrelet, ed. L. Douët-d'Arcq, 6
vols, Société de l'histoire de France, Paris, 1857-62
Chronique du Mont St Michel, ed. S. Luce, 2 vols, Société des
anciens textes français, Paris 1879-83
Chronique de la Pucelle ou chronique de Cousinot, ed. M. Vallet de
Viriville, Paris, 1859
'Documents relating to the Anglo-French Negotiations of 1439', ed.

C. T. Allmand, *Camden Miscellany*, xxiv (Royal Historical Society, 1972), pp. 79-149

'Enquiry before Juvenal des Ursins on the taking of Fougères', in T. Basin, *Histoire des règnes de Charles VII et Louis XI*, iv, pp. 290-347, Paris, 1859

The Essential Portions of Nicholas Upton's de Studio Militari, ed. F. P. Barnard, Oxford, 1931

d'Escouchy, M., *Chronique*, ed. G. du Fresne de Beaucourt, 3 vols, Société de l'histoire de France, 1863-64

Gruel, G.. *Chronique d'Arthur de Richemont*, ed. Achille le Vavasseur, 1890

Hall, E., *The Union of the Noble and Illustre Famelies of Lancastre and Yorke*, 1809

Hall, T. W., *Sheffield Manorial Records*, Sheffield, 1926

Hunger, V., *Quelques actes Normands des XIV^c, XV^c et XVI^c siècles*, 3 vols, Paris, 1909-11

Issues of the Exchequer, ed. F. Devon, 1837

Journal d'un Bourgeois de Paris, 1405-1449, ed. A. Tuetey, Paris, 1881

Letters and Papers Illustrative of the Wars of the English in France during the reign of Henry VI, ed. J. Stevenson, 2 vols in 3, Rolls Series, 1861-4

Tito Livio, *Vita Henri Quinti*, ed. T. Hearne, Oxford, 1716

Narratives of the Expulsion of the English from Normandy, 1449-50 (Robert Blondel, 'de Reductione Normandie', and Berry, 'Le Recouvrement de Normandie'), ed. J. Stevenson, Rolls Series 32, 1863

Nortier, M., 'Les sources de l'histoire de la Normandie au département des manuscrits de la bibliothèque nationale de Paris: le fonds des Nouvelles Acquisitions Françaises', *Cahiers Léopold Delisle*, 16, fasc. 3-4 (1967): *Répertoire périodique de documentation normande*, no. 5

The Paston Letters, ed. J. Gairdner, 6 vols, 1904

de Pisan, Christine, *The Book of Fayttes of Armes and of Chivalrye* trans. William Caxton, ed. A.T.P. Byles, Early English Text Society, 1937

Political Poems and Songs relating to English History, ed. Thomas Wright, Rolls Series 14, ii, 1861

Proceedings and Ordinances of the Privy Council of England, ed. N.H. Nicolas, 6 vols, 1834

Public Record Office, *Reports of the Deputy Keeper of the Public Records*, Nos xxxvi, xli, xlii, xliv, xlvi, xlviii

Recueil des croniques par Jehan de Waurin, ed. Sir William Hardy, Rolls Series 39, 5 vols, 1864-84

Rotuli Parliamentorum, 6 vols, 1767-77

Rotulorum Patentium et Clausorum Cancellariae Hiberniae Calendarium, i, Part 1, Dublin, 1828

Rouen au temps de Jeanne d'Arc et pendant l'occupation anglaise, ed. P. Lecacheux, Société de l'histoire de Normandie, Rouen-Paris, 1931

Rymer, T. *Foedera, Conventiones, Litterae etc.,* 10 vols, 1704-35

Sheffield Estates Documents, ed. S.O. Addy and A.H. Thomas, in *THAS1* (1918), 2 (1942) and 6 (1950)

The Shropshire Peace Roll, 1400-1414, ed. E.G. Kimball, Shrewsbury, 1959

Testamenta Eboracensia, ii and iii, Surtees Society, xxx, xlv, 1855, 1864

Three Books of Polydore Vergil's English History (Henry VI-Richard III), ed. H. Ellis, Camden Society, 1846

The Tree of Battles of Honoré Bonet, trans. G.W. Coopland, Liverpool, 1949

'The Will of John Talbot, First Earl of Shrewsbury', ed. G.H.F. Vane, in *TSAS* 3rd series 4 (1904), 371-8

II: SECONDARY WORKS CITED IN FOOTNOTES

Allmand, C.T., 'The Relations between the English Government, the Higher Clergy and the Papacy in Normandy' (unpublished Oxford University DPhil thesis, 1963)

_____ 'The collection of Dom Lenoir and the English occupation of Normandy in the Fifteenth Century', *Archives*, 6 (1963-4)

_____ 'The Anglo-French Negotiations, 1439', *BIHR*, 40 (May 1967)

_____ 'The Lancastrian Land Settlement in Normandy 1417-50', *Econ HR*, 2nd ser, 21, 3 (1968)

_____ (ed.), *Society at War: the experience of England and France during the Hundred Years' War* (Edinburgh, 1973)

_____ 'The Aftermath of War in Fifteenth-Century France', *History*, 61 (Oct 1976)

Barber, R., *The Knight and Chivalry* (London, 1970)

de Beaucourt, G. du Fresne, *Histoire de Charles VII*, 6 vols (Paris, 1881-91)

Bois, G., *Crise du féodalisme: Économie rurale et demographie en Normandie orientale du début du 14ᵉ siècle au milieu du 16ᵉ* (Paris, 1976)

Bossuat, A., *Perrinet Gressart et François de Surienne, agents de l'Angleterre* (Paris, 1936)

_____ Le Rétablissement de la paix sociale sous le règne de Charles VII', *Le Moyen Age*, 60, (1954); reprinted as, 'The Re-Establishment of Peace in Society during the Reign of Charles VII', in *The Recovery of France in the Fifteenth Century*, ed. P.S. Lewis, (1971)

Boutruche, R., *'La Dévastation des campagnes pendant la guerre de cent ans et la reconstruction de la France', Mélanges 1945, 3: Études historiques* (Paris, 1947); reprinted as 'The Devastation of Rural Areas during the Hundred Years' War and the Agricultural Recovery of France', in *The Recovery of France in the Fifteenth Century*, ed. P.S. Lewis, (1971)

Bridbury, A.R., 'The Hundred Years' War: Costs and Profits', in *Trade, Government and Economy in Pre-Industrial England*, ed. D.C. Coleman and A.H. John (1976)

Brill, R., 'An English captain of the later hundred years' war: John Lord Talbot, c1388-1444' (unpublished Princeton University PhD thesis, 1966)

_____ 'The English preparations before the treaty of Arras: a new interpretation of Sir John Fastolf's Report, September 1435', *Studies in Medieval and Renaissance History* 7 (1970)

Burne, A.H., *The Agincourt War* (1956)

Burney, E.M., 'The English Rule in Normandy, 1435-1450' (unpublished Oxford University B Litt thesis, 1958)

Charles, R., 'L' Invasion anglaise dans le Maine de 1417 à 1428', *Revue historique et archéologique du Maine* 25 (1889)

Contamine, P., 'Les Armées française et anglaise à l'époque de Jeanne d'Arc', *Revue Soc. Sau. Hte. Normandie, Lettres et Sciences Humaines* 57 (1970)

———*Guerre, état et société à la fin du moyen âge* (Paris, 1972)

Cosneau, E., *Le Connétable de Richemont* (Paris, 1886)

Cronne H.A. & Hilton R.H., 'The Beauchamp Household Book', *University of Birmingham Historical Journal* 2 (1950)

Curry, A. E., 'The First English Standing Army? - Military Organization in Lancastrian Normandy, 1420-1450', in *Patronage, Pedigree and Power in Later Medieval England*, ed. Charles Ross (1979)

Curtis, R., *The History of Medieval Ireland* (1938)

Dickinson, J.G., *The Congress of Arras* (Oxford, 1955)

Dictionary of National Biography 19 (1890)

Dubuc, A., 'Le Tabellionnage rouennais durant l'occupation anglaise', *Bulletin Philologique et Historique* (année 1967, 2, Paris 1969)

Dugdale, W., *The Baronage of England* 1 (1675)

Egerton, W.H., 'Talbot's Tomb', *Transactions of the Shropshire Archaeological Society* 8 (1874)

Ferguson, A.B., *The Indian Summer of English Chivalry* (Durham, North Carolina, 1960)

Fowler, K.A., *The Age of Plantagenet and Valois* (1967)

Gray, H.L., 'Incomes from land in England in 1436', *EHR* 49 (1934)

Griffith, M.C., 'The Talbot-Ormond Struggle for Control of Anglo-Irish Government', *Irish Historical Studies* 2 (1941)

Griffiths, R.A., 'Duke Richard of York's Intentions in 1450', *Journal of Medieval History* 1 (1975)

Higounet, C., 'Bordeaux sous les rois d'Angleterre', *Histoire de Bordeaux* 3 (Bordeaux, 1965)

Holmes, G.A., *The Estates of the Higher Nobility in Fourteenth-Century England* (Cambridge, 1957)

Hunter, J., *Hallamshire: The History of Sheffield* (Sheffield, 1819)

Jacob, E.F., *The Fifteenth Century* (Oxford, 1961)

Jarry, L., *Le Compte de l'armée anglaise au siège d'Orléans, 1428-29*, (Orléans, 1892)

Jouet, R., *La résistance à l'occupation anglaise en Basse-*

Normandie, 1418-1450, Cahiers des Annales de Normandie, 5 (Caen, 1969)

Keen, M.H., *England in the Later Middle Ages* (1973)

_____ *The Laws of War in the Late Middle Ages* (1965)

_____ & Daniel, M.J., 'English Diplomacy and the Sack of Fougères in 1449', *History* 59 (1974)

_____ 'Chivalry, Nobility and the Man-at-Arms', in *War, Literature and Politics in the Later Middle Ages,* ed. C.T. Allmand (Liverpool, 1976)

Kingsford, C.L., *English Historical Literature in the Fifteenth Century* (Oxford, 1913)

Lewis, P.S., *Later Medieval France: the Polity* (1968)

Lloyd, Sir John, *Owen Glendower* (Oxford, 1931)

Lodge, E.C., *Gascony under English Rule* (London, 1926)

Lydon, J.F., *The Lordship of Ireland in the Middle Ages* (Dublin, 1972)

_____ *Ireland in the Later Middle Ages* (Dublin, 1973)

Marchegay, P., 'La rançon d'Olivier de Coëtivy, seigneur de Taillebourg, sénéchal de Guyenne, 1451-77', *Bibliothèque de l'École des Chartes* 38 (1887)

McFarlane, K.B., 'Bastard Feudalism', *BIHR* 20 (1945)

_____ *The Nobility of Later Medieval England* (Oxford, 1973)

_____ 'The Investment of Sir John Fastolf's Profits of War', *TRHS* 5th Series 7 (1957)

_____ 'William Worcestre: A Preliminary Survey', in *Studies Presented to Sir Hilary Jenkinson,* ed. J. Conway Davies (Oxford, 1957)

McKerrow, R.B., *Nashe* (Oxford, 1910)

Marshall, A., 'The Role of English War Captains in England and Normandy, 1436-1461' (Unpublished University of Wales MA thesis, 1974)

de Molandon, Boucher, *L'armée anglaise vaincue par Jeanne d'Arc sous les murs d'Orléans* (Orléans, 1892)

Newhall, R.A., *Muster and Review* (Harvard, 1940)

Otway-Ruthven, A.J., *A History of Medieval Ireland* (1968)

Palmer, J.J.N., 'The War Aims of the Protagonists and the Negotiations for Peace', in *The Hundred Years' War,* ed. K.A. Fowler (1971)

Perroy, E., *The Hundred Years' War* (1965)

Pollard, A.J., 'The Family of Talbot, Lords Talbot and Earls of Shrewsbury in the Fifteenth Century' (Unpublished University of Bristol PhD thesis, 1968)

Postan, M.M., 'The costs of the Hundred Years', *Past and Present,* 27(1964)

Powicke, M.R., 'Lancastrian Captains', in *Essays in Medieval History presented to Bertie Wilkinson,* ed. T.A. Sandquist & M.R. Powicke (Toronto, 1969)

Prince, A.E., 'The Indenture System under Edward III', in *Historical Essays in Honour of James Tait,* ed. J.G. Edwards *et al* (Manchester, 1933)

Pugh, T.B., *The Marcher Lordships of South Wales, 1415-1536* (University of Wales, 1963)

_____ & Ross, C.D., 'The English Baronage and the Income Tax of 1436', *BIHR,* 26 (1953)

Ramsay, J.H., *Lancaster and York,* 1 (Oxford, 1892)

Ribadieu, H., *La Conquête de la Guyenne* (Bordeaux, 1966)

Roskell, J.S., *The Knights of the Shire of Lancaster,* Chetham Society, new series 96 (1937)

_____ 'William Burley of Broncroft', *Transactions of the Shrophire Archaeological Society* 56 part 3 (1960)

_____ 'John Wenlock of the Someries', *Publications of the Bedfordshire Historical Record Society* 38 (1958)

Ross, C.D., 'The Estates and Finances of Richard Beauchamp, Earl of Warwick, *Dugdale Society Occasional Papers* 12 (1956)

Rowe, B.J.H., 'A contemporary account of the Hundred Years' War', *EHR* 41 (1926)

_____ 'Discipline in the Norman Garrisons under Bedford', *EHR* 46 (1931), 194-208

_____ 'John Duke of Bedford and the Norman Brigands', *EHR* 47 (1932)

_____ 'The *Grand Conseil* under the Duke of Bedford', in *Oxford Essays in Medieval History presented to Herbert Edward Salter* (Oxford, 1934)

Rudder, S., *A New History of Gloucestershire* (Cirencester, 1779)

Shakespeare, William, *Henry V*

_____ *Henry VI, Part I*

Sharpe, R.R., *London and the Kingdom,* 3 (1895)

Smyth J., *The Lives of the Berkeleys,* ed. J. McLean, 2 (Gloucester, 1885)

Steel, A.B., *The Receipt of the Exchequer, 1377-1485* (Cambridge, 1954)

Storey, R.L., *The End of the House of Lancaster* (1966)

Vale, M.G.A., *'The Last Years of English Gascony, 1451-53',* *TRHS* 5th series 19 (1969)

_____ *English Gascony, 1399-1453* (Oxford, 1970)

_____ 'Sir John Fastolf's Report of 1435: A New Interpretation Reconsidered', *Nottingham Medieval Studies* 17 (1973)

Vaughan, R., *Philip the Good: The Apogee of Burgundy* (1970)

de Villaret, A. de Foulques, *Campagnes des Anglais dans l'Orléanais, la Beauce Chartraine et le Gâtinais, 1421-28* (Orléans, 1893)

Virgoe, R., 'Some Ancient Indictments in King's Bench referring to Kent, 1450-52', *Kent Archaeological Society Record Publications*, 18 (1964)

Wedgwood, J.C., *History of Parliament – Biographies of the Members of the House of Commons, 1439-1509* (1936)

Weyman, H. T., 'Shropshire Members of Parliament, 1393-1584', *Transactions of the Shropshire Archaeological Society*, 4th series 9 (Part 1, 1927)

Williams, E.C., *My Lord of Bedford* (1963)

Williams, G., *Owen Glendower* (Oxford, 1966)

Wright, N.A.R., 'The *Tree of Battles* of Honoré Bouvet and the Laws of War', in *War, Literature and Politics in the Later Middle Ages*, ed. C.T. Allmand (Liverpool, 1976)

Wylie, J.H., *The History of England under Henry the Fourth*, 1 (1892)

POSTSCRIPT

Several works have appeared since the typescript of this book was delivered to the Royal Historical Society in 1980. The following are of direct relevance to this study:

English suits before the Parlement of Paris, 1420-1436, ed. C.T. Allmand and C.A.J. Armstrong (Camden Fourth Series, 26, 1982).

Contamine, P., 'Rançons et butins dans la Normandie anglaise (1424-1444)', in *La France au xive et xve siècles: Hommes, mentalités, guerre et paix* (Variorum Reprints, 1981).

Curry, A.E., 'L'effet de la libération sur l'armée anglaise: les problèmes de l'organisation militaire en Normandie de 1429 à 1435', in *Jeanne d'Arc: une époque, un rayonnement* (Centre National de la Recherche Scientifique, 1982)

Griffiths, R.A., *The Reign of King Henry VI; the exercise of royal authority, 1422-1461* (1981)

Herbert, A., 'Herefordshire, 1416-61: some aspects of society and public order', in *Patronage, the Crown and the Provinces in Later Medieval England,* ed. R.A. Griffiths (1981), pp. 101-23

Jones, M., 'John Beaufort, Duke of Somerset and the French expedition of 1443', *Ibid.,* pp. 79-102

Talbot, H., *The English Achilles: the life and campaigns of John Talbot, 1st Earl of Shrewsbury* (1981)

Vale, M.G.A., *War and Chivalry: Warfare and Aristocratic Culture in England, France and Burgundy at the end of the middle ages* (1981)

Wolffe, B.P., *Henry VI* (1981)

INDEX

Abbeville, 49
Abrahall, John, 10
Agincourt, battle of, 76
Alençon, 13, 79
Ambrières, 12
Andelys (Les), 48
Andrews, Richard, 133
Angers, 14
Army, English, in Normandy, 32-8, 62, 73-4
Arques, 71
Arundel: John, earl of, 19, 20, 36, 79; Thomas, earl of, 10, 81
Arras, congress and treaty of, 21, 26-7
Ashton, Thomas, 82n
Auge, 107
Aumale, 80
Avallon, 19
Avranches, 41, 52, 92

Bailly, Watkin, 86
Banaster: Hugh, 79; Richard, 78-9; Thomas, 84n
Bannes, Richard, 86-7, 89, 91
Barbazan, Arnaud-Guillaume, lord of, 17, 114
Bascaille, 93
Basin, Thomas, bishop of Lisieux, 6, 30, 44-5, 56, 62, 126-7, 139
Baudemont, 49
Baudwyn, Simon, 89
Baytmont, Jean de, 74
Beauchamp, Cicely, duchess of Warwick, 111
Beauchamp, Richard, earl of Warwick: campaigns of, 12, 18; captain of Rouen, 96; captain of Château Gaillard, 97; death, 51, 132; governor of Normandy, 28, 39, 49, 109n; relationship with Talbot, 8, 11, 40-1, 114-15, 118n; retainers of, 80-1, 88; participation in tournaments, 122
Beaufort, Edmund, earl and marquis of Dorset, earl and second duke of Somerset: deputy lieutenant for the matter of the war, 52n, 53 and n; feud with York, 131, 133-4; governor of Normandy, 63, 65-6, 111; relationship with Talbot, 63, 81-2; retainers of, 80-2, 111
Beaufort, Eleanor, duchess of Somerset, 81
Beaufort, Henry, cardinal and bishop of Winchester, 26, 39, 51, 117
Beaufort, John, earl and duke of Somerset, 39 and n, 40n, 51, 52-3, 53n, 60, 79

Beaugency, 14, 16, 88, 139
Beaume, Jean de la, marshal of France, 37
Beaumont-le-Roger, 58, 65
Beaumont-sur-Oise, 19, 56
Beauvais, 20, 48
Bedford, John, duke of, regent of France, 11, 12-13, 17, 89; campaigns
    of, 12, 18; death, 21, 28; retainers of, 78-9, 88, 97
Berkeley, 99
Berkeley: Isabel, lady, 132-3; James, lord, 131, 133
Bernay, 52
Bieta, Mathew, 90
Bishop's Castle, 9
Bishopton, Sir William, 97
Blakemere, lordship of (near Whitchurch, Salop), 7, 75, 76n, 87,
    112n; manor house at, 119; receiver of, 89; steward of, 76n, 78, 81;
    tenants of, 84 and n (see also Whitchurch)
Blondel, Robert, 66
Bolt, Richard, 82
Bonet, Honoré, 123, 125-7
Bordeaux, 104, 119, 135-8
Boston, 111
Boulers, Reginald, bishop of Hereford, 134
'Bourgeois of Paris', The, 19, 58
Bourges, 18
Bowland, Edmond, 84n
Breton, Sir William, 82
Bretteville-sur-Laize, 106
Brid, Robert, 82n
Brigands, 32
Brill, Reginald, 6, 20n, 44n
Brittany: Francis I, duke of, 63-4; Gilles of, 63; John V, duke of, 12,
    114, 119
Brosse, John de la, 90, 92
Bueil, Jean de, 129, 137
Burdet, Nicholas, 22n, 80-1
Bureau, Jean, 136
Burgh, Hugh, 114
Burgundy: John duke of, 21; Philip, duke of, 12, 18, 20-1, 25, 41, 49
Burne, A.H., 6
Burley, William, 76n, 81
Butler, James, earl of Ormond, 10-11

Cade's Revolt, 131-2
Caen, 20, 29, 31, 93

Calais, 82, 134
Camoys, Roger, lord, 62
Camvill, John, 84n
Canterbury, 131
Cantock, Edmond, 87, 91
Castillon, 136-7, 139
Castillon, battle of, 1, 112, 123, 137-8; mass celebrated before, 124;
    Talbot's retainers at, 77, 99; Talbot's tactics at, 5-6, 128-9
Caudebec, 22-3, 49; garrison of, 72, 79, 88, 95-6, 109, 115, 141;
    links between garrison and Talbot's personal retinue, 22n, 91;
    Talbot as captain, 22
Caxton, William, 2, 130, 139
Chabannes, André, 87
Chalouns, John, 78
Chamberlain, Sir William, 52
Charles VII, king of France, 14, 18, 21, 30, 37, 50, 61-2; acquires
    Talbot as his prisoner, 17-18, 113-14; and recovery of Pontoise,
    54-8
Charlesmesnil, 59
Chartier, Jean, 56, 60n, 125
Chartres, 14, 18
Château Gaillard, 17-18, 23, 80, 97; garrison of, 83, 92, 106, 142
Cherbourg, 93
Chester, 77
Chesnebrun, 93
Chevreuse, 48
Chichester, 111
Cholmondley, Richard, 78
Churchill, Winston, 5
Clarence, Thomas, duke of, 88
Clay, John, 81
Clerc, Thomas, 98
Clermont, 20, 106-7
Clermont, Jean, count of, 136-7
Clifford, Sir Henry, 73, 82
Clifton, Gervase, 135
Clinton, John, lord, 57
Clyn, Edward, 90n
Coëtivy, Olivier de, 104
Coeur, Jacques, 27
Cokesay, Hugh, 11
Compiègne, edict of, 30
Conches, 50, 64, 97; campaigns to recover, 35, 54, 58-9, 73, 86, 88;
    loss of, 53-4

Conflans, 56
Conningston, Richard, 91, 95
Cooks, Thomas, 99
Corournaille, William, 90n
Council in Normandy, 29, 39-40, 42
Countryside, devastation of, 30, 41-2, 44; *see also* Pays de Caux
Courteilles, 93
Coutances, 78, 91-2, 141
Coventry, 114, 133
Cowley, 132
Cravant, 19
Creil, 19-20; defence of, 20n, 24, 44, 50-1; garrison of, 78, 141; loss of, 54-5, 58; Talbot as captain, 49
Crépy-en-Valois, 20, 126
Crich, 120
Cromwell, Ralph, lord, 120
Crotoy (Le), 39, 49, 105
Curson, Sir Richard, 80-1

Dalton, Thomas, 90, 93-4
D'Arcy, Sir Philip, 82n
Dartford, 134
Dartmouth, 136
Dauphin, the, *see* Charles VII, and Louis, dauphin of France
Dieppe, 22, 45n, 50-1; abortive siege of (1442-3), 45, 59-61, 77, 80, 97
Domfront, 38, 91n
Doudeley, Henry, 87
Doule, William, 92
Douville, 115
Dowe, Thomas, 87-8, 98-9
Dreux, 60
Duchesman, Hans, 74
Dunois, Jean, count of, 59, 65

Escorchebeuf, 106
Escouchy, Matthieu d', 137
Elbeuf, 54, 57
Emond, Richard, 84n
Eu, Charles, count of, 50, 53, 65
Everingham: Thomas, the elder, 75, 76-7, 81, 89, 97; Thomas, the younger, 77, 85, 89, 99
Évreux, 38, 50, 58-9, 91n
Eyton, Fulk, 22, 71, 79, 80-1

Falaise, 66, 71, 82, 96-7; garrison of, 75, 83, 141; Talbot as captain of, 49, 64, 72
Fastolf, Sir John, 12-13, 15, 17, 77n; his proposals of 1435, 125, 142; his quarrel with Talbot, 123; his profits of war, 103, 107, 108n, 118
Faversham, 131
Fécamp, 22, 45
Ferrour, Walter, 84n
Ferté Bernard (La), 13, 89
Fevre (Le), Jean, 112
Foix, Gaston, count of, 136
Folville, 53, 105
Fougères, 62, 96, 105
Fresnay, 81
Fronsac, 136
Furness, Lawrence, 90

Gaillon, 59
Gallardon, 59
Gascony, 27, 99-100, 112, 135-7
Gavray, 82
Gerberoy, 24, 64; battle of, 21
Gisors, 19, 23, 48, 105, 126; garrison of, 23n, 82, 88, 91; Talbot as captain of, 19, 49, 95, 109n, 142
Gloucester, Humphrey, duke of, 12, 26, 28, 39, 107-8
Glyn Dŵr, Owain, 8, 83
Good, Richard, 82-3
Goodrich, 10, 77-8, 119
Gougeul, William, lord of Rouville, 104n
Gournay-en-Bray, 49
Governor of Normandy, 28-9, 35-6; see also Beauchamp, Beaufort, York
Gracieu, Jean, dit Guy, 86-7
Granville, 41, 120n
Graville, 50
Graville-Sainte-Honorine, 106
Green, John, 78, 93
Griffin, Sir Robert, 82n
Griffith, Sir Thomas, 82n, 97
Gruel, Guillaume, 56
Gwyn, Griffith, 87

Halford, Geoffrey, 110
Hall, Edward, 2
Harcourt, 65, 139

Harfleur, 49-51, 55n, 58-9, 73, 79, 93, 106; garrison of, 75, 77, 85, 87, 89, 91, 99, 142; siege of (1440), 32, 44-5, 53-4, 71, 73, 85, 92, 132; Talbot as captain of, 53, 66, 72, 107
Hasildene, Henry, 131
Hasteseld, Richard, 82
Henry V, king of England, 7, 8, 9-11, 34, 115n, 127, 128n
Henry VI, king of England, 26, 28, 111, 116, 123, 127-8, 131
Hensacre, John, 85, 94, 99, 115
Heugeville, 106
Hire (La), Étienne de Vignolles, 12-13, 23-4
Honfleur, 53, 106
Hoo, Thomas, lord, 23, 82, 88, 91
Hore, Geoffrey, 87
Hull, Sir Edward, 135
Hungerford: Robert, lord Moleyns, 114; Sir Walter, 113
Husee, John, 84n

Indentures of retainer, 68-9; *see also,* Talbot, John, first earl of Shrewsbury
Ivry, 45

James, Sir Robert, 82n
Jargeau, 14, 16
Joan of Arc, 3, 15, 17
Jouy, 19, 126
Jumièges, 49, 59, 72, 96
Juziers, 55n, 56, 97

Katherine of Valois, queen of England, 9-10
Kenilworth, 133
Kent, Henry, 116
Kersford, John, 84
Kirkham, John, 84n
Kyriell, Sir Thomas, 23, 50

Lagny, 18
Lancaster: house of, 7; John of Gaunt, duke of, 69
Langons, 136
Lannoy, Hue de, 26
Laval, 13, 105, 126, 131
Laws of war, 126
Legett, Richard, 110, 114
Leighton, Edmund, 84n
Leland, John, 119

Lensedit, Gerrard, 98
Libourne, 136
Lihons, 53, 105, 126
Lillebonne, 22-3, 45
Lisieux, 54, 82, 107
L'Isle Adam, *see* Villiers
Lokkay, Richard, 83, 84n
Longchamps, 50
London, 27
Longempré, 71, 106, 112
Longueville, 50
Louis, dauphin of France, 55, 61
Louis of Luxembourg, archbishop of Rouen, 24, 29, 35, 38, 40, 42
Louviers, 18, 53, 57, 64; attempts to recover (1440-1), 35n, 58-9, 67;
    troops for the recovery of, 73, 86, 88, 95
Ludlow, 118, 134

McFarlane, K B, 102
MacMurrough, Donagh, 77
Mailly, 17
Maine, 11-12, 25, 41, 63-4, 107n
Malory, Thomas, 139
Mans, Jean du, 74
Mans (Le), 13, 61, 105
Mantes, 24, 48, 55-7, 71
Mantes, Jean de, 74
Mannessier, Rimon, 87-8, 90, 96-7, 99
March, Edmund, earl of, 11n
Mare, John de la, 89
Maretz, Charles de, 22
Margaret of Anjou, queen of England, 61, 98, 112, 122, 128
Mark, 136
Marshalcy of France, 37-9
Martignas, 136, 139
Massy, William, 93
Mayre, Thomas, 84n
Meaux, 10, 44, 48-50, 51-2, 54, 105
Meaux, Jean de, 74
Melun, 9
Meung, 14, 16, 88
Minors, William, 49n, 79-80, 82, 93, 97
Monstrelet, Enguerran de, 105, 126-7
Montague, Thomas, earl of Salisbury, 15, 88
Montargis, 12, 44, 49

Montereau, 39, 44
Montfort, John, 87, 91, 93, 99
Montgomery, 9, 83
Montivilliers, 22, 50, 53, 107, 142
Monyn, John, 90n
Morelet, Jean, 106
Motte-Fontaines (La), 106

Naas, 116
Nancy, 61
Nashe, Thomas, 5
Neufchâtel-en-Bray, 19, 80, 90n, 91-2, 95, 109n, 143
Neufmarché, 50
Nevill:Richard, earl of Salisbury, 33, 39; Thomas, lord Funival, 7-8
Nevill, William, lord Fauconberg, 33, 38, 49-53, 57-9, 71; retinues
    of, 33n, 41, 86n, 91n, 92n, 94
Newhall, R.A., 68, 94
Norbury, Sir Henry, 23, 82
Northampton, 134
Nôtre Dame de Talbot, Castillon, 138

Orbec, 107
Order of the Garter, 123-4
Ordonnance of 1445, 62
Orléans, Charles duke of, 26, 42
Orléans, siege of, 14, 70, 88, 139
Orville, 21
Oswestry, 79
Overton, Hugh, 84n; Nicholas, 94, 98
Owain Glyn Dŵr, see Glyn Dŵr

Pacy, 19
Painswick, 77, 100
Paris, 18-21, 23-5, 44, 48, 70, 105
Partisans, see Brigands
Pasquier, John, 95
Patay, battle of, 6, 17-18, 88, 120n, 139
Pays de Caux, 22, 30-1, 44-5, 49-51, 53-4, 59
Peasant risings, 22-3, 31
Perpoynt, Henry, 114
Peyto, Sir William, 60-1, 80-1, 95
Pierre-Perthuis, 19
Pigot, Thomas, 59
Pisan, Christine de, 113, 123, 125

Poissy, 56, 72, 142
Pole, William de la, earl, marquis and duke of Suffolk, 14, 16, 33, 61, 63, 66, 113
Pont-Audemer, 53-4, 64-5, 85-6, 93, 107
Pont-de-L'Arche, 54-5, 57, 59, 64
Pontoise, 20n, 23, 44-8, 51, 97, 105; siege of, 1441, 54-7, 67, 71, 87, 95n, 126
Porchester, 134
Portsmouth, 134
Pontorson, 12, 72
Pont-Sainte-Maxence, 20
Postan, M.M., 102
Prince (Le), John the elder, 87, 93, 96-8; John the younger, 93, 96-8
Profits of war, 36; *see also* Talbot, John, first earl of Shrewsbury
Plymouth, 136

Quesnel, Guillaume, 115

Rainford, Ralph, 87, 93, 99
Redman, Alice, 75
Richemont, Arthur de, constable of France, 21-2, 24, 28, 41, 45n, 52
Rieux, Pierre de, 22
Ripley, Sir John, 60n, 61, 97
Rochester, 131
Romilly, 106
Rotheram, 77
Roque, Cardinot, 64
Rouen, 19, 20-5, 29-30, 45-50, 52, 54-6, 65, 93, 112n; Talbot as captain of, 36, 40-1, 58, 72, 95, 98, 107; Talbot's retinues, 71-2, 75, 80-3, 90-2, 95-6, 109, 143-4
Ry, 23
Ryons, 136

Saint-Denis, 21, 57
Saint-Emilion, 136
Saint-Germain-en-Laye, 23, 45, 50-1, 82, 107, 142
Saint-Lô, 38
Saint-Makeris, 136
Saint-Sever, 136
Saint-Vigor, 78, 97n
Sandford, Bryan, 84
Sandwich, 83
Savill, William, 83-4n

Scales, Thomas, lord, 36-7, 51, 67, 91n, 94, 120n; his campaigns, 14, 16-17, 21, 23-4n, 38, 52-3n, 55, 57, 61n
Sercy, John de, 93
Shakespeare, William, 3-5, 130
Sheffield, 75, 77-8, 84, 89, 100, 116, 119
Shrewsbury, 118; battle of, 8
Shrewsbury Book, The, 123, 128
Simondshall, 132
Spring, Edward, 90n
Stafford, Henry, 89
Stafford, Humphrey, duke of Buckingham, 110
Stafford, Robert, 13, 87-9, 93, 95-9, 109, 115
Sterky, John, 48, 99
Stewart, Alan, 90n
Stuych, William, 84n
Surienne, François de, 63-4, 94, 107
Sutton, William, 84

Tait, J.A., 6
TALBOT, Ankaret, Lady, 7; Beatrice, Lady, 10; Sir Christopher, 122; Gilbert, fifth lord, 7-8; Sir Gilbert, 138; Henry, 115; John, second earl of Shrewsbury, 77, 99, 120, 132; John, lord and viscount Lisle, 132-4, 136; Margaret, Lady Talbot and countess of Shrewsbury, 8, 11, 61, 81, 97, 99, 104, 112, 114, 119, 131-3; Maud, Lady Talbot, 7, 10; Richard, fourth lord Talbot, 7; Richard, archbishop of Dublin, 10; Richard, 84, 89; William, 11
TALBOT, JOHN, FIRST EARL OF SHREWSBURY:
bastard sons, 61 (see also Talbot, Henry)
birth, 1, 7, 19
campaigns (in chronological order): Shrewsbury (1403), 8; Wales (1404-9), 8-9; Ireland (1415), 9; France (1420-1), 9-10; Verneuil (1424), 11n; Maine (1427-8), 12; Orléans (1428-9), 14-16; Patay (1429), 16-17; Burgundy (1433), 18-19; Île de France (1434), 19-20; Île de France (1435), 20-1; Rouen (1435-6), 21-3; Gisors (1436), 24; Pontoise (1437), 45, 48; Tancarville (1437), 49; Le Crotoy (1437), 49; Pays de Caux (1438), 50; Meaux (1439), 51-2; Avranches (1439), 52; Picardy (1440), 53; Harfleur (1440), 53; Louviers and Conches (1440-1), 53-4, 59, 95; Pontoise (1441), 54-7; Dieppe (1442-3), 59-61; Fougères (1449), 62-5; Normandy (1449), 65-6; Bordeaux (1452), 135-6; Castillon (1453), 136-8
commands and offices: captaincies, 19, 22, 35-6, 40-1, 45n, 49, 51, 53, 58, 68, 105-7 (see also Caudebec, Creil, Gisors, Harfleur, Rouen); commander of the fleet (1452), 134; constable

of France, 38-9; governor of Anjou and Maine, 12; lieutenant-general, 19, 36, 39, 41, 58, 103; lieutenant of Guyenne, 135; lieutenant of Ireland, 8-9, 61, 110-11; marshal of France, 37-9, 97, 103, 106-8, 127

creation as earl of Shrewsbury, 8, 41, 59, 121

death, 1, 123n, 138

estates and finances, 8, 103-4, 106-7, 116-19

feuds, 10-11, 107, 123, 131-3

gains of war, 104-6, 125

household, 98, 100, 104, 112-13, 124

imprisonment, 17-18, 65-6

marriages, see (1) Talbot, Lady Maud, (2) Talbot, Lady Margaret

as merchant, 119-20

military abilities, 5-6, 9, 24-5, 128-9, 138-9

military achievement, 50-1, 57-8, 66-7

mutiny against, 59-60

officers, retainers and servants: his archers, 90; his 'adjutant', 97-8; his clerk, 96-7; his captains and lieutenants, 75-83, 99, 103; his feedmen and annuitants, 75-6; his heralds, 122-3; his men-at-arms, 74, 83-101; musterers, 97; his paymaster, 95-6; their ransoms, 115 (see also household)

personality, 124-9, 133, 139

pilgrimage to Rome, 66, 124, 131

and piracy, 119

as poet, 128

ransom, 17, 113-15, 117, 120

reputation, 1-3, 9, 13, 66, 125-7, 133

retained by the crown, 18-20, 72, 85, 110

retinues: creus, 72-3, 88, 90, 92, 144; garrisons, 72, 91-2, 141-4; personal retinues, 20n, 34n, 40, 61, 69-71, 133, 140-1; reinforcements raised in England, 58, 60, 73-4; (see also officers, etc)

and suppression of popular revolt, 131, 135

his will, 116-20, 124, 128n

Tancarville, 22; siege of, 35n, 45, 49, 67, 96; army for siege, 68, 72-3, 79, 82, 97n

Taxation, 32

Tewe, Ryse, 133

Thouars, 106

Tonbridge, 131

Tours, truce of, 27, 36, 44, 61

Trollope, Andrew, 81-2

Troyes, treaty of, 9, 26

Trumpet, William, 90n

Valmont, 22
Vavassour, Duvant le, 90
Vendôme, 61
Vergil, Polydore, 3
Vergy, Antoine de, 37
Verneuil, 18, 38, 65, 91n, 93; battle of, 11n, 76, 78-9
Vernon, 48-9, 52, 55, 88, 144
Vignolles, Amadeo de, 19; Étienne de, *see* Hire
Villiers, Jean, lord of L'Isle Adam, 19, 37, 48
Vire, 38, 91n

Warbretton, Thomas, 90n
Warwick, 80
Waurin, Jean, 16, 53, 56
Wenlock: John, 84n, 89; William, 84n
Westminster, 20, 60, 62, 134
Wexford, 77
Whitchurch, 100, 124, 138 (*see also* Blakemere)
White, James, 84n
Wilkins, John, 135
Williamson, Thomas, 119
Willoughby, Robert, lord, 19, 21, 38
Windfield, 120
Woodford, Jenkin, 87
Woodville, Sir Richard, 82
Worcester, William, 2, 130, 139
Worsley: Seth, 78; William, 78, 91
Wotton-under-Edge, 132
Wynne, John, 116

Xaintrailles, Poton de, 17-18, 23-4, 113-14

Ynde, John of, 90
York, 35
York, Richard, duke of, 24, 45, 54-6, 63, 97, 110, 116, 118; as
    governor of Normandy, 28-9, 35-7, 60; his feud with Somerset, 66,
    131, 133-4; his relationship with Talbot, 40-1, 58, 61, 70, 80-1,
    87, 111, 134; his retainers, 33, 38-9, 42, 69, 79, 80-2, 100
Young, Thomas, 90n